A Diary to My Babies

Journeying Through Pregnancy Loss

by Carmen Grover

DEMETER

A Diary to My Babies
Journeying Through Pregnancy Loss
by Carmen Grover

Copyright © 2022 Demeter Press

Individual copyright to their work is retained by the authors. All rights reserved. No part of this book may be reproduced or transmitted in any form by any means without permission in writing from the publisher.

Demeter Press
PO Box 197
Coe Hill, Ontario
Canada
K0L 1P0
Tel: 289-383-0134
Email: info@demeterpress.org
Website: www.demeterpress.org

Demeter Press logo based on the sculpture "Demeter" by Maria-Luise Bodirsky www.keramik-atelier.bodirsky.de

Printed and Bound in Canada

Cover design: Emily Melo
Typesetting: Michelle Pirovich
Proof reading: Jena Woodhouse

Library and Archives Canada Cataloguing in Publication
Title: A diary for my babies : journeying through pregnancy loss /
by Carmen Grover.
Names: Grover, Carmen, author.
Identifiers: Canadiana 2022044398X | ISBN 9781772584233 (softcover)
Subjects: LCSH: Grover, Carmen. | LCSH: Miscarriage–Patients–Canada–
Biography. | LCSH: Parental grief. | LCGFT: Autobiographies.
Classification: LCC RG648.G76 2023 | DDC 618.3/920092–dc23

G9 T2 P2 A4 L3

The light in you forever shines through us.
It was then that I carried you.
It is now that I carry you onwards with me.

Disclaimer

This is a work of nonfiction. I have tried to recreate events, locales, and conversations from my memories when writing my diary entries. To maintain anonymity, in some instances, I have changed the names of individuals and places or omitted or replaced personal names with pseudonyms. It is an honour to share the names of the women who wished to use their names—the courageous women who supported us on our journey and who shared their own stories of loss. I have also changed some identifying characteristics and details, such as physical properties, occupations, and places of residence.

To the babies I never held on the outside,
to the babies I held in my hands,
to the babies who I hold in my heart,
to the babies I hold in my life,
and to the babies who live on in my mind and dreams.
I do this for us.
Our story, the diary of our babies,
will go on—their stories that became ours.

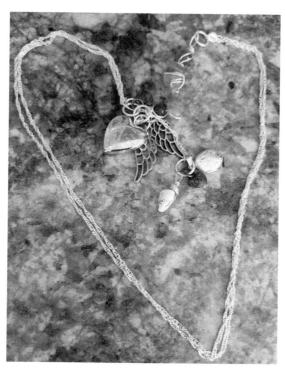

My Locket of Hope that holds Kaia & Jude.

Contents

A Love Letter to Grieving Mamas

From loss before having;
to having after loss;
to loss after having;
to having.

Dearest Mama,

You might crave your baby and the expectations you had of what your future might have looked like. You don't crave the pity party. You might anger at the happy families who seem to have babies so haphazardly. You might cherish your luck in the child or children that you do have and that might cause you to feel more of what you have lost.

You might know there is nothing you could have done differently to save your baby. But it doesn't stop you from searching for reasons. You might know that in life, there is so much we cannot control. But you might crave that control.

You might feel selfish for wanting more.

You might think that our children are not our children. They might come through you but not from you. You might house their bodies but not their souls.

You might believe that the babies who do not stay have the potential of becoming intercessors and guides for the children who are to come.

You might lean into the symbolism. You might take these messages as comfort even if it feels woo-woo or crazy. They might be reminders that there is some bigger force at play.

Mama, the loss never goes away, but the suffering gets softer. As we go through our worst nightmares, our darkest days, so much love is beneath it all.

May you feel all the love and support that surrounds you, seen and unseen. And know that your tears can be healing.

Love from a mama who has lost,

Carmen Grover
(Amity, Will, Kaia Belle, x), Case Emerson, Maelie Lynn, (x, Jude Simba Joy), and Ayda Catherine.

Preface

My name is Carmen Grover, and I am thirty years old. I am a married mother of three beautiful children, Case, Maelie, and Ayda, and our fur baby, Nola. I grew up on a farm and adore being able to give a taste of it to my children. I work as a paediatric nurse, which is where my true passion lies, working with super-resilient kiddos—what a true honour. I am also a bereaved mother of two infants and have had four miscarriages (six losses in total), and I wish to share our story while processing my own grief. I am beyond sympathetic to the families I get to serve as a nurse and wish to offer support and community by sharing our story of grief.

In my spare time, I teach yoga in our backyard (my happy place). I love to do any and all kinds of outdoor activities and have had the opportunity to travel to such places as Peru, Guatemala (helping out with scholarship and school programs), Africa, and recently the Grand Canyon (with our littlies). I am fortunate to visit family in Holland, France, and Manitoba, which always brings me back to my true roots. Our children are our entire world, and we get to show them adventure and the paradise and miracles of life that exist right in our backyard and our lives each and every day. I tinker on the piano, and my husband plays the fiddle, so our children are constantly twirling to the music of life.

I am a first-time writer but have been journaling for years (if that counts). I write to document what my babies' lives meant to me, for myself, and my loved ones, and that is enough reason to keep writing, knowing their story—our love story—has been told.

Pregnancy loss can be a dark, isolating, and lonely time full of despair. Sadly, it is a stigmatized topic as no one wishes to hear about the loss of a baby; it is just too horrible. However, it doesn't have to be, as we begin to more openly share our stories of loss.

There is a movement happening. My hope is to shine light on the darkness of this taboo and unspoken topic, to normalize our feelings about it, and to offer support. Everyone has a story that they don't need to hide or keep locked up.

After the loss of our son Jude in August 2020, I wrote in my journal, as I always had, and it helped me to cope. I was writing in the book that was supposed to be for my boy, and it hit me. As I thought of the five other journals sitting under my bed, of all the other diaries that were supposed to be for the babies I had lost, and how this diary, too, would end up there, I thought to myself: *What is the point of all of this? Why am I doing this?*

My son's death sparked something in me, and I began to compile all those diaries to my babies into a book. I never planned to be a writer, and where this inspiration came from, I owe to my babies. The journey that my babies wanted me to tell suddenly became my purpose. Every circumstance is different, but those lost children and their stories will remain with me for a lifetime.

This is not a guidebook on how to do pregnancy loss, nor is it a self-help book (though in writing it, it helped me heal myself). But it does show the story of a mother's undying love for her babies and what it was like going through it, from rolling in the grass like a primal animal to convulsing in tears on the kitchen floor. It shows the nonlinear, erratic, and nonsensical timeline of grief, one deeply rooted in hope, and the day-to-day roller coaster that I have been on these past five years. All that I have written, even though it is scattered all over the place, accurately describes my experiences and how everything felt. Like most people, I have experienced grief and situations in life that made me realize how quickly it can all change and all be taken away. I also realize that I cannot live each day in fear that I will lose everything.

Each day I recite to myself: I am alive. I have a beating heart (in honour of Kaia). I have working kidneys (in honour of Jude). I am surrounded by a family that loves me. I have a job, a house, and a simple yet adventure-filled, beautiful life.

Because I so fortunately have living children (this memoir in itself would be a whole other story had I not had children), I grieve whole-heartedly and collectively, in an unknowing and unimaginable place, with those who wished to and never could have children. Grief is always changing and is always present in varying degrees. We simply cannot skip over pain (if only there was a fast-forward button). We have to move through it, not over it. Our love comes out in tears and written stories, dreams, lost hopes, and wishes for our babies; it is exhausting and part of the process. It is also life changing in devastatingly beautiful ways.

Part 1
Dreaming of Flight

During my early miscarriages,
I wanted new adventures and experiences to escape.
Hiding from what was happening to me.

Before Kids

I kept many journals before having kids. I feel it is important to go back to the beginning, when life was more selfish, to revisit old entries that formed the backstory of my life and the journey to starting our family.

August 17, 2010 (Age Nineteen): Ponderings at the Tree

I sit here with the grass beneath me, the sun beaming overhead, lively corn husks swaying in the wind. I can hear the sound of the crickets, feel the warm breeze on my skin, and I'm enjoying our dog running freely under the fluffy clouds. This is how life should be. The corn's liveliness and ability to stand tall as well as the sun's incredible strength to emit such warmth and brightness guides me on my journey. The sharpness of the grass reminds me it is there, yet it is able to cushion me. The wind's gentle push comforts and moves me along to my next dream while at the same time blows my worries away. The dark clouds represent my problems. I learn that eventually the rain and my tears will fall and that the clouds will pass by. The next clouds move in, but each time, I am stronger, more rooted in the ground and more equipped with guidance from the sun, the trees, the grass, and the breeze. The natural world comforts me with a newfound confidence to face the next challenge.

August 23, 2012 (Age 21): Considerations about Life

I am at a bit of a crossroads in deciding what I would like to do with my nursing career. I would absolutely love to work with babies. They are adorable. It is usually a happy and exciting time for the parents, so they are not particularly upset. The doctor delivers the baby, and I would get to be there providing support and witnessing joy. Also, it is in my thinking that losing a baby, although extremely hard and so sad, is not as difficult as losing, let's say, a seven-year-old to cancer. By then, the child is already a little person, and the parents have developed that unconditional bond.

In both situations, milestones will always be a trigger. One would wonder who that baby, that person, might have been or what they would have done. But, and this is just my opinion, the loss of a baby, as terribly horrible as it is, is not as hard as watching a young child die.

The next option for my nursing career could be home visits to young families starting out to offer teaching and resources. This work would be less stressful; I am a nutball when it comes to stress. Although each child and family would be different, I worry it might become too repetitive.

Lastly, I think it would also be neat to work with adults with various conditions and teach or care for those people with general health problems. With such work, I could continue to learn and keep it interesting. Also, since I am essentially an adult, their concerns could apply to me, and I feel I could better relate. A drawback might be that I come to believe I have every disease and illness in the book.

So that is where I stand: all over the place. But I have a general direction, right?

I like how I am beginning to better understand the person I am; however, I also wish I could be more independent. Still, it is good to know what I can and can't handle. I don't want to take on too much.

That's enough of the professional mumbo jumbo, now for the family bit. I don't want my profession to affect the number of kids I want to have (that is if I am able). Right now that number stands at three or four; however, Phillip is right that we need to have the time and means to provide for each child. We don't want to half-commit to raising our kids. Also, I don't want to be a mom who is never there. Phillip and I should have the same parenting beliefs, and there are so many things to consider. This will be an incredibly hard challenge for me, as I can't seem to punish or lay down rules, so a lot of self-work will need to happen. Maybe a dog first?

I think about having enough wellness and time for myself. This means a lot to me. Lately, I love time to be active, read/write, reflect, be spiritual, play piano, and be creative. These things will likely stop with having children. I worry about that. But the greatest accomplishment in life is your children, right? That is what I will gain, the greatest reward and pride. Also, my passion and ability to help others tie into parenting. Sounds like a win-win situation.

I would love to travel and do humanitarian work into my retirement. I think I am asking for too much, but for now, I have big goals and dreams. Life really is too short, and if my dreams fall short, I won't be disappointed because at least I always dreamed big.

October 31, 2015 (Age Twenty-Four): Last Day in Cuzco

Today in Cuzco, my husband and I explored the markets, and it led us to locals selling Peruvian hats and rubber sandals. The market is a place where you can find absolutely anything, and the smells were overwhelmingly sweet, like flowers, yet also pungently fishy. Pig heads were hanging from the ceiling, and every vegetable and root imaginable were placed delicately under the heads. What a sight to see. We went to a chocolate museum and stocked up on cocoa tea (not to be confused with coca leaves . . . when combined with alcohol—look out!). We shared a sundae on the balcony and watched young love, merchants, and sellers working. The chocolate was the strongest—the most delicious chocolate we have ever tasted.

On our second walk, we came across a fabric shop. We were shocked that it only cost twenty-five American dollars for three Peruvian cloth throws. The women in the shop were not pushy at all and, in fact, showed us how to make a throw into a baby holder, so one day we can just carry a baby on our backs like they do. This excited me. I am starting to feel as if Phillip and I are getting ready for the idea of children. The woman sewed up the fabric right there in front of us. We ended up getting three cloth throws, but I wanted more.

Later that night, we partook in what we thought would be a cute Halloween activity: handing out candy to the children. Phillip was swarmed, buried in a kiddy pile, and it was hilarious. Turns out, Halloween is a big deal in Peru, and there were no last calls for candy; it went on all night. At least the kids were super cute.

Babe #1
Amity Ella Lynn Grover

January 28, 2016: Sleeping Beauty

Today, we found out our truest, deepest love was sleeping forever. Last night, I started experiencing some cramping. We went to the hospital, and the doctor took my blood to monitor my hCG level for a baseline. The doctor said that many women have cramping all throughout their pregnancies so he wasn't too worried, but just in case he booked us for an ultrasound the following morning. This morning at 5:00 a.m., I woke up writhing with cramps, and I grounded my body into the bed. When I went to the washroom there it was—bright red blood. And even still, I couldn't believe it was a miscarriage, and I remained hopeful.

During the ultrasound, when the technician left the room, I peeked up at the screen. I saw "no fetal pole" written and remembered researching this previously. The absence of a fetal pole can mean that a miscarriage has happened. Phillip and I waited, still naively hopeful. But then the doctor came in to tell us we were having a miscarriage and explained to us how our baby had stopped developing at nine weeks but that my body was still holding on to the baby at twelve weeks, believing it was still pregnant. This is known as a missed miscarriage.

Go home, and it will pass, the doctor said. Take Tylenol or Advil for the pain. And that was that.

Home, we went. I immediately opened my laptop and began to write everything and anything to honour all that you are and were to me, sweet darling child.

Phillip brought me a Kleenex box as my tears flowed, and again later that day as I cried on the toilet in pain, not knowing what to expect when it happened. You let go as a giant thunk in the toilet. I imagined you as the size of a small mandarin. I screamed and squeezed Phillip's hand while sitting there with him. Stunned, I told him what had happened, urging him to flush the toilet. I didn't want to look. I couldn't. He flushed you two times.

Second Entry: Later this Same Day

After this miscarriage, I realize just how naïve I was. I was shocked when it happened, as the thought of a miscarriage had truly never crossed my mind. My mom has never talked about it, and now that we've had that conversation, I've found out she never had one herself. She apologized to me for not being able to empathize.

Statistics show one in five women (roughly 10 to 20 per cent) experience miscarriage, so we have just got ours over with first. Next the healthy babies will come. Earlier, some friends comforted us by telling us that their parents' first pregnancy ended in miscarriage, as sometimes the body just doesn't know what to do in the beginning and later figures it out.

Today, as I commemorated you with such love through my writing and then collapsed in overwhelming anger as we neared the end of the night, Phillip said to me ever so gently, "Remember it's a bad day, but it is not a bad life." It is something that I find myself repeating so often. It is a truth that has been with us every step of our journey.

January 21, 2016: A Tribute to Babe #1, Forever Our Peanut

> *The great art of life is sensation,*
> *to feel that we exist, even in pain.*
> —Lord Byron

Dear Babe #1,

Although you were only around three-months gestation, you were so well loved already and referred to as Peanut by all of Mommy's friends. If you were a girl, which Mommy thinks you were, your name would have been Amity Ella Lynn Grover. Amity means friendship and harmony, which you brought to our lives. Ellie stands for bright shining star, which we had wished upon. You get the Ella from Belle, your dad's grandma's last name. Belle for beauty, of course. Lynn you get from the middle names of three generations on Mommy's side. Also, surprisingly, (I just learned) it means lake. I love the lake! My August baby, it was my plan to sit with you by the lake all summer long and forevermore.

If you were a boy (your Daddy says he just knew you were a boy). you would have been named Sawyer Ewen Case Grover. Sawyer means woodcutter, which is what your Daddy loves to do, and it does keep us warm. Ewen means from the yew tree, which goes well with wood-cutting, eh? Case because we want to just put you in our suit(Case) and take you all around the world with us. Also, that was Great Opa's name. Grover you get from Daddy and the Sesame Street character, naturally. So there is the name story. Wow—for all the love that goes into a name.

Where You Began

We had just returned, happily and very in love, from Peru (our official honeymoon). To celebrate, we thought we would make you. Humans are just so crafty; we can make a person. I happen to think that is pretty cool. I believe you were conceived November 21, 2015, as that night the bright stars aligned. It was a good night of movie watching in the bedroom and one or two alcoholic drinks each. My drink was called Tempt No. 9, and that was my favourite drink of the year for the record. The next night we went bowling with my brothers and their girlfriends and that would have been your first real adventure.

On December 4, we took our first official First Response pregnancy test. I could see two lines, although I must admit they were faint. I blurted out the obscure pregnancy reading to my girlfriends at Skeets (our small-town hangout spot, which would have been your favourite restaurant) and I ordered a pitcher of iced tea. What? Yup, I was that obvious.

I kind of joked with Daddy that, hmm . . . maybe I'm pregnant. Look, two lines. Daddy did not see a second line, and we let it slide. (Note to self: Always go with the pregnancy test that displays a plus sign for a positive pregnancy, as there's less chance for misinter-pretation.) December 7 was the official day when pregnancy test number two showed positive. I leapt from the toilet like a frog off a log and screamed in excitement. Nola, your big sister, (she is a dog but we truly believe she is human) stared at me. She seemed kind of frightened by my actions, but she then proceeded to wag her tail.

While in the Green Earth store, I read a quote by Buddha: "Happiness increases when being shared." That was when I knew I wanted to share all the happiness in the world with you and that you in turn would give me even more happiness. Daddy got the news on December 12. How I managed to keep that secret for five whole days is beyond me. And there is even a video to go with it. I will tell you this story so you have an idea of the kind of people you would have been spending your life with.

Telling Daddy

Mommy had a grand idea on how to be cute. I decided to announce your arrival into this world by displaying you as a bun in the oven. Daddy was cooking chicken, and I watched him diligently while shaking in nervous excitement. Oh, so many emotions and hormones. He checked the temperature, and I presumed he would be taking the chicken out in roughly two-and-a-half minutes. It was a perfect opportunity for me to toss some garlic bread in the oven with your purple positive pregnancy test on the cooking sheet. I was giddy with anticipation. To my surprise, your Daddy's favourite song came on the radio: "Your Man" by Josh Turner. Daddy started belting out the tune as the timer sounded. Mommy tried to wait patiently but was thinking, like seriously, *check the chicken already!* I wanted him to take the garlic bread out of the oven so I didn't have to. *Oh dear,* I thought, *maybe people do this without having the oven on.* (I will have this down next time for sure.) But by that point I had the camera cued for the cutest moment of life.

What did Daddy say when he opened the oven?

"What the..."

Okay, let's just leave it at that. I told him what the purple melted blob on the cooking sheet meant. He said, "It's not positive. I don't see a positive." Sadly, it was true, as we couldn't see much of anything besides smoky white and purple goop. So that was super cute.

Finally, your Daddy said he would not believe I was pregnant until he saw a belly. He is just one of those guys who can't believe it at first. He was in shock, and it really was hard for him to believe it. I think some men have a hard time believing until they actually hold the baby because unlike women, they are not the ones carrying the baby.

January 16 was the official belly-seeing date. He did congratulate me on January 4, though, when my first medical appointment confirmed the pregnancy. Daddy was just as shocked as Mommy, especially during the last few weeks. We had been getting so excited to meet you. I admit that writing all of this does make it a little harder to say goodbye to you, sweetie.

Those Who Knew You

In early December, a coworker in the paediatric critical care unit (PCCU) predicted my pregnancy when she pulled out a big booger from a patient while saying, "Here comes a gummy worm." I will never forget it. Out it came from one of our patient's nostrils, and I almost had to make her suction my mouth out because I thought I was going to throw up.

"Oh, you must be pregnant," she said.

It was my first sign you were on the way. Other nurses made comments, such as "Don't stare at the babies, or you'll be pregnant tonight" and "Ovulation station over here." They were right.

On December 16, more of our friends found out. We were making Christmas cookies, and it took me way too long to answer the question "Are you pregnant?" I tried to cover it up by sticking a cookie in my mouth. They were not fooled. Mommy is super subtle, don't you know?

On January 15, I was driving some girlfriends home, and my friend Jess exclaimed, "Anyone who wants to get preggers, do it now or wait." She was getting married the next summer. *Perfect,* I thought, *done and done.* I tossed the girls their New Year's presents, which were chocolate-filled shot glasses with diapers as wrapping paper. I got some thank yous and kept driving, when finally my friend Nicole asked, "Do you have something to tell us?"

Tee hee hee. I just said, "You will have to use the diapers in August."

Oh my goodness, the hugs you and I received were incredible! You brought me so much love from others. It was unbelievable. I enjoyed and basked in every minute of it.

Next up, I told my mama, your Gramma. On January 16, we had our usual Cora breakfast jab-jab session. After our date, as we sat in my mama's vehicle just prior to her follow-up echocardiogram (an ultrasound of the heart), I decided it was a good time to tell her. I gave her a watch necklace that was also a locket, one that had four places for pictures. Inside I had placed pictures of my granny, my mama, and me with my tongue out as a baby, and a little spot for you that read "Baby coming soon to a home near you this August 2016."

My mom burst into tears. I thought, *Oh no! Oops. Maybe now was not a good time.* She must have screamed "What?" four times and then "Oh my goodness! What? Really?" It was absolutely priceless and a moment I will always cherish. You also gave your Gramma so much excitement that she scored the highest recorded blood pressure reading yet on the excitement radar scale. Good work kid!

Later that night, my elementary school friends all gathered for Jenn's birthday party. I shared the exciting news in the bathroom, just as we high school girls had always liked to do in the good old days. All good stories start in the bathroom. They touched my belly, and we all screamed in gleeful harmony. I was thankful I could share the exciting news with so many of our close friends, but sadly some remaining close friends and family had to find out today, January 28, that we were devastated by the terrible news.

Your Daddy and I have received nothing but amazing support. Even though the time that you were in my belly was the shortest of time, you touched us infinitely and in more ways than you can ever know, sweet little child of ours.

My Favourite Cutest Baby Story for You

I have proof that you were a girl—an event that took place on December 21. Your mama actually works with kids, which is probably what led to my strong desire for you because kids are the absolute best. Everyone knows kids are so intuitive. I was playing the board game Sorry! with my five-year-old patient, and he asked me, "Can I touch your belly?"

I asked, "Why?"

He replied, "Cause there's a baby in there."

"Oh, is there?" I asked. "How do you know that?"

"Because I just know there's a baby in there."

Later in the day, when he was in the washroom taking the biggest poop of his life, I pointed to my belly and asked if it was a girl or boy.

He nonchalantly said, "Girl."

He stepped on the stool to wash his hands and then grabbed my hand to run back to his room. I had to share this with you, since Daddy is convinced you were a boy. But, for the record, you and I both know what we know.

We Love You Forever and Always

Wow, it's amazing what you remember and hold on to when you're in love. August 15, 2016, was your official due date. As you can see, in just three short months, you provided us with a lifetime of sweet memories. You were our first real child, and now we know we are ready. You were well loved.

Yesterday, the last song I listened to was "Everything Is Making You."

All these memories help make us stronger. For everyone, life is not without struggle. You will always be our first little sweet Peanut, and the initial excitement we shared with the universe was all because of you. What an amazing time we spent glowing with joy, which is definitely the way we want to be in this life. Like your name says, you lit up our life for a short while, and we will carry that light forevermore. It is incredible that with tragedy we discover the friendships and amazing supports we all have in our lives.

We love you always little Peanut,
Mommy and Daddy Grover xoxoxo

Babe #2
Will Grover

May 10, 2016: I Am Losing You

Today a song called "I'm Done" came on the radio.
I spotted a mommy bird in the tree with her babies.
If the next baby lives, I'm naming it Hope.

On April 1, I took five pregnancy tests to find out it was no joke.
We were pregnant.
Phillip said, "Hmm, I guess you are... so + means you're pregnant?"
You were due December 4, 2016.
You were roughly at ten-weeks gestation.
You were definitely a boy, as I ate all the time.

We did not pick names or name you, but liked William for a boy
and Everleigh for a girl.
I am amazed at how each new pregnancy brings with it a
new tailored names list.

This time I only told three friends we were expecting.
I told my sister Selena by lifting up my shirt that read
"I'm going to be a mommy."
(A shirt I had secretly and eagerly purchased when we were pregnant with
our first baby.)
A shirt I never got to use.
We took you to the East Coast with us.
When we left on our trip, I started to have a little cramping.

*I planned to run our eight kilometre annual road race on
Victoria Day with you.
Instead I would run with you, my baby, in my ever racing mind.
We planned to announce our pregnancy on our second wedding
anniversary, July 12, to the song
"You Are My Sunshine" played as a duet,
featuring Mommy on piano and Daddy on violin.*

*This grief is too raw to put together a nice story, like I did with
our first miscarriage, so I wrote it in dash points, turning it into
a lyric that only my heart will sing.*

*Maybe things do happen for a reason, and later you find the gifts in it?
Life is not that bad. It can always be worse . . . accept what you have.
My husband would do anything for me.
Love all that you can.
Everyone is there if you ask for them.
You were worth it.
Shine through the darkness, find a way.
Do what makes you happy.
Let creativity blossom and begin to let go.*

*When I was feeling gloom, I painted our bedroom.
That is where you'll find me: in our bedroom.
I'll be sitting under our new backdrop-painted cherry blossom tree with a
tea.
Thinking of you and your blooming spirit.
Listening to my heart's song of you.
Praying for one day.
I am naming you Will, as I believe . . .
We Will try again.*

May 16, 2016: A Tribute to Babe #2

Recollecting on this pregnancy, I am reminded that I was newly pregnant when Phillip and I went on one of our most favourite trips yet—Newfoundland. I do not recall this pregnancy announcement to Phillip being anything special, as I was trying to protect myself from the pain of getting so attached, like I did with our first. I am pretty sure he came home from work one day and while sitting on a stool in the kitchen I blurted, "So I'm pregnant."

Phillip simply said, "We'll just see how it goes."

It was clear how losing Amity had changed Phillip as well. I sorrowfully recognized that the excitement was dampened for not just me but for him, too. Just prior to leaving for our trip, when I was seven-weeks pregnant, I had two internal ultrasounds so the doctors could try to find the heartbeat. You would think that a light bulb would go off in me, but no, I grasped on to you. Despite our previous loss, I said to myself, it's just too early to get an accurate reading. I hoped that my dating was off, even though my cycle has always been pretty regular.

I remember at Gros Morne National Park jumping in pure giddy excitement at the beauty and enormity of the mountains I never expected to see out east. I was running through the tall grass. I later kicked myself for jumping, as I believed this is what caused the miscarriage. Or was it the coffee I had at Robin's Donuts, healthfully balanced with ice cream?

On the Cabot Trail, we took pictures, and I could already see the early stages of my baby belly. Everything was spontaneous. We stopped at every type of rock along the way: Devil's Footprints in Newfoundland, rainbow rocks in Bonavista, Hopewell Rocks in New Brunswick, rocks with holes—thinking about how everything rocks. We saw icebergs, and we ate the best lobsters (my first ever) at a local bagel shop, believe it or not. We planned nothing. But we stayed at amazing places where locals promoted us to the honeymoon suite. They fetched and fed us crab, and we walked right into a local fiddle festival. Phillip plays the fiddle and would have serenaded you one day, as he did me.

On our final night before heading home I started to see the brown staining in my underpants. I remembered how some women (one in three) have some bleeding during pregnancy and only when cramps accompany the bleeding is there cause for concern. Well, the cramps came, and so we decided to fashionably party hard in a bar on George

Street, St. John's, sitting and talking with some young, music-adventure folk. I was in shock and needed to put this loss out of my mind with enticing conversation of travel and lots of alcohol.

It was so quaint. We all sat near each other and were able to talk to the performer while he was singing. It was a certain kind of magic. We ate mussels, and then we stood up and nearly fell down. How we got home, drunkards on those wickedly inclined roads, I have no idea. When we awoke, I found Phillip in a corner changing his pants, trying to hide the fact that he "may have just peed the bed," and me trying to hide that I, too, "may have just peed the bed." This may just be one of my happiest, sloppiest memories, as I wasn't going to let myself hurt this time around. I didn't want to think about the fear, which kept creeping in, that I may never carry a baby to term. Understanding pregnancy loss and learning to be protective of myself this time, I just drank my worries away but also criticized myself the entire time, hanging my head while I also hung our peed-up sheets to dry out the window.

I started to wonder if maybe I was one of the unlucky ones, which contrasted with my hope that I couldn't possibly have any more losses after this. I thought that I was definitely set to not have any more miscarriages. Our one in five statistic of miscarriage was now two out of five. We had almost conquered all odds, right?

When we came back from our trip, I took a week off of work sick, explaining to the clerk we had lost another baby. Upon my return to work the following week, my "nurse mama" took me into a patient room, put a baby in my arms, closed the curtains, and said, "Take as long as you need. We will cover for you." I held that baby boy—unlike my own babies. I rocked, wept, and smiled at his cuteness. I changed the baby's outfit twice, not because they were soiled by normal baby happenings but from my constant tears.

June 25, 2016: Safe Zone

I wish I had told more people that we were pregnant. My first baby I told everyone too soon, and this baby I didn't tell anyone soon enough. We all wait, the dreaded twelve weeks, as then we think that we are in the safe zone. We may do this especially after a previous miscarriage. If only we could have enjoyed the pregnancy (like we had our first pregnancy) rather than holding our breath as some protective mechanism. Had I shared my pregnancy with others, I would have had a support network that could have shared in our excitement and would have helped us as we grieved—so that we didn't have to go it alone. I hid our pregnancies, with lost naïveté, to save others from the pain, embarrassment, and shame I felt. Instead, I ridiculed myself in harsh silence.

Even harder was telling people who didn't even know we were pregnant that we miscarried, as they simply couldn't share the whole cycle with us. They were left processing it all without having shared the excitement of hearing the initial news. Instead the initial news for them was filled with sadness. In that case, I found it was just easier not to say anything. Yet it is so important to create a comforting community for yourself and your baby to honour their short life. It is difficult to go back and honour a life, other than with your husband, of course, when no one else was there for it with you. Especially when you are grieving, you forget the beautiful moments that did occur, and sometimes you need friends and family to remind you of them. Such a struggle.

Part 2
Finding My Wings

I couldn't learn to fly until I discovered my wings,
extending them, with the wind that lifted them up.

Babe #3
Kaia Belle Grover

July 31, 2016: Possible Date of Conception

Tonight after a friend's wedding, I swear I felt the sparks of the stars colliding.

August 11, 2016: Here We Go

Today, I found out I am pregnant! Now I really know. How fitting, as today we are going to see the play *Mama Mia* with Gramma.

October 19, 2016: Our Announcement

We are overcome with happiness, love, gratitude, and every greatest emotion ever imagined to welcome our little pumpkin Baby Grover in April 2017!

December 9, 2016: 50 Per Cent Loaded

Today marks a year to the day we found out we were expecting with our first baby, the day we would have been expecting our second baby, and the halfway mark with this baby, our third. This year has given us such precious gifts, memories, and life lessons that we will hold on to forever. At the time of our heartbreak, I would have said much differently, but here I am now, and I wouldn't have it any other way. Our first baby made us happy, our second made us travel, and this baby is allowing us to be doing what we love. We are so eagerly waiting to meet you, our most precious gift.

January 2, 2017: Love of My Life

We worry about what a child will become tomorrow,
yet we forget that he is someone today.
—Stacia Tauscher

Today marked the saddest and happiest day of our lives. We were happy to be your parents but sad it couldn't be for longer. You are gone too soon, but you were held and loved for every single second of your beating life. You are the most beautiful and purest soul I have ever honourably met and that is something I will carry with me for a lifetime.

You are the love of my life.

How crazy it is that we track our lives so closely when we are pregnant, knowing we are with another soul, yet we don't do this in our day-to-day life. This shows the love, new hope, and excitement we have for the lives we are able to hold.

January 15, 2017: A Message from a University Classmate

You have been in my thoughts and prayers all week. I am so sorry for your loss. Coming from experience, it's something you will carry forever. My words are not adequate to express the sorrow I feel for your loss. You sharing your story online is an inspiration, with such courage. I want to thank you, as it gave me the opportunity to remember my twin girls and the struggles that I have overcome. You truly are a beautiful person.

The strangers and strangers-turned-friends that have found me, and I them, along the way during these dark days are dazzling. As I recount everything, I see how much support I had the entire time, even when I felt like no one was there. We are not alone.

January 17, 2017: Supernatural

Tonight, while chatting in bed about Kaia (as we did in the wee hours of the night because I would often wake up crying), the dresser next to Phillip fell over completely. How did that happen; we hadn't touched it, and the way it fell was like it was pushed, and it would have taken a great deal of effort to flip it. We both started laughing freakishly, and were convinced you, dear Kaia, were forcefully haunting us in a friendly way. Something we both can never explain, but we both witnessed, just like our love for you.

January 25, 2017: Taking Flight

My elementary-school friend Tasha and I went to Nashville to escape; I was in desperate need of flying away. Tasha had just gone through a breakup and me a broken heart. We were both experiencing loss. We drank too much, partied too hard, and it felt just right. We made friends in the streets, with spontaneous outbursts of laughter and tears. I got so drunk on the Sprocket Rocket Party Bike, and then I got kicked out of a bar after I puked on their floor. Then I found myself on a church bus instead of our shuttle bus; we were kicked off.

We drank away our pain, danced on the table at Coyote Ugly bar, did shots with the server, wore hats that said bad words, and enjoyed a meal at Dick's Last Resort restaurant. We really enjoyed drinking our extra big beers that we never ordered. There were beautiful moments, too, as we sang together at the Country Music Hall of Fame, went to the Grand Ole Opry, and listened to the song "Love Me More" by Maggie Rose. That song was in our heads for the remainder of the trip.

We listened to live music at the famous Tootsies Orchid Lounge and found the Parthenon replica as we tried to look for the Nashville show set. One day, as we walked the streets, we came across angel wings painted on a wall. Next to them were baby wings painted as well. I found the symbolism powerful and started to cry. Together, we learned to find our wings so we could continue to fly.

January 27, 2017: Marked

This morning I got a tattoo of Kaia's little feet placed on my left ribs. I went, laid down, and heard the buzz of the needle, but I felt nothing, completely numb. I smiled and snapped a picture and jumped in my car, loaded up at the liquor store, and headed for Collingwood, Ontario.

The nurses I worked with in the PCCU had planned a fun girls' weekend getaway at a cottage. Many of the girls did not have kids of their own, and I realized I was one of the first to try to have a baby out of most of my friends. The minute I got there I started hammering back the drinks. My theme of numbing myself continued as I jumped in the hot tub with my clothes, forgetting my freshly inked tattoo. I vaguely remembered that I was not to submerge it in water for up to six weeks... whoopsies! I was reckless and it felt so good. At the bar I was flipping drinks, doing flips on the dance floor, getting flipped off with a warning not to dance on chairs, and basically bringing a taste of Nashville honky-tonk to my girls.

Once back at the cottage, I showed off my tattoo to some of the girls and they all said, full of compassion but not knowing how to relate or what to say, how beautiful it was. I couldn't hide anymore. Where was my numbness now when I needed it most? As I started to speak, my voice faltered as I said, "It's so cute, isn't it?" The words came before I could even hold them back and then the tears. Thinking of those tiny feet, I was a blubbering mess and had to run to my room and drift away to sleep into an unconscious, numb abyss again. It was all just too much.

The rest of the weekend no further words were spoken of my girl Kaia, and I pretended to be having the time of my life, but all I wanted was to not be drunk, nurturing my baby, and having quaint conversations with my work friends about the excitement I had for the future —the plans, the baby room, the names, the dreams I had for her. And to eventually share her birth story.

February 3, 2017: Face Plant

I had booked a facial to do something for myself. When I arrived, my aesthetician said, "Oh wow did you have your baby already? You look great." It had completely slipped my mind to let her know. My relaxing experience had abruptly become uncomfortable. I thought about how I never wanted to do another errand, let alone a self-care errand, again. She said she was sorry for our loss, though I quickly downplayed it. I remembered our last session, where the whole spa staff was buzzing with excitement about the baby. Today, I lay there in silence, covering up in my own mask, smiling, and doing small-talking nonsense, unable to stop the thoughts of Kaia. The exciting baby ramblings were now just deadened, faint memories.

A Tribute to Baby Kaia

*I was nurturing, carrying, and feeling a baby I loved,
even if it was for a short time.*

Kaia: Pure, Hawaiian for sea.

Belle: Feminine, French for beautiful

February 11, 2017: My Pure Beauty

Oh my dearest sweet Kaia, there is so much to reflect back on and to
say about you.

We had been asked at our next obstetrician (OB) follow-up appointment if we wanted to be referred to a fertility clinic. Usually after three
miscarriages, they suggest this path, but the doctor was willing to
make the referral after two miscarriages in our case. One hundred
times, yes please . . . I didn't want to wait and miscarry one more time
before I was seen. How horrible that the medical professionals act
like it's just one more miscarriage, but to us, it is another baby lost.

Both Phillip and I had bloodwork done, which was done for all
couples going to the fertility clinic, to check for any chromosomal
abnormalities. We were both fine. We went home and were to discuss
options in the next month, but in the meantime, I was to start taking
baby aspirin in case I had a clotting disease that causes miscarriages. I
was also prescribed progesterone in case I had a weak uterus. It all
sounded promising.

The week prior to our appointment at the fertility clinic, I found out
I was pregnant again. I continued to take all the pills. I announced the

pregnancy to Phillip, still cutesy and hopeful, by putting car-themed baby clothes in the laundry basket as we folded them together. I wanted to have a little fun this time. When we met the doctor, she said, "Well, hello there, Fertile Myrtle."

I chuckled at this but also felt kind of guilty. My hairdresser, who had been trying to conceive for several years, came to my mind. In fact, I even saw her at the clinic during one of our visits. Although she would say she couldn't imagine losing a pregnancy, I sincerely couldn't imagine her experience, as I still felt we had hope every time we got pregnant. Getting pregnant was never our problem, yet here we were at a fertility clinic. It was keeping the babies that I needed all the help in the world with.

So we went for weekly ultrasounds until we were ten-weeks along. I remember bawling when I heard your heartbeat for the first time; you were already making our dreams happen. As I left with a bounce in my step, there stood another couple in tears. They were just told they had a miscarriage. How awful it was to cross the same hallways when you are given a clean slate of health and when others are handed their worst fear. I was feeling sorry and tremendously sympathetic. Quietly though, I said to myself: *Been there, done that. We finally dodged that bullet. Now is our time to have the happy ending.* Little did I know that in a matter of weeks, I too would have to walk those same dreaded hallways on the OB floor with those going home with healthy babies.

But at the time, there was a heartbeat. We had graduated from the clinic, and I had the right drugs. All would go dreamily. There were also challenges, though. I sometimes found it difficult to work in the paediatric intensive care unit with babies who had Trisomy 18, cerebral palsy, hydrocephalus, or hypoxic-ischemic encephalopathy, to name a few. Sometimes those babies had severe brain damage and had tracheostomies done soon after birth, leaving the nurses to take care of them until their time came and the families having to make unimaginable decisions. I said to Phillip that I couldn't imagine ever having a child with special needs. Did I subconsciously plant that seed, or did the aspirin and progesterone (the drugs that in my mind were helping us keep our baby) end up working so well to keep a pregnancy that should have ended in miscarriage?

On October 10, we announced your presence to our family, with specially made t-shirts for each relative, such as "I'm the Crazy Uncle,"

"Special Auntie," "Super Uncle," and "Workout Buddy for Auntie." We made shirts for our parents to symbolize their promotion to grandparenthood, with "Grandma EST 2017" and "Classic Car Opa." I wore one that read, "I can't keep calm I'm going to be a mommy," and Daddy wore "I am your FATHER." Baby Grover cupcakes were a hit; green and pink soothers were placed in the mouth of each Sesame Street Grover. The future was bright with you in our lives. We were so thankful for you that we shared you with the whole family on Thanksgiving.

I remember being Little Red Motherhood for Halloween and into December feeling your kicks for the first time (not knowing they could ever be taken from me). I was working eagerly, carolling cheerily, decorating for Christmas, and laughing all the way. Excitement was in the air. All was falalala lovely. I was working and so excited to finally post our first pregnancy picture on social media, with "Loading: 50 per cent complete" painted on my belly. Just as we made it to the halfway mark, and I was rejuvenated after coming home from up north, I was told on the phone that the ultrasound showed our baby's heart was backwards.

We had waited the safe thirteen weeks to tell family and even waited for the halfway mark to announce on Facebook, yet we were not in the so-called safe zone at all. Immediately, I called my mama in hysterics. She replied, "I am sorry. Perhaps it is my fault." My mama, too, had been born with a congenital heart defect.

We began to research our own families, looking at everyone in a way we never had before, asking questions we had never inquired about before. My mom had an aortic valve replacement in January 2013. My cousin had open heart surgery at birth. Oma's niece lost a four-year-old to heart problems. Phillip was born with "a silly foot," which is apparently common from where his family is from in France.

But in that moment, would you believe, I blamed my mama even though my brothers, sisters, and I had all gone for echocardiograms, knowing that there was a one in five chance we could have the same issue. The odds had been in our favour. There were five of us, and none of us had it. Yes, there were times that I felt lucky to not have a defect myself, although I think I would rather have it if I could spare my baby. But then I thought, *Do I carry the trait? Is this my fault again?*

The weeks to come were a blur. We went for a fetal echocardiogram to get a closer look and confirm that the heart was backwards. To me, the blood flow looked great, but we were then told all of the things wrong with our baby's heart. Many babies did not survive these challenges, but the doctors said they could refer us to SickKids Hospital in Toronto.

On a side note, we were told that we were having a girl, and this was unwelcome knowledge. It was not the gender reveal we had envisioned. We had previously, before hearing the diagnosis, wanted to wait until the birth to find out our baby's gender. A seemingly simple wish that many expecting families get to make that now wouldn't happen for us. Phillip and I left through the long hallways of the hospital where I work, the ones I have walked many times before bringing patients to these same tests—the hallways I was praying none of my coworkers would see me in. We faced those hallways, tightly holding hands, unable to look at each other; no words could be spoken. All we had was each other to hold on to.

We had been told that the problems that were presenting on ultra-sound had many characteristics of DiGeorge syndrome, although we wouldn't know this for sure until we did an amniocentesis. I found out that DiGeorge syndrome happens when part of the DNA of chromosome 22 is missing, and it can cause developmental delay in many areas of the body.

The second issue was that an amniocentesis entailed sticking a big needle into my belly to obtain a fluid sample for genetic testing—joy to the world. We shared all of the news with our family, pleading for them to make the decision for us.

That night, I borrowed a friend's log-in at a university so I could spend all night reading anything and everything to save my baby. Most studies I found had very few participants and too many factors to count, such as infection from surgery and the high number of surgeries required, not to mention the other issues related to DiGeorge syndrome. My mama tried to be helpful by saying that her friend's sister had a little girl with DiGeorge syndrome who was high functioning, but she had needed many surgeries.

I remember Phillip and I looking at each other in a new light since going for testing to see if we were carriers of DiGeorge syndrome. We asked each other if we maybe had the syndrome, but since we were higher functioning, we never needed to complete the testing. Phillip's ears suddenly looked small and lower set, and I noticed how my eye openings were kind of small, and my upper lip was on the thinner side—some of the distinct facial features associated with DiGeorge syndrome. We both also weren't the best in school. This served as a kind of comic relief for us, although it also was not funny in many ways.

This would be the reality if we carried the baby to term. Our baby would need to be delivered by a scheduled C-section so that they could take her straight to surgery, without me even holding her and without me even knowing if she would survive the surgery. Four or more surgeries would be needed in the first year of her life. We would spend our daughter's entire life in hospital. While it was something we would have done in a heartbeat, it was not the life we wanted for our daughter. After talking about if we ever were to leave the hospital and the fear of her heart giving out at any moment, I remember Phillip saying, "I don't want to be shoveling snow with her one day, and she spontaneously dies." In most of the studies I had read the life expectancy was seven to eighteen years, maximum, assuming no complications. It was just too much to wrap our heads around. But we trusted our high-risk obstetrician when she said the heart complications were just the tip of the iceberg of the health problems our baby would have.

Another part of the nightmare was that inductions for therapeutic abortions had to be done prior to twenty-four weeks gestation. We were running out of time to decide. We had done the amniocentesis to be sure that the DiGeorge syndrome diagnosis was accurate, but the results would arrive after the decision needed to be made for an induction. How could we decide without the facts?

Did I mention it was Christmas? So here we were, almost a year after our first loss, very pregnant and pretending to be cheery as we celebrated a baby that would never live. There were presents for our baby. There were presents for all the children—hockey sticks that my sisters had given my cousins—and for some reason that is what set me off. The hockey my child would never play.

I drank some Baileys at Oma's and felt my little sister, Selena, was secretly judging me for it, even knowing that our baby would die. But the truth was I didn't care. I thought our sweet girl should at least get to enjoy some booze in her life because not drinking felt like the one thing I had done right in the pregnancy. I also remember Phillip saying, "We are not pregnant, and we do not have a baby until it is alive and in our arms."

That was hard to hear when I was still pregnant with our baby, even though I understood where he was coming from. The thought of a live baby in my arms seemed less and less possible. She might be the only baby of ours that I got to hold, and she would soon be dead in my arms.

On Boxing Day, and before we had to make our final decision about keeping the pregnancy, my sisters and I spontaneously left for Chicago for a weekend getaway. My mother-in-law was livid, asking, "How could you do this? What if something happens to the baby while you are away?"

My response: "I wish that something bad would happen to the baby. Then we wouldn't have to make this unimaginable decision. And also, what worse thing can happen to this baby?" I was furious at everyone and everything. I just wanted to run away from the nightmare that was my current life.

Yet we had the best time in Chicago, walking the streets, taking pictures with headless statues, eating Lucky Charms, almost running into people in the streets, and watching Netflix in our super-hot hotel room. We went to the play *A Charlie Brown Christmas*, as that was all we could get tickets for on short notice. We were the only ones without kids, and the cast members asked us, "Hey guys, what do you think is in Snoopy's doghouse?" Thinking of the trip still makes me belly laugh. Sure, there was so much pain, but it disguised itself in a form of hysteria and laughter.

Sometimes, when someone you love is about to die, you hear these stories of such triumph in their final days: The day before their final day they were at their best, a day of ultimate zest, and then the next day, gone. That was how I felt—so full of life, so indestructible, and a little too silly, before the day that came and killed a part of me.

We had made the excruciating decision to have an induction, and we knew that our planned induction day would be the day after the New Year's holiday (which we certainly did not celebrate). We were instructed to wait for the hospital's phone call when a bed became available, and they were ready for us. As we prepared for the inevitable, we tried to keep busy. On the morning of January 1, Phillip and I went for a walk, together but alone with our thoughts. When we got back, I insisted we take a picture of us in the Chevelle. Although it felt and seemed strange, I needed to know and have proof that our family had a chance to be together in our family car. Later that day, I invited my sisters over, as I couldn't take the waiting any longer and needed their distraction. I had been in my hospital clothes all day when they finally called us at 10:00 p.m. The phone call that we had been waiting for and dreading all day, yet we still did not believe it when it actually came, waking us up to the reality of this unreal event.

We arrived at the hospital at 11:00 p.m., at which point I was oddly excited to meet our girl and finally deliver our baby, having made it so much further along in a pregnancy than ever before. However, even having looked at pictures of babies born at twenty-four weeks (our girl's gestational age), the preparation still left me with no idea of what to expect.

They triaged us, took us to our room, and popped in the pill that would start the induction right away. As we waited for the pill to take effect, Phillip and I ordered pizza so we could focus on casually eating rather than on what the pill meant and what we were about to do.

It didn't take long before I began to writhe in pain. From a tripod position on the bed, I looked up at Phillip with tears in my eyes. Although I wasn't complaining, Phillip quickly called the nurse. I cried with the physical pain but knew it was heightened by the emotional pain. As I pleaded with Phillip not to tell the nurse I was in pain, he said, "You don't need to be tough," although I felt like I deserved all of the pain.

Drained, I listened to Phillip, who again reminded me that I didn't need to suffer more than I already had. I decided to get an epidural quite early in the process, and quite frankly Phillip was right; it was all too unbearable. I had no energy left to try and be strong.

As we waited for our daughter's birth, I lay comfortably in the bed, chatting with my husband, somehow cracking jokes with him and drinking tea as the sun dipped under the clouds and shone on us through our fifth floor window.

The on-call doctor who delivered our girl was a urinary and gyne-cological doctor, one that did not specialize in this kind of thing. As our daughter was born, he just said, "There it is." No sympathy. No nothing. I felt like we were being judged as he left the room. It was horrible.

They directly put our girl in my arms. *Our baby girl has been born with a heartbeat,* my brain screamed out. *Somebody save her.* What if all the ultrasounds were wrong? Selfishly, we wanted you so badly, but it was also selfish to make you suffer all of your life just so we could have you for a little while. I had to try to remind myself that the plan of the early induction was for you not to go to surgery.

Kaia Belle was born on January 2 at 6:56 p.m. and died at 8:50 p.m. She had a heartbeat for what felt like at least an hour, although I will never know this for certain as time stopped, sped up, and disappeared. I remember feeling when Kaia went cold in my hands, when her colour drastically changed from dark to light as her circulation stopped, but I do not and will never know the time this happened. She was pronounced much later, which I wasn't aware of until I saw the time written on her death certificate. I couldn't give her up, so they could take her away to pronounce her. I never once looked at the clock. I never took my eyes or hands off her the whole time she was with us.

Oh, Kaia. I felt your heart beating on my thumb; I felt your warmth and peace. I looked into your innocent soul that had such unconditional beauty. You were never tainted by the power-hungry world we live in, and we can forever keep our memories of you pure. You were the epitome of perfect in our eyes. I relished every part of you and will never forget how I could open and close your mouth with my pinky finger and how you curled your whole hand around my index finger. I loved your button nose, healthy big cheeks, your Daddy's hands, and your Mommy's toes. It's so amazing how you encompassed all that we are.

My Oma, my parents, and Phillip's parents joined us after Kaia had died. I took pictures, and I eagerly showed off our girl. As I look back, this gives me chills, as I was happily replicating a mother with a newborn who was celebrating her baby. Phillip didn't want the pictures. At the time, when I took those photos of our daughter, I don't even think my mind registered that my daughter was dead. I was just so proud and so in love with her in that moment. I wanted to shout her arrival over the mountaintops.

Now I see that we took photos of our dead girl; however, those pictures speak such truth. We were both excited and grieving, in love and in complete heartbreak. We had given birth, new life to death— our first and only birthing experience. That is how it looked for us. It was not like any feeling I can ever explain. It was horrifyingly beautiful.

The nightmare continued. The day after the passing of our daughter, the funeral home called. We went to the funeral home together, something we never thought we would have to do. In the days following, we had to go to the hospital to pick up our baby's little feet moulds, and the cardiac surgeon at SickKids Hospital called us about our missed appointment, a consultation that was never cancelled. I had to register her birth, since she had a heartbeat at birth. A new health card came in the mail. I didn't know how to register the birth and then death. There was nowhere on the registry website to indicate the baby died. We were called and asked if we wanted the Canada Child Benefit. Yes please, only there is no child. I was maddened that the world went on with day-to-day life, hounding us at a time that was so sensitive.

We had an autopsy for our girl. Weeks later the results came back, and everything was confirmed. We found out in the autopsy that her heart and brain were even worse than they had expected, and her thalamus was also severely affected. The medical care team said her life would have been tragic, and we truly felt we made the right decision. Going forwards, we have a small chance of a DiGeorge syndrome diagnosis happening again, at 1 to 4 per cent. We were offered more genetic testing, and again we said we wanted to do everything we could.

Kaia, your legacy brought joy to many lives. You left a beautiful footprint in our hearts. For a short time, we could reevaluate what really mattered and that was an amazing gift.

We were so lucky to make memories with you. "Experiences and memories" is our motto, and, oh golly, you are a memory we will never forget. The six months I spent with you were an important and memorable part of my life. Even now, I still wake up in the middle of the night convinced I feel your kicks. It amazes me how the body remembers.

You are forever in my thoughts in all that I do. I have not stopped feeling your determination and strength, which makes me miss you more. You were so perfect, and the feeling of you in my hands was like none I have ever experienced. Please don't ever feel like we gave up on you. You fought for every second of your triumphant life.

You always will be our little angel. How do I move on when I just want you now? You will never ever be forgotten, and you live on in each of us. Thoughts of you make me smile, and I feel honoured to have met you, as I never met your siblings. You definitely were my favourite hello and my hardest goodbye.

Every morning, I promise I am going to wake up and tell myself we are going to have a beautiful, healthy baby. I want you to see the parents we could have been to you. Your dad and I are so happy, so in love, and so eager for a family. Please be with us in this time and be the best sister, one looking over your future siblings. We are still holding on to hope that one day we will meet your siblings, ones that I know, from deep in the sacred part of my heart where you live, your siblings that you will send us.

Family Day is coming up, and we are excited to start trying again. You gave us that gift, but trust us, we would rather have you. I feel that everything is going to work out, as I have newfound compassion, enjoyment, priorities, and insight in how to live my life. I am getting help, and I'm going to be the best me I can be, in this life, forever, and as I live for you and through you always.

Forever yours,
Your mama

February 10, 2017: Screaming in My Mind

It is honestly incredible what the human body is capable of. Phillip and I supported each other as we went through extremely tough things. He came with me to return my maternity clothes. When the clerk asked what was wrong with them, I yelled to the poor woman, "I don't need them anymore."

She asked no further questions.

Phillip admitted that walking through the mall and seeing what seemed like every single person with a baby in a stroller was unbearable. How come they could all have healthy babies? How come our friends could announce their pregnancies with no fear of anything going wrong?

We thought we were in the clear, having previously gone through two losses. Kaia was supposed to be our rainbow baby (a baby that comes after loss, which she was, just not how we expected). This was our time. We had been through the bad; we couldn't possibly have more bad. But, yup, that was us. As our friends had babies, Phillip and I were almost mad at them. Of course, we weren't really. We were just so jealous that everything went so smoothly for them.

As all our family and friends said they were thinking of us and praying for us, I would scream in my mind: *What does praying about this fix?*

Pray for what? They would also say it happened for a reason. They said all the things people say when they don't know what to say and are truly just trying to be helpful. What reason could there be for this? My husband and I are good people. We've been saving for a baby, working on providing the perfect house, always planning trips, and daydreaming of projects and activities to do with our kids. I recall the fun we had coming up with and listing Celtic names, like Declan (with my sister Selena saying, "like a duckling?") and Ivan Aveni. Then more traditional names, like Isabella (Is-a-bell-ringing?) or Justin Case. My mother would ask, "Just in case of what?" We did this so often, clearly wishing for kids to name.

Our dark humour started to get a hold of us. Phillip would say, "Maybe if we just become meth heads, our next pregnancy will work out." We had to use humour, as these miscarriages and the birth of Kaia were starting to affect us and our relationship. We no longer talked like we used to, and when we did, it was usually about things we wanted to do for ourselves, reverting back to the selflessness of prekids and even predating. We didn't talk about what we used to enjoy together or what we wanted to do together as a couple. Without even realizing, Phillip buried himself in side-jobs, and I took more nursing contracts up north. I made arrangements to go on more trips with friends, trips that were not with my husband. It was clear that we no longer knew how to be together like before, when we filled our days with date nights, movies, and adventures, as now making plans seemed to lose their original and loving purpose. There was now a new loneliness. Being together reminded both of us of our lost children.

I had been seeing a counsellor named Janice, who specialized in fertility issues and pregnancy loss. We talked about our loss, our relationship, and the things people would say to try and make us feel better. A personal favourite comment we heard was "Have some faith. It will all work out." We did have faith with every pregnancy and look how well they turned out. How in the world was I supposed to have more faith? But the crazy part is that I still do. I think back to the families I used to see in the intensive care unit (ICU) with tragic events changing their lives forever, and they were grounded in faith.

People also said to us, "At least you can get pregnant. Just try again." Yes, this was reassuring, but I also felt like it invalidated my previous pregnancies and like a future pregnancy would just replace them.

Phillip said it so well: "Yes, there are people who have it worse. But right now, this is our worst, and it doesn't make it easier to think of others who are worse off. This is our struggle right now."

At one point, I honestly thought the reason it wasn't working for us was because we weren't meant to be together or weren't meant to have kids, and I worried about a failed marriage as a result. Some days, it just seemed easier to give in to "it's just not supposed to be." Phillip again reminded me that many couples don't have kids together and still make it work. Phillip was trying to reassure me that our relationship was strong and not defined by kids before this, and I was comforted that he was not going to leave me if we could not have children. But this put a whole new kind of stress on us, one we never knew before. We were entering new territory and had to learn how to flap our wings together, harder and stronger.

February 11, 2017: Letters

A Letter from Your Gramma

Dearest Kaia Belle,

You brought your Mommy and Daddy so much joy and happiness. At six weeks, four days, your Mommy got to see your heartbeat for the first time. It was so exciting to hear all about the ultrasound updates. Your Mommy was so thrilled when she could see and hear your heart beating and knew that you were growing into your own little person.

As the weeks went on and your Mommy got to see your little hands, feet, legs, arms, cute button nose, and everything about you, she knew she was falling deeply in love with you, and that love will be with your Mommy and Daddy forever. You were known as the little dancing bean, and you were moving and grooving a lot inside your Mommy. Your Mommy got to even see you sucking your thumb, and you waved at her.

Experiencing this bond with you and feeling your every movement, your Mommy was reminded every second that she was never alone. and she knew that you would always be with her.

We had such a nice celebration together at Thanksgiving, when your Mommy and Daddy announced to all the family that they were expecting with you. Although we will never get to have you with us Earth side, you will always shape who we are and who we become. In the short twenty-four weeks that you were with your Mommy and Daddy and all of us, you taught us all the greatest amount of love and happiness. May you shine through all of us to make us better people and may you help us to hold on to the love that we have for each other.

Kaia Belle, your inner beauty will always be with us all. Thanks for being a big part of our lives and giving us the wonderful great memories.

We love you forever, dearest Kaia Belle Grover

A Letter from Great Oma

To my Sweet Angel,

You always will be my first great-grandchild. I made you a little hat with love. Take care of your Mommy and Daddy from heaven. Love you so much, sweetie.

Great Oma

A Letter from Your Auntie

Hey Kaia,

You know how everyone has that one crazy relative that they think is so weird. Well, I think you know hands down I was that relative for you. Remember the feeling you had when you were so hyper and wanted to kick and dance like crazy? Yeah, that was because your crazy Aunt Kerrie came to town. I will admit I might have a slight addiction to a glorious beverage called an iced cappuccino, and basically I can convince anyone around me to have some too, so your Mommy couldn't really say no. She may have had one or two, and these drinks contain a wee bit of coffee, so I am sorry for getting you a bit wound up on that, but at least you were able to tell if I was around or not!

Also as an aunt, I feel it's my duty to teach you some rebellious ways, which I did do! I may or may not have smuggled you into America for a crazy adventure in Chicago against grandma's wishes. I know that was a pretty risky move, teaching you to disobey your grandma like that, but it's fun living on the edge sometimes, right? I think so. I had a great trip with you tagging along, and it was pretty cool showing you around another part of the world. So thanks for being there.

You brought a lot of sunshine to a lot of people and know that a whole whack of people love you, especially your Mommy and Daddy. Thanks for teaching all of us to live life to the fullest.

Love you,
Crazy Aunt Kerrie

Babe #4
Chemical Pregnancy

February 13, 2017: False Hope

After delivering Kaia, I was still testing positive on pregnancy tests. This may have just been circulating hCG levels remaining high; however, it was distressing. On February 8, I saw a bald eagle. Bald eagles have a particular significance to me because it is a bird I always seem to see before I experience loss in my life. Today, I am bleeding again. I think I may have had a chemical pregnancy—a very early pregnancy loss that occurs because the fertilized egg never attaches to the uterus.

How quickly I had already started thinking and fantasizing about how we might be pregnant again. I even started painting rooms upstairs trying to distract myself, finishing the nursery, pretending like I was painting it for an office room but knowing full well I was still working on it for Kaia/my future baby.

Weeks of tears after the loss of Kaia, I was still researching helplessly. Was there anything else we could have done? Phillip took my hand and brought me to the couch, and there we sat with his laptop as he researched things. What unfolded was the booking of an impromptu trip to Africa. Phillip said we needed to get away; we needed this. Not that Africa would ever heal the loss of our daughter, but it gave us excitement in our life, excitement for the future. I sometimes don't believe we still deserve to have adventure and moments of happiness, but suddenly we were together in the moment and that was all that mattered.

February 16, 2017: Addressing

I remember driving home from getting groceries and seeing a bald eagle seconds before my phone dinged, and my work friend Claire asked me if I could come over. As I entered her house, it was noticeably quiet, which was odd as she has two kids. I met her up in her bedroom. There she was, set up with a book, her knitting, and a tea, and she was deeply upset.

After a few introductory words she blurted out, "I am having a miscarriage." The words came out so fast and so sharp in my ears, but I could tell she just needed to say it and couldn't hold it in any longer. My friend was crying to me, saying how she just didn't understand how this was happening to her. She was in shock—she really believed it would never happen to her—as they, too, thought they were in the clear having never had problems before. After all, miscarriage only happened in the beginning of a pregnancy, right? I totally felt the pain she felt, but as she was crying to me, I felt a deep-pitted bitterness course throughout me. Here was my friend who already had two healthy beautiful babies, and I couldn't help but judge her. I felt awful. I should have been able to empathize with her, but my grief was too raw.

I thought to myself: *Well, at least her grief is not as bad as mine. At least she already has children. How nice it must be to have the chance to have another.* Here I was, feeling like I truly had nothing as I sat empty handed a mere two months after losing Kaia. Sharing her miscarriage with me, without warning, and expecting my support felt like my friend was saying I should have been over my grief by now. She spoke of how she had told everyone around Christmas, but she didn't want to tell our family with all that we were going through waiting for our induction day. Wow, how bloody considerate.

I understood just how excited she had been, as she had been with every pregnancy before, as all women should be. She wanted to blurt out her excitement the same way she needed to blurt out her grief. I understood, since I, too, once felt excited about those things. But at that time, I just couldn't understand it.

As I went to leave, my friend said, "At least now I finally understand what you have been through." She had joined the club, so to speak— the club that nobody wants to be a part of. This left me speechless. *Finally understand? You have no idea what I've been through.* I left in a fury, angry and defeated, but still trying to appear empathetic.

In the depths of heartache, nothing we say is right. That is the truth. Nobody really understands another person's hurt; every experience is so different. I was consumed by my own grief and couldn't realize her grief was real and valid. How dare she ask me to be with her just because I got it. I was still processing my own loss. She, of course, didn't see it that way, and I did only because I was hurting so much. She was looking for support when she needed it most, and I was looking to be alone when I needed support the most. In the end, we both just wanted our grief to be validated and to talk about our babies that lived within us for a short time, wanting to honour them and fill that deep, dark hole that was left within.

February 20, 2017: Hiding

Here I am, hiding upstairs in our guest bedroom, staring at a framed picture of Kaia—a picture I keep hidden in the closet so that Phillip won't see it. He doesn't like seeing her picture or like me having it anywhere visible around the house. I also don't want to appear weak or that I am still lingering on something that I can't do anything about. But I can't help but look. Look and wonder, staring at the magnitude of her deep beauty and purity that touched the hollows of my soul. I need to remember all of her; I can never let her image ever slip away from my mind. I feel I owe her this. I am so terrified I will forget the littlest details, and if I do, then I will have failed her and her abiding memory.

Your Mommy loved you way too much to throw this picture away, although others make me feel like I must heal and move on. The constant debate: I can do this, I have to, but I can't. I can't let go. I feel I have already failed you.

I meditate on you, and I sob and end up just wanting you even more. I feel I have to hide this longing and heartbreak from the people I love and from the world. I lock you up inside of me, never to release you from the intense, cavernous grip you have on my heart.

March 2, 2017: Living

One . . . Two . . . Three . . . Take Off!
To Africa, to leave everything, every judgment,
every comment, every thought,
every everything behind.

We arrived in Swakopmund, often called the adventure capital of Namibia. We upgraded to a couples room, reviewed the activities, and decided to sign up for skydiving—no thinking, no regrets, and within thirty minutes we were on a bus headed for the thrill of our lives. There was no going back. Wow, how do I explain when adrenalin awaits? My stomach did flip flops as I contemplated what I was about to do—jump out of a plane. In the distance, we watched as members from our group went before us and were little dots falling from the sky—their rush of exhilaration and one of our group mates saying "What did I just do?" as he landed. Well, you just voluntarily decided to jump out of a plane. And we were next.

The jump included getting into a jumpsuit and harness, walking up to a little bush plane with the side of the plane completely open and sitting with our feet feeling like they were out of the plane. As we lifted up, I felt sick. Ten thousand feet! As we got higher and higher, and twenty deep breaths later, I actually started to feel relaxed. For a moment so brief, we were free before the rush. Our instructors and jumping partners read their e-books and ate sandwiches on the ride up, using our backs as tables. After we got higher in the air, we were eventually attached to our guides—yup, we didn't realize that we would not be strapped in the entire time before the jump. Yet not knowing that prior was helpful and so freeing.

When our time came, we stuck our feet over the edge, put our heads back, and prepared for one of the greatest and most vomit-inducing (or last) moments of our lives. I watched as Phillip literally just looked like he got sucked and whipped out of the plane, like a vortex took him. Oh, wow, goodbye Phillip, hope to see you on the other side. You can hardly scream as you get sucked out of a plane because your belly goes into your esophagus and the pressure is far too great. Whether it was a moment of irresponsibility because we felt like we had nothing to live for (which of course wasn't true) or of pure thrill, we knew this was something we needed to do together before kids. Yes, we still held on to the thought of having children, and we knew we would never be this irresponsible once we had kids, but for now, we were and could be those irresponsible kids.

When it was my turn, the air took hold of me, bearing my weight. I felt weightless, like the air was holding me in some way while I was falling free like a bird. I didn't even fight the air as my arms shot up, and I embraced it in its full force entirely. I was done resisting. Thirty-five seconds of pure free fall and five minutes soaring through the sky, overlooking the purples hues of the salt pan, the white desert, the sand dunes, and the varying blues of the Atlantic. Such incredible magnitude and sharply contrasted colours, all within eye shot. Earth, water, and sky as far as the eye could see, and I had a fire within.

What a pure rush—being able to live in the moment by releasing, letting go, and being free, even if only temporarily. This was our FTW (fuck the world) trip, and we were literally on top of the world. I honestly didn't think of anything else. You can't even begin to think of anything else when you are falling to your (non)death. Phew! We may just have had lots to live for after all.

We were both bouncy and giddy at the end and so happy to see each other. I felt that life was good being able to experience adventure like that, and it made me want to experience more and more. I tried to appreciate what was granted to me and right in front of me at that moment. We emailed the family to speak of our grand survival and for the first time in what felt like months, we were reignited, alive, and refuelled by our love for each other.

It turns out that it was a time to be reunited together, the three of us. A time to bask in Africa's vastness, purity, and beauty. Phillip and I jumped out of a plane and leaped towards the future together, letting go and being purely in the present, something we never thought we would do. Kaia gave us that strength to dream. As the sun beamed on us, we knew it was her saying hello and telling us she was okay. After the jump, the sun hid again, but it was now time to believe again.

When we came home, I put pictures up in the office/nursery of the majestic baby animals with their mamas that we had seen in Africa. I decorated the room in African memorabilia, knowing it was a theme I wanted for our baby. A theme, a memory, where we were alive, happy in love, in the wild, and free, as we wished for a future Simba cub to be.

March 27, 2017: Rebirth

Phillip confirmed that he in fact did see a bald eagle in the small village where we live. Finally, he believes me. This is the day that I believe is your rebirth, Kaia.

March 29, 2017: Forwards

As I left my counselling session, Janice's last words as she hugged me were "Good things will happen for you." I stepped out of her office, and the first thing I saw crossing my path as I walked out of those doors was a woman pushing her baby in a stroller. The father walked next to her with the dog, and the sun was beaming down, highlighting them. I recalled Christmas shopping and being utterly pissed off at every person pushing a stroller. This time something felt different. This time, I did not feel anger or hate for those parents. Instead, I felt love, joy, and hope. I knew things were beginning to change.

March 31, 2017: Hope

My elementary school friends got together with me to celebrate my birthday prior to me leaving for a nursing work contract up north. As they tried to take my picture, a light speck kept interfering with the picture taking. My friend Amanda said those flecks of light are usually a spirit. As a birthday gift, I received a Hope bracelet and a Heaven Sent bracelet that I put on to take with me.

April 1, 2017: Hopelessness

Today, we celebrated our friend Jess's stag and doe. There we were, partying with many shenanigans, when (no joke) my Hope bracelet broke. All I could think was that surely all hope was lost for a future baby. Remembering the eagle, I prepared myself to go up north to hopefully forget all about this horrendous "no hope" omen.

April 4, 2017: Twenty-Six

Oh my darling sweet light,

It is my birthday. As I write this, I think about how I should be celebrating this month with you, but instead I am up north in Attawapiskat Ontario. I signed up for a month contract, to fly way up, away from home and my thoughts, escaping it all. I didn't want to be swarmed by the people I love for my birthday while remembering that I should be at home joyously awaiting your arrival.

The first work event I encountered here was an eight-month-old who had been sexually assaulted and killed by an uncle while the parents were away delivering twins. Immersing myself in this terrible tragedy served to numb out my own pain, and my plan worked, as all I could think about were the horrors of the world.

I feel lost without you. You were my biggest celebration of all. How overjoyed I was to get to share my birthday month with you. I am overcome with sadness and can't understand why I lost you. Why I can't hold you and love you come the end of April. I hold you in every ray of the beaming sun that comes my way, even more all the way up here in the great white north, where the light reaches us much longer. You bring peace to my day, even for a moment, and I know you are with me. You will guide me on my path; I have total faith in that.

Although I had hoped to be pregnant this month, in honour of your due date, I have now lost hope in that. I lost hope in the job I thought I wanted. I lost hope in my every ability—my career, health, finances, and life's purpose. Nonetheless, I hold on to the hope that the purity I felt through you will come through me in remarkable ways when I least expect it, and I can find comfort in that.

Today you sent me hope through a three-year-old girl. I got to join the staff in singing happy birthday, and we had birthday brownies. I find hope when I come across things that I open myself up to. I am currently reading a book that shows that our journey through life requires hope, passion, courage, independence, self-discipline, and perseverance. You, my love, are in some ways helping me to conquer all of the above. Shine all your light on me.

Part 3
Learning to Fly

Every bird has to balance, run, leap,
and flap before it first learns to fly.

Babe #5
Case Emerson Grover

April 12, 2017: 360 Degrees

I took a pregnancy test with a colleague while I was up north. We stole a bunch from the clinic when looking for something fun to do. We both peed on a stick to ease our boredom. I was pregnant! What? My colleague thought I was totally joking. I called my mom to see how things were back home, and she randomly told me, "I fixed your Hope bracelet."

I was overjoyed with emotion, as things all seemed to be working out. I was recently offered the easier-for-our-lives, nine-to-five job, which was so helpful to me, since the ICU was too triggering. Also, we wanted a baby so badly, and the thought that the new baby's birthday would be around Kaia's birthdate, January 2, was incredible. But I didn't want to get my hopes up. Still, I felt positive things for us. To think that in one year we could do a total 360.

April 18, 2017: Future

*When an eagle appears, you are on notice to be courageous
and stretch your limits....
Be patient with the present; know that the future holds possibilities
that you may not yet be able to see.
You are about to take flight.*

—*Fly Like the Eagle*, Trish Phillips

I had eagle moccasins made for me while up north, which I will wear in the cold winter months while thinking of you, dear baby. You will one day hear the story of your mother's obsession with bald eagles.

While wearing them, I have been creating my own art, crocheting a zebra, saying to others that it is for a friend's future baby but secretly wishing it can be for you, our next potential baby. With a positive pregnancy test, I decided to write to you.

To Baby G Jr.,

As you may know, I struggle deeply with what I am currently doing, putting pen to paper. I don't want this to just be another memento to add to a memory book for all the sweet babies I have lost. You have four guardian siblings already to start with in your life. I would say you are doing pretty well so far. As I wonder about you, I think often about my other children: how they would have been, their features, their ages, and personalities. Although I can't call you our miracle child yet, I can share with you the story of your beginnings. A story I will keep with me.

Mommy and Daddy had just returned from a trip to Africa. During that trip, we focused on living in the present, and we did many exciting things, like jumping out of a plane. Your little seed came to us perfectly after our lovely adventure. In Africa, we had the time of our lives. But we knew the ultimate time of our lives would come when we could share this life with you, our forever treasured pride and joy.

April 27, 2017: Brighter Days

My flight home from working up north was delayed a day due to the weather, but it didn't matter, as I was always thinking of Kaia, my head in the clouds. As I prepared to leave the following day, I noticed that on the ground it was dreary, blustery, and snow covered, yet as soon as the plane rose up, breaking and bursting through those clouds, the sun filled the sky. The sun that just couldn't get through the clouds to reach the ground below.

April 28, 2017: New Hope

The day I returned from up north, which was the day prior to starting my new clinic job at the eating disorder service, was the day I told dear hubby the news. I couldn't bring myself to do it when I was away from him. A part of me was scared that if I said it to him, not only would it make it real for us, but it would also make it scary for us again. I said it just nonchalantly, no special antics, just sitting at the kitchen table again.

His response: "We will just wait and see what happens."

This was secretly how I felt as well. We were both trying to be ever so protective of one another. I told my mom in the same way but did reference the Hope bracelet and what it meant to me that she fixed it when I was up north.

April 30, 2017: Kaia's Due Date

Dearest Kaia,

As I ran the half marathon today, I reflected and thought about you. Today is the date you were due to enter the world, your original birthday. You showed us that in this life, we cannot control anything, and we truly have to appreciate what we have in each moment. In this moment, I have you with me in my heart and mind. I am grateful that I had the opportunity to experience one of this world's greatest miracles, in the love and happiness a mother feels for her child. It is the kind of love and happiness I hope for all humankind. Now I take one day at a time, meditate, and try to enjoy the little moments.

On every step during my run, I said, "I am pregnant now, and everything is going to be okay." I have learned to say, "I am pregnant today" and enjoy it for now. I am grateful and mindful of right now. I am healthy and alive with every stride.

Your sibling's due date is December 23, 2017. Please be with us in this time and please be the best sister looking over your sibling. You are our greatest guardian angel. I run with you, to you, and for you, with new life inside and a new life to live.

It was the best run I have had in a while.

May 14, 2017: My First Mother's Day

Today, I felt like no one acknowledged I was a mother, even though I felt like I had experienced the undying love for my baby, the love that every mother has. I still had the gift of becoming a mommy.

What I also found hard today were the older folks in the nursing home where I work asking me if I had any children. This seemingly harmless question was followed by "Do you have a husband?" In their minds, I was at an age where I should have kids to celebrate this day with, as they had during their generation. Saying no tore me up inside but seemed easier than saying I had been trying. Yet in an effort to avoid awkwardness, I found I was more likely to say, "Yes, I had a girl" to strangers.

Maybe it would have been different had I been able to tell them I was pregnant (still too early with our history), but I still felt like an utter failure, with all the tried and failed attempts to bring a baby into this world, not knowing if this baby would ever live.

I was also sad this day, as I couldn't be celebrated the way I had wished to. I tried to celebrate thoughts of our daughter, remembering the warmth and endless love that she brought us, but it still came with such pain that felt exacerbated on this day. I had said to Phillip when he asked what was wrong: "I am just sad because you never have tears."

Phillip said, "I don't know. I've been to the bathroom a few times after you and had some tears."

We both laughed and cried, and he said, "You are and will be an excellent mother."

May 28, 2017: Recalling

The ultrasound tech told us that you looked like a healthy little baby. I was haunted by the following thought: *So did your sister. Her heartbeat sounded perfect.*

June 2, 2017: Denial

Jess's wedding night ended with me bawling in the bathroom. I drank virgin Caesars throughout the day, ordering when no one was looking. I also drank some alcohol to cover up any unnecessary rumours of a pregnancy and felt absolutely guilty about it. The guilt seemed more bearable somehow than sharing the news; we were still too early. Yet here I was thinking I should know better, and what if my selfish drinking to protect myself from disclosing our pregnancy actually affected our final chance at a baby. I desperately wanted to hide from everyone that I was pregnant. I couldn't deal with the questions. I was still thinking this baby was likely going to end in a miscarriage or terrible diagnosis.

June 9, 2017: Relief

An extensive ultrasound said no defect seen with the heart.

July 4, 2017: Backwards

The amniocentesis has been booked, and all I can think is *What if we get bad news again? What if we are the unlucky 1 per cent where the amnio causes us to lose the baby, and what if this is the baby that was actually one that could live?*

Here we are with our fifth pregnancy, and one in five women is known to have a miscarriage. With my math, five out of five this time, we should now be granted a full and whole baby. I don't want anything to mess this up.

I am currently being followed by geneticists, high-risk obstetricians, and radiologists. I'm freaking out and hope to complete this story as a Christmas miracle.

July 7, 2017: Concealing

We told the family of our exciting pregnancy on Gramma's fiftieth birthday. We didn't do anything special; we simply told everyone that we are waiting for an amniocentesis to make sure everything is okay, and we will keep them posted. The hardest part of having waited until the twenty-week anatomy scan was that I wasn't fooling anyone. Everyone already knew we were pregnant—there is only so much that skirts and dresses and flowy shirts can hide in the summer. That is also why we decided to make it official by telling everyone, but everyone was smart and sensitive enough to never bug us or ask us.

July 8, 2017: Different

My hopes shot up the minute they said the preliminary testing looked good, but that testing does not include DiGeorge syndrome. I am terrified and will be completely crushed if you don't work out. What will I do if I have to lose you, too, in just two weeks? I want you so badly. The fun we three will have, my little son. We found out you are a BOY, kind of by accident. I was eager to know, and the geneticist gave me an example using XY, which I equated to you being a boy!

To be honest, I was initially kind of sad when they said you were a boy. I think I had subconsciously hoped for a girl—a girl to replace my hopes for Kaia's life, the ones that I had planned for in my heart and mind. I secretly wanted and hoped to restore the loss of Kaia, my wished-for daughter. Janice had advised for us to find out what we were having this time, so we could mentally prepare for what that would look like. We concluded that a boy would be good, since then I wouldn't transfer my aspirations for Kaia onto a boy baby. They would be different sexes and different individuals with different hopes and dreams.

Keep on fighting for me, and I will fight for you, sweetie. I just need you to know that. I got ahead of myself again and have all my pregnancy announcement cards made for your family. I love you very much and am trying to balance work, life, and my excitement for you.

July 13, 2017: Victory

No DiGeorge syndrome! We shared the news with our family and friends. We couldn't be happier. You have raised me up. A great weight has been lifted. Thanks so much for fighting with me.

July 15, 2017: Therapy

Wisdom means to choose now what will make sense later.
—Tracee Ellis Ross

Once I knew we were DiGeorge free, I told my eating disorder clinic colleagues that I was pregnant, although they all said they had known. What I loved about working at the eating disorder clinic was that I was not tied to any one patient, and no one really knew me. I could hide my pregnancy for quite some time, which I loved and needed. I also learned a lot from my experience there, teaching cognitive behavioural therapy and listening to my patients' stories.

I would joke that pregnancy made me experience binge eating and puking, but it was truly no joke. What people go through in life is unbearable, and the need to have control over one area of your life made total sense to me. It was the loss of control over my pregnancies that completely shattered me. I wanted to control and do everything I could to make my pregnancies nothing less than perfect.

One of the ladies I worked with mentioned to me how she had lost her twins at twenty-three weeks, and she was such a support to me. It always amazes me how life lends me these different stories and supports that I would never have known if I didn't share my own story. She told me she will never forget them but is so grateful for the two kids she has now. She understood how hard it was going through it all, feeling completely alone. She understood what I was going through. Many of my clients had children themselves and were trying to get the help they needed with their eating disorders, with their children being their motivating force. Or it was motherhood and the difficulties of navigating it, the loss of control, and their changing bodies that led them to an eating disorder. One client got better because she was pregnant and needed to be healthy for the growing life inside her. We do what we have to at the time. We all fall down and are shattered in life, but we do begin to pick up the pieces, putting them together the way it makes sense for our lives.

July 20, 2017: Joy

I got to watch you on ultrasound; you gave your stone-face smirk and hysterical laughter. Oh, you make us smile. We cannot wait to meet you. The fact that you are already laughing in there is the best medicine for us. Love and laughter mean happily ever after... or it is gas!

August 24, 2017: Nourishment While Up North

The bush plane didn't have any seat belts, and during the emergency briefing, the pilot said, "The emergency box is somewhere in the back under all your shit." We had to learn to soar, trust, and let go.

When we landed up north that night, I went for a walk. I found myself lying on a rock with the water, birds, and trees surrounding me. With my wild hair, calm heart, and no sense of direction, I had my baby with me, and the sunshine trail lay ahead. Setting out on my walk back, I pointed myself in the direction of the medicine wheel (also known as the Sacred Hoop that is used for health and healing in Indigenous cultures), which guided my life and soothed my spirit with new healing perspective. My mental and physical wellbeing was aligning with the sky, earth, water, and trees and being nourished. You have and will show me the way.

August 28, 2017: Moments to Reflect

Today, I am overcome with emotion as I reflect upon a déjà vu moment I had. I am exactly twenty-four weeks pregnant, as far along as I was when I delivered Kaia. Hubby says that we are off to a better start, but it still hurts. I am recalling how we posted about your sister, "Loading 50 Per Cent," as we were halfway through our pregnancy. I, of course, haven't done any of that with you, as it is all just too emotional.

I also came back from a contract up north, a place I once shared with your sister right before we received the bad news. I got to share time up north with both of you. Time for just the two of us, in the north, by the lake—a memory I will always hold on to. Thank you for sharing the moment with me. You gave me time to reflect, and it's what I need more than ever right now. I'm excited for what the future brings and for the moments shared with boys and their toys.

I feel so guilty for not taking any photos or really enjoying this pregnancy with you, but I continue to grieve the loss of your sister. Janice said, "It's the pictures of Kaia that got you through your loss of her. Do not be afraid to take pictures now."

I'm so sad, as I now realize I have no belly shots of you, my boy, but I remain torn. Psychologically, I feel if I take photos, they will only end up in a memory book. The possibility that I may, in fact, one day make a baby book does not occur to me.

September 12, 2017: Somatic Pain

A Message to My Counsellor:

> I am just at work and was so looking forward to our session. I was speaking to the nurse practitioner here, as I have been having this sharp right upper quadrant pain for a week. I thought it was just pregnancy symptoms or growing pains, but she said I should get it checked out, so I am going to head to the OB triage around lunch. I will see how long it all takes, but I may have to cancel our session for tonight. I will update you on timing when I'm in the hospital.

Later that day:

> PS. The results are back, and they think it is just muscular pain, so that is good. And they think it just may be in my head. This

makes me feel crazy, like I am just making up symptoms at this point.

October 1, 2017: Cruising

Today was the first time I didn't stall the 1968 Chevelle, and I know I had you helping me. Soon you will come to know this car very well, Daddy's first baby. This car is our life-mobile car, the one he started working on when we started dating. We drove it on our wedding day; it was our Sunday cruiser to the beach and for ice cream adventures, and now it will be our one-day fam-mobile with you, little one. I still hold on to the pictures we took as a family in the Chevelle when we were pregnant with Kaia. I needed to know our baby experienced the ride of her life—the family fun ride we still dream of.

October 17, 2017: Guarded

Well, kiddo, you officially scared the crap out of me! But what pregnancy doesn't?

I went for my check-up appointment, and you had a deceleration (heart rate drop). Then I fainted, so you had another deceleration. But once they looked at you on ultrasound, you looked perfect; you were doing your practice breathing, getting ready, which was reassuring to see.

This pregnancy has not been easy for me at all. I can't get attached. I am riddled with a deep-rooted fear of talking about your future, as it is unknown and not guaranteed. Yet today's events frightened me because, as it turns out, I'm attached. How can I not be attached? I love you very much and can't bear the thought that anything could happen to you.

Our OB said that we never expect the cancer, or the baby loss, or the heart attacks that will happen to us. No one really gets it until they have gone through it themselves. Of course not—merely living is unexpected. If we expected things all the time it would not be a fun life. But when things are expected, the pain of the cancer returning or another impending loss or heart attack, the experience is so different. I am being protective of myself right now so I can be protective of you one day. Happiness is the key to life, and one day you will be the key that unlocks all the happiness this world has to offer me. I may be locked and guarded right now, but when I am open, my heart will swell, and the love I have for you will envelop me entirely.

November 21, 2017: Choosing

I used to say to myself: "Take a moment to look around. You never knew you would be where you are today." There was a point when I didn't know what school I would go to, what job I would have, where I would live, what house I would own, who I would marry, what dog I would pick out, or even if I would do or choose any of those things at all. Suddenly, I am here in this moment. I am sitting on our couch, pregnant, in our home, with my husband and dog. I have a job that I love back at the paediatric ICU, and I am friends with people I care for deeply.

This is now our life. Life is all sorted out, and I feel contentment. These are all decisions we made, obstacles we conquered, dreams we had. They were choices we made along the way that got us to right here, right now. With this pregnancy, we will not know what our kid will look like or be like or even how many more we will have. We feel like you have been with us all along, all part of the mystery of living life. Soon our life will change, and only then will we know life as it is right then, dreaming of it no other way. We will love it. But right here, right now, I am choosing you and enjoying this life that is ours.

December 4, 2017: My Christmas Wish

Santa visited me today while I worked back at the PCCU. He asked if I had any kids at home. I said, "I have one coming at Christmas time."

"That's the best gift ever," he said.

I couldn't agree more, Mr. Claus!

December 13, 2017: Chasing Rainbows

Today, I received a rainbow blanket from Becca, a dear colleague and friend, for our rainbow baby. After the rain comes the rainbow. I love the idea of wrapping our baby in colour, no longer in black and white like the photos of our past deadened dreams. This baby has and will brighten our every day.

December 14, 2017: Anticipating

Hey little man,

Today I found out I am three centimetres dilated, which means your grand entrance into this world is fast approaching. I touch my belly, feeling and constantly counting your movements, which reminds me to persevere and that you are still here. Each passing day that brings us closer to your delivery also has moments of me not believing you are real or that a potential delivery will happen. My anxiety creeps up when I allow myself to daydream about you, as I did in my other pregnancies; it is hard for me to believe I will truly get to take a baby home. After so many losses, I fear so strongly that even though I have made it further, I will lose you as well. At this point, I have visited the OB triage three times for false labour, and although every time I am embarrassed, I just want to be admitted for close monitoring of every moment I don't feel you, every cramp, every mucousy discharge, every pregnancy symptom. The nurses assure me that with my history they would never fault me for going in to get checked out, even if it is just for my peace of mind. I know, though, that to them I have become a frequent flyer. But they are still compassionate towards me, and for that, I am indebted to them.

Today, I decide to write for the future. I will have a healthy baby boy. You are a beam of light and every person in our lives is overjoyed to meet you. You, little wonder, will fill our days with so much joy. It is hard to believe I haven't met you, yet I know you so much and can only picture a world with you in it. I also know that in all the excitement and love and your amazingness, I can't ever imagine raising my voice with you, but I know that day will come. Please know it will come from a place of compassion and of caring too much and of just wanting all things good for you in this world. You, dear son, have already changed my life for the better by just being. I have a sense of calm, unlike any I've had before, and I just know life will be everything I've dreamed of, and more, with you.

Daddy told me to start jumping, as we are just so eager to meet you. Today, I took you on our very first date, lunch at a coffeehouse. Then I laminated some artwork in memory of the many angels that you will have in your life, and we walked in the fresh sparkling snow as I talked to you. We visited Great Oma for tea and Gramma for a brownie. We love you more than anything.

December 16, 2017: Appreciating

We went out to a Christmas party with friends, and I literally wore my oversized Christmas boxers that have turkeys with Santa hats on them. My belly was used as the drink table for many. One of my friends yelped, "Whatever you do, do not have a forceps delivery. I've watched *Call the Midwife* after all!" Maybe this evening will get the party started for our own little turkey.

December 17, 2017: The Love of My Life

I did this whole pregnancy one day at a time. I am pregnant today. I think of the parents of the children in the ICU, when they're asked how they do it. One day at a time they respond. They have to. I have to keep going, taking it one day at a time. That is the only thing I can do, the only thing I can control, showing up for myself, my family, and this baby of ours.

Daddy went hunting, and I sorted sheets with Gramma. Who even does that? Your fur sister, Nola, was anxious. We were ready.

Life is full of unknowns. With every end, there is a new beginning. It is unbelievable to think how you can do a complete 360 in a year. Almost the same day a year ago, on December 21, we received the worst news of our life—news that caused me to just lay in bed, waiting for the walls to cave in and barricade me so I never had to leave and face the world or life without a baby in it again. Yet on this day a year ago, I was unexpectedly the most happy I've ever been. Today you are the best news of our life.

I recall my colleague Shannon saying that after they had an unimaginable loss, they moved their bed into the living room and just stayed there for days, closing the blinds, and not moving. Now I wish to move our bed to the living room but to open the curtains and put you on full display for all to see, so when anyone walks into our house, they will see our family of three, cozy as can be, the light spotlighting us, our bed as our proud stage.

It takes tremendous hope, trust, and faith to believe this could all be possible—that your very worst day one year could, in fact, become your very best day another. Being headstrong, tough, and bullheaded also helps—strong Dutch traits of mine. We could not have predicted this year and now with you, we cherish every possible moment, for in these moments, we are so blessed. We also hold a deep love for our babies who were born sleeping; we never forget they were here, and they mattered. Today, we get to show our outrageous love for our son through the love we have held for every baby, the love we have saved for our newest addition to the family.

Every living child's birth is scary. The entire process, before the baby is in one's arms, is scary. There is simply no guarantee. And it is forever scary after that moment. The scariest part is just how long we have wished, obsessed over, and wanted this kind of scary. We have longed for the terrifying journey of parenthood. We are ready and want to be parents, taking in full stride everything being a parent encompasses. Somehow, the fears of actually parenting feel less than the fears we held in getting to this point.

Case Emerson Grover's Birth Story

Case: Irish for brave, observant, alert, and vigorous.

Emerson: German for "son of Emery," a dignified, serious name. In honour of Grampa, who was German, and Emerson, the town in Manitoba where my mother grew up.

December 23, 2017: Your Actual Due Date

It all started at Gramma and Opa's on December 17th at 4:27 p.m. I had finished watching the season of *Life in Pieces*. I made your birth announcement card for work. In the hospital, we have a tube delivery system for sending things rapidly, which is how I let my workmates know I had delivered. And I quote the actual card I wrote: "Guess what? Chicken butt... just kidding. Whoop, here he is."

As mentioned, I was sorting sheets with Gramma and feeling very accomplished. Your Daddy was out hunting, yodelling with coyotes, and he remembers that afternoon as being quite eerie. I will let you know that your dear mother has been like the woman who cried wolf all through the pregnancy. So when I called your Daddy, of course he asked, "Is your yodelling for real this time?"

Since I had to stop talking mid-sentence to brace my belly, grunt, huff, puff, and blow you out, Gramma said, "If this isn't labour, I don't know what is."

The timing of your labour and delivery couldn't have been better. Auntie Kerrie and Uncle Ryen were heading home for the holidays from Manitoba (our second home). Their trip started with a flat tire, followed by Uncle Ryen's dog suddenly dying. (That is another story in itself but a tragic one.) Then Auntie Kerrie announced: "Watch. Carmen will go into labour tonight." I followed suit, of course, because all things come in threes.

Uncle Evan was in Grimsby, Ontario, for a work-related course. Your dear Auntie Selena (who teased that you would be born on Christmas because I was always late for Christmas celebrations) thought, lo and behold, the family would all have to go to the hospital over Christmas. But you spared her this. She was studying for her final exam and didn't want me to deliver until she was done. She finished that day. Since Opa was picking up Great Uncle Ricky from the airport, Gramma was going crazy without a vehicle, since she wanted to be at the hospital the second you were born. She would have caught you if she could. It was amazing how all your family was home for your birth, as they were all coming home for Christmas. The stars had aligned—a Christmas miracle.

We arrived at the hospital at 10:00 p.m. and, boy, were you ready to join us on Great Opa's birthday. We had picked your name about six weeks before your due date. Your due date, December 23, was close to Opa's birthdate, so it was pretty special for Oma to hear you were named after Opa and also that you were born on his exact birthdate. I promise: I had no control over these things—okay, maybe some increased jumping.

It was all so magical.

During my contractions, your father had a few interesting motivational words that weren't so magical. There's nothing like "Good job. You're really killing it." Words to live by from philosophical Phillip. You'll get to know your dad and his humour, and that is all I am going to say for now.

It turns out I set a record for the quickest delivery, going from four to ten centimetres dilated in just thirty-three minutes. (PS your Daddy just adores the word dilated . . . not!) The whole team and the neonatal ICU were called, as your birth was a little dramatic. You were having decelerations, and I believe your heart rate was fifty-seven beats per minute at one point. I heard them say, "If we don't get him out in five minutes, we have to do a C-section." This was serious business. I grabbed the side rails, shaking them, pushing with triumphant might, and that worked. Then I heard them yell, "We are going to have to use forceps."

Immediately, my friend's words from the night prior came blaring to my mind. Whatever you do, don't use forceps. All I ended up saying was "Just b-b-be careful."

With just five minutes of pushing, you came out (mommy's friends refer to you as Pop-Tart), crying (truly the most beautiful sound we have ever heard) and squirting pee everywhere. Meanwhile, apparently your Daddy cut the umbilical cord, something I wasn't even slightly aware of as I was in such awe of you.

Daddy said, "That's my boy!"

You were born on December 18, 2017 at 3:33 a.m. How simply hilarious, as I must repeat, that all good things come in threes.

To us, seeing the number 333 meant you would receive divine guidance, protection, and help. I will admit, though, we didn't always believe this given our history. You were born in the same room as your sister and you had four other angel siblings watching over you as well as Great Opa (of course), Great Grampa, Great Granny, and second cousin, Janelle.

Grandma and Grandpa came to visit as soon as they could, which was 6:00 a.m., and Gramma, Opa, and Great Oma all came to visit at 9:30 a.m. They obviously all thought you were just so precious and handsome. The nurse we had after your delivery was the same nurse we had for your sister Kaia. (Your Daddy and I went to high school with this nurse.) And Janice's husband was your pediatrician, so it was unimaginable how full circle everything became.

As we headed home from the hospital with the greatest joy in our hearts, the first song that came on the radio was "All I Want for Christmas Is You." This couldn't have been more perfect or true as you are our best gift ever. The rest is history. You better believe I belted that song out, ripping my stitches all the way!

When we arrived at home, I remember Daddy just plunking your car seat down on the floor. We both couldn't stop staring at you and we both simultaneously said, "Wow, there's a baby in this house."

Here was another human we would get to share this life with in our home. How surreal and beyond wondrous. We stared at your every move, in total disbelief and not wanting to miss a single moment of the miracle that was before us. We marvelled at you and were completely awestruck and dumbfounded by how amazing your little sounds, features, and movements were. You were real. You were ours. And you were here.

We have never been so in love, and thoughts of you keep dancing in our heads as we cheer. As my friend Erin perfectly said, "It's crazy how much you can love someone. I don't think you appreciate it until you have your own baby—you'd do anything for them."

January 1, 2018: A Message from My Counsellor

Dear Carmen,

I am so happy that you and your new little family are getting settled. I will think about you tomorrow and reflect on all the milestones you have reached in this past year. It has been a whirlwind for you, and I feel privileged to have known you at such a special time in your life. Please keep in touch and know that you are an amazing young woman with the courage to do absolutely anything! With my best wishes for an amazing new year ahead, filled with the joys of motherhood!

January 2, 2018: Written in Kaia's Memory Book

The year 2017 brought us Kaia and Case, two sweeties. We have been lucky in two very different ways. Our year was a year of total heartbreak, a year of hearts overflowing with love, and a year of growth, commitment, and perseverance. Although 2017 was not at all what we expected, it taught us a lot about living, finding purpose, and supporting each other.

I sometimes find myself thinking that if we had not lost Kaia, we would not have had you, Case. This is a chilling thought, one that is hard to digest, as I could not wish for one over the other. As parents, we want to honour our children. As I laid my babies to rest, a weight was lifted; we moved on towards an exciting future, knowing they had been here, and they changed our world forever. We will keep them always in our hearts; they are the stars that shape us.

A Tribute to Baby Case

When asked if this was my first baby, I would say my first boy.
That seemed to work out well because I wasn't lying.

April 15, 2018: My First Boy

This story has been written before by every mama; nonetheless, let us embrace it. When I throw you in the air, I adore the way you squeak with the most enthusiastic giggles. I marvel at how you hold my hand so tightly when you are feeding. You are most content when you sleep with your arms fully stretched up and meeting at the top of your head. I hear your soft breath, little whimpers, and laughs as you sleep. I notice your rapid breathing as you dream. Dream big, my son! You nuzzle my arm and tickle it with your tongue, giving me the cutest baby hickeys. You babble to yourself and make farting noises with your mouth. You hold your hands together for comfort, like your great grandpa did before you. (They were hardworking farming hands.)

Thank you for letting me do yoga on a spring day, cry free, while you watch me. You take big unapologetic yawns and stare at me wide eyed with such astonishing wonder and curiosity—if only all life moments may be free, as seen through the eyes of a baby. You freely let out your bottom lip and grin. You are so focused, picking up and spotting the tiniest of threads on the carpet, reminding us to be mindful. You stop what you are doing when the camera is rolling, which reminds us to take in the current moment. But, boy, I don't want to miss a thing. When you laughed during the church service to commemorate Great Opa, you taught us not to be so serious.

A baby's laugh is so innocent; a baby does not yet know the pain in this world, which is a treasure to witness. You look deeply into the soul of each person you meet. You, my son, are a beautiful soul. We love you more with each passing day. Just looking at you, I see that you are pure excellence. I say this with no bias. How did we get so lucky?

"What are you thinking?" I often ask. You look at us with such knowing and you are fully there in each moment. You take in each new thing that comes your way. Your fluttery eyes rest when they are tired and awaken when they are rested. Simple. No alarm clocks necessary, although you are our alarm clock. You place your hand on my chest as you snuggle into the nook of my shoulder. The flawless fit. I want to remember your rosy cheeks, soft skin (especially your wrists), ticklish toes, and strong chunky legs. How you twirl your hair when you're feeding and grin as if to say, "What now in this adventure that is life?" That smile of yours lights a fire in my heart and makes me want to live fully. We are in this life together; your hand is on my heart, and my heart is full of you. There's one thing I know for certain in this life and that is that I have you.

The saddest cries you give are when you want to be cuddled. Cuddling you makes the world a better place; all the problems spontaneously combust. Sweet Case, thanks for letting me live and know a life of sunshine and joy. You are all I need.

How are we so blessed to get to know a love like this one? When we went to the retirement home to visit Great Oma, you held so many hands. The grins and happiness we saw in the seniors' eyes was so touching. You took them back to earlier days of babies in their lives. It is the circle of life. Every person always knows a baby in their lives that changed their world forever. Don't ever let go of the many hands that you grace in this life. Connection to something, to each other, is why we exist. We love you forever. And that is a connection unbreakable.

April 30, 2018: Exploring

I dreamt of taking you in my suit(Case) and travelling the world, and we made that dream come true. We visited relatives out west who adored you. You actually licked the snow caps off the mountains! You also threw up all over dear Auntie Kerrie at what seemed like the one and only gas station in Saskatchewan. You are the best traveller. When we hit turbulence and couldn't land, the men behind us puked. I offered them wet wipes (which come in handy for everything). You laughed uncontrollably while bouncing. You make travelling fun.

May 13, 2018: Loss is Never Lost: My First Mother's Day with a Living Baby

The dream of becoming a mom when I grew up has come true! Everyone has a purpose in this life, whether it's helping children overseas or in your backyard, fostering, adopting, babysitting, volunteering, steering the children you teach, cuddling your pets/fur babies, being a loving devoted aunt, or mothering and caring for yourself, your partner, or your own parents. Just plain being a loving person in this life is what we were put here to do. Let's celebrate that. I had no certainty in my future, but I always knew one way or another I would be a mother. Today, let's honour women everywhere for the nurturing and loving kindness they bring to this world.

June 10, 2018: A Bird Taking Flight

Dearest Kaia,

This morning we awoke to the sound of a bird trapped in our closet. This has never happened before. Kinda strange?

Today, Gramma, your brother, and I went to a butterfly release ceremony in memory of those we have loved and have lost. This was the first year we went since losing you, sweet Kaia. The first reading at the ceremony talked about how spirits come to us in different ways, whether it's by way of a butterfly or a bird. I honestly could not believe we woke up to a bird this morning in our house! I was waking up to your strong spirit. These things don't just happen every day and have certainly never happened before. As I went to release our butterfly at the ceremony, a dad next to us yelled, "Kaia! Kaia, come to the pond to see the fishies."

I jumped, catching myself, and I had to look. That is when I knew you were with us today and every day. But when we commemorate you and look for you, we find you even more fiercely in every turn we take. To finish our night off, Daddy and I drank a Savanna cider, the same drink we had in Africa while we grieved for you. Today, we drank to new life and to the most beautiful soul we were lucky enough to meet. You prove you are with us when we need you most. What a beautiful day to be with my truest loves and for Case to witness your great and mighty spirit. May we find peace in these unexplainable moments, welcome them always, and rejoice in them.

Babe # 6
Maelie Lynn Grover

Notice and cherish life's surprises.
Just because it's not what you were expecting, doesn't mean
it's not everything you've been waiting for.
—Angel Chernoff

July 5, 2018: Welcoming

We took a trip to Manitoba to visit family and to show off Case, but most importantly to welcome your first cousin, Weslee, into this world.

July 25, 2018: Crossing

Sweet Case,

Today we took Gramma and you to the Pinawa Suspension Bridge in Manitoba. The journey was about conquering fears: Gramma's fear of swinging bridges (her dad used to jokingly swing them when she was a child) and my fear of another pregnancy going wrong. I just had a feeling that I might be pregnant.

In life, we always look at what lies ahead or lies beyond what we see. On a bridge we might worry about its possible destruction, but instead we should focus on the path right in front of us that we have paved for ourselves. The bridge is there to hold us and support us in that moment. We don't need to worry; life is too short. We must cross each bridge as we come to it.

July 30, 2018: Positive

A new pregnancy. I have to admit: We never really tried for you. You just kind of happened. With our history, we had talked about wanting to try for another pregnancy sooner rather than later so that we didn't lose more time if there was another miscarriage. That is how our new minds are wired. But we didn't need to try. We are happy, and we welcome this pleasant surprise.

August 2, 2018: Going Slow

I saw a dragonfly. I've read that dragonflies can represent change. I already feel like I am seeing things differently with you and starting to slow down. This slowing down might also be related to you loving when I eat anything potato based. I approve.

September 5, 2018: Hearing

Dear little one,

I heard your beating heart at 143 beats per minute. Such a beautiful, powerful sound.

September 8, 2018: Seeing

I came across a bald eagle today—a sign. And a bird we have seen with each of Mommy's pregnancies.

September 14, 2018: Feeling

First ultrasound. Ten weeks and three days. You're moving like crazy.

September 28, 2018: Chancing

I told Gramma that we are expecting you in April, and I ordered a classic virgin Caesar (sticking with tradition). The age gap will be close, although we never really believed we would make it this far again. Too good to be true. I am loving our current odds.

October 22, 2018: Carrying

I was twenty-weeks pregnant and had the greatest time with you in Brittany, France, our next great traveller in the making. I could no longer hide my French-food baby belly, and I ate so much and felt nauseous on the cobblestones and great winding roads. We celebrated the news of you with loved ones, watching them slurp mussels and champagne. Everyone was so excited.

To think I carried your brother in his carrier while I carried you inside of me. Please remember this trip, okay? We took you to cool places, even though you don't know it. I have photo proof of my belly in historical places.

October 23, 2018: Dying

The day after returning from France, we were called with bad news again. We thought we were in the clear and would not have another miscarriage, but the twenty-week curse seemed to be present again. Before hearing what the news actually was, I lost hope and wrote, "You were just too perfect to be true, as per usual."

A voicemail message had been left when we were in France with no cell service, saying there were some concerning test results and that we were booked to see a geneticist. We had missed the appointment while on our trip.

Phillip had just left to go to school in Ottawa. I am alone and helpless, and I have fallen to the ground. I had originally planned to return to work early, since I'm pregnant and need to get my maternity hours in. But I fear that it is DiGeorge syndrome again. I want to stay off work, as going back and then having to terminate the pregnancy would be that much more devastating.

My Stages of Grief—Despair, Hopelessness, Frustration, Shock, and Loss of Self

My worst nightmare repeats itself in the same way.
I guessed you were a girl.
Is that why you are destined to the same fate?
What is the point of it all?
We are too greedy to want more kids.
Are we really that bad to deserve this?
But everyone already loves you.
And I love you.
Can't we just have another lovely kid like Case?
I can't go on like this.
One really starts to understand just how fragile life is.
I hate this.

October 24, 2018: Processing

The news was relayed—we tested positive for Down's syndrome. My immediate thought was *It's not DiGeorge. And Down's syndrome is something we can live with.* I care for many adorable, funny, kind kids with Down's syndrome at work.

Case and I walked outside to see the sunrise. In this life sometimes I need to live moment to moment, walking out of the darkness to see and feel the sun. Later that day, Gramma, Case, and I went to the hospital so I could get more testing done. Fingers crossed. You are too precious to us, even though you came to us as the greatest surprise.

November 1, 2018: Breathing

The lab technician called with comforting news. Our baby doesn't have Down's syndrome. Remind me to never do this testing again, as it mostly seems to test positive. It is not worth the fear. Just three more weeks until the anatomy scan. You have given us our breath back. We love you so much and will do anything to protect you.

November 12, 2018: Thankful

We officially announced our sweetest joy—that we are pregnant with a healthy baby. We told our friends and family the news and that we are keeping the gender a surprise. We announced to our loved ones by placing a nut in a diaper, as in, another peanut is coming soon. Psst... your Gramma's maiden name is Knutt, and everyone thinks the K is silent, so we get it, honestly. We also included your ultrasound picture at the end of a picture book that we gave to each relative, which showed the times we were most thankful for this year. We kept our tradition of thankful announcements, but we couldn't bring ourselves to do this at Thanksgiving again. The memory of having announced our pregnancy with Kaia at Thanksgiving still comes woven with so many emotions.

November 16, 2018: Fearful

Today was ultrasound day. Oh, what a bundle of emotions Mommy was. The ultrasound tech started crying during the ultrasound. It made me nervous; crying in the past has meant many things. I was on heightened alert. Note to self: Next time I will wear eye protection so I cannot see the tech's reactions. In the end, I think it was happy tears because you are perfect. With Phillip still away at school, your big brother and Gramma got to see you moving and grooving on the ultrasound.

All the tech had to report was that you had a double vessel cord. This means that instead of having two arteries and a vein, the umbilical cord has one artery and one vein. Pffft! We would have taken you even if you had Daddy's silly toes. (And they are pretty silly, always cuddling each other.) I left feeling assured, and we went to cheer on Auntie Selena at hockey.

Later, I looked up the risks associated with two-vessel cord—genetic abnormalities, sometimes life threatening and sometimes not, and higher risk for not growing properly.

November 29, 2018: Strength

Your heartbeat was the most gorgeous sounding whoosh! Such a strong, triumphant, full, pumping heart.

December 7, 2018: Moving

You are flutter kicking in there. Case loves playing with you, slapping my belly, and nuzzling you, saying "ba" for baby.

December 18, 2018: Case's First Birthday

My endless love Case,

From before you were born to the moment you entered this world (and onwards), we knew you were a miracle. My boy, you bring endless joy to all those you grace. We have been on so many adventures in your first year: to Ottawa where your dad was in school; to Florida with Gramma and Opa; to Edmonton (by accident), when you ooo-aaa'd at the flight attendants and giggled at the turbulence; to the Rockies with your aunties; to Manitoba to meet your cousin, Weslee; to the Toronto Island and day trips to Rock Glen, Grand Bend, and Highland Glen. Did I mention France with Grandma, where we have documented you as the best world traveller ever? You literally put yourself in our suitcase, packing yourself up and playing peekaboo in there. I love the spontaneity of travel, always making do wherever we go with you and changing you on every cashier's table. I promise they found your fancy derrière endearing. You were so happy as long as we were exploring.

While in France, we watched a family recreate an old picture. We dream of doing this with you one day. We have tons of pictures to choose from.

We have so many memorable moments with you—you roaring back at Dad and laughing at Nola and scaring her. You love being scared by us. You love pointing and putting your index finger in my mouth and grabbing my nose and you love grabbing Dad's thermometer that is always in his pocket.

You hate your car seat, as you would rather be out and about than strapped down. You giggle your head off when you see yourself in the mirror. You also like finding the littlest objects that adults can't even see and putting them in your mouth. You love being roughhoused and thrown in the air by your aunties. You have no fear, as you leap from any height and would leap down the stairs if we didn't catch you first.

You are your own person and can't be bothered with toys. You prefer pens, spatulas, paper, printers, and knives; you want to experience how the real stuff works. You bop to Bob Marley and twangy music. You are very cuddly yet show your affection by smacking everyone.

The Lessons of Being

Grin with your two teeth ... you won't always have them.

Enjoy the little things, like threads coming out of doormats.

Beat to your own rhythm, as you hammer your drum.

Follow your own path, as you try to meander your way through every chair or obstacle.

Laugh at dogs, because animals are fun and always love you no matter what.

Stand up for what you believe in, even if you need to hold the couch for encouragement.

Breathe rapidly when you get excited.

Do things that get you exhilarated and your heart beating.

Never stop investigating, even if it is electrical outlets, tapes, and cords.

Point and say ooh to the sky ... the sky is the limit.

We love you, Case Man

Reflections on Loss and Other Things

January 10, 2019: The Car Seat

Life throws us many moments that teach us lessons; sometimes they are small, and often we are too busy to notice. As a nurse, I work every day with people dealing with unexpected events. These unexpected events sometimes serve to cancel the daily noise in our heads and force us to focus. It is then we find time for family and realize what the most important part of life is.

Recently, driving to work, I unexpectedly fell asleep at the wheel. You hear of it happening to people, but then you always think surely it will never happen to me. My speed climbed to 130 kilometres per hour, and I zig-zagged across the road into the ditch. When I woke, I quickly pulled myself out to the other side of the road and back again in the appropriate lane. I was shaking. How did I not hit anyone? Moments later, lights started flashing and I pulled over. I was completely numb. The police officer who pulled me over said that what he witnessed was unbelievable. He did not know how I survived. The saying "Jesus take the wheel" was very real in that moment.

We chatted as I tried to come to grips with what happened. He was so grateful he didn't have to deal with an accident or call my family with bad news. Then his eyes fell on the empty car seat in the back of my car. We both started crying. After all the times I feared losing a child, this time an entirely different kind of fear settled in. This fear seemed greater than any other—the fear of not being there for my children.

I was beyond grateful for my life and that no one but the police officer and I were on that road at that time. The police officer made me pause for a moment and see just how lucky I was—lucky I could get into work safely and have the pleasure of working with the strongest people I know and to go home to my own son and husband with my very round belly. Joy can be so profound in just those simple thoughts.

I have to admit that the night before, I was busy with cleaning the house, prepping meals, being pregnant and tired, worrying about getting my hours in before maternity leave, and worrying about the week ahead, and all those things that I thought mattered so much. May I also mention that I had not been sleeping.

I take Gravol or Benadryl most nights to fall asleep, as recommended by my doctor. I could say that my not sleeping is from the normal restlessness that accompanies pregnancy, but it is deeper than that. It is my extreme anxiety about how incredibly difficult pregnancy is after loss. How I have tried to show excitement, smiling until my cheeks hurt, although my eyes hurt from crying (which I pretend is the lack of sleep from eager anticipation). How this pregnancy especially has brought up a lot of old hurt, as it so closely follows a similar timeline to Kaia's. Then there has been the stress of the test earlier on and then finding out about the double vessel cord, which was a smaller thing, but it still caused me to spin deeper into dizzying delirium, despair, and sleep deprivation.

I've been overthinking about all the jobs that need to get done when the most important things have always been right in front of me. All I want is to be with my family, but I was so blinded by those many other things to do. I can't be mindful of these moments all the time, as life does pull me in so many different directions (just as my car had done), and there are always frustrations. But now, anytime I'm feeling overwhelmed, generally by thoughts I bring on myself, I will look at my car seat and stop. STOP. Take a pause, observe, and proceed, knowing I have a purpose and what an incredible reward I am granted in having it.

In reflection, there was something particularly different about that night before I fell asleep at the wheel. Phillip and I were actually talking together about life and death before bed. In the morning, I kissed Case's head, cuddled my husband, and patted Nola, something I'm usually too rushed to do in the morning. Why those specific things transpired, I don't know. I do know those were the moments that appeared before my eyes as I awoke behind the wheel. Those are the moments I want to fill my life up with.

February 20, 2019: Trust Your Gut

The most beautiful moment happened today. The little boy patient (the same one who said "there's a baby in there" prior to our first pregnancy loss) was back at the hospital, and I went to visit him. He touched my belly again and guessed the baby was a girl. Then he said, "It will go well this time." He told me he would never forget me. This is a connection that has brought me so much amazement and has somehow lessened my anxiety. I have full trust in him. I believe that children can see what we can't, and they have an even greater intuition and insight than us adults.

March 4, 2019: Dreaming

Sweet little one,

Mommy had a dream in the middle of the night—of a name that astonishingly appeared and spelled itself out in white writing: M-A-E-L-I-E. So I did what any logical dream interpreter would do. I started Googling.

Maybe I was reading too much into this. Nope. I think not. The spelling comes straight from Brittany, France, and means "princess." Brittany is where your Daddy's family is from and where we took you in October. Your sister Kaia's middle name is Belle, meaning beautiful, and is the last name of your paternal great grandmother. As you will learn one day, Daddy and I went to South Africa to honour her. In South Africa, "Maeli" means most beautiful, strong, joyful, and graceful. How perfect is that? The name is Sanskrit in origin. Mommy practices yoga with you and even started a yoga instructor course right when I found out I was pregnant with you. I'm also a bit of a hippie, and "Maylie" also means wildflower. So perhaps this is your name if you are a girl. If you're a boy, though, Daddy wants to simply name you Jack Grover because it is a good, solid name and sounds like a pirate. Aaaarrrggghhh.

March 11, 2019: Measuring

Today, I took belly measurements because who doesn't measure their belly across the button whilst at work? Measuring in at 101 centimetres, or 39.5 inches round.

April 1, 2019: Freedom

So . . . no joke. Today, while your brother and I went for a walk in the sunshine, we saw our first bald eagle of the year flying high overhead. Case kept saying "up." An eagle has always appeared at times of need and to me represents your siblings and your great grandparents. The sight gave me a bit of an alarmed feeling, but I have to remember that the eagles have appeared both in times of life and death. When Daddy and I found out we were pregnant with Case and with you, we saw a bald eagle; now being due with you, we saw one again. There is symbolism in every step. Remember, the eagle bestows the freedom and strength to look ahead. We can't wait for you, and we so look forward to meeting you.

April 4, 2019: Twenty-Eight

Mommy had a wonderful birthday with you.
A swim with you.
Breakfast with your gramma and aunties.
Yes, at twenty-eight I asked for and got a special rainbow-toes pedicure. It looks great!
A Starbucks venti green tea Frappuccino that was free for my b-day.
A peaceful waddling walk to my favourite tree and a nice talk with you.
An ice cream cake with family, which I ate all of.
Your brother's first haircut. He has to look dapper for your big entry.
Saw the play *Mamma Mia!* (the play we went to see when I was pregnant with Kaia) at the local high school with Great Oma, Gramma, and Auntie Kerrie.
Everyone is eager to meet you.
A birthday is a gift in this beautiful life.

Maelie Lynn Grover's Birth Story

Maelie: Princess, most beautiful, strong, joyful, and graceful.
Lynn: Living near a lake, waterfall, or pool. The fourth generation.

April 13, 2019: Our Little Princess

On April 8, the sun was shining; it was a beautiful day, and I took you and Nola for a walk. You waited just perfectly for your Daddy to finish his motorcycle course on Sunday, for Mommy and your brother to get over our colds, and for Daddy to get treatment for his strep throat. We were apparently in rough shape. You, my girl, were already the most generous sweetie for thinking of all of us.

On Monday night, Gramma had your brother for the night so your parents could have a relaxing night in. We eagerly awaited your arrival. At 2:00 a.m., Mommy went to the bathroom and noticed some bright red blood (a sign that has always scared me), and since you were usually a wiggly girly in there, I was worried when I didn't feel any movement. We headed for the hospital. By the time we arrived, you were moving up a storm, and your heart rate was great. Daddy and I walked a lot and got the new Tim Hortons drink called a London Fog, a glorious, fluffy taste of heaven. You introduced me to that drink, and I am so thankful to you for finding my calming tea. Tea will forever be our thing—high teatime with the butterflies.

At 8:00 a.m., we let the family know that we were in the hospital and eagerly awaiting your most amazing arrival. Surprisingly, we found out from Gramma that Case had woken up at 5:00 a.m. and couldn't go back to sleep. We think he knew you were coming.

At the hospital, we had an older British nurse named Linda (to go with the theme of London Fog, said in an English accent), and we had a lot of fun with her. Linda had a student trainee and was excited for an easy patient (cue Mommy). We hoped it would be like Case's birth. Step one: Take an epidural. Step two: Break water. Step three: You would be here in thirty minutes flat. Linda concurred and said, "Okay, let's do that."

At noon, they broke my water. I ate popsicles during my contractions, and nurse Linda would ask, "Don't you feel that?" No. That's the incredible thing about epidurals. I was pretty much just sleeping and eating popsicles. But you were not progressing.

Then your heart rate started to drop, just like your brother's had. We told the medical staff and felt we were prepared for that event. When your heartbeat dropped, they kept referring to you as a little turkey. I think I said out loud to your Daddy, a little disappointedly, "You're going to be a boy now, too, aren't you? A turkey just like your brother." The medical student thought maybe you were posterior. Your dear Gramma called it "sunny side up." We knew from the start you would be bringing rays to our days.

As they continued to monitor the situation, your heart rate continued to drop. You weren't recuperating well after each contraction, so they rushed us into the operating room for an emergency C-section. I'd be lying if I said I wasn't scared to death. It was surreal for me to be on the patient side of the gurney; I am the one usually reassuring patients.

My stretcher crashed into walls, with me still being attached to wires that were plugged into the wall. I could see the terror in the medical team's eyes when someone yelled, "We need an OR, STAT!" Right then, they couldn't even tell us we were going to be okay. They put the oxygen mask on me, and I knew they were scared. All I remember is going completely quiet. I was stretched out, with my arms pinned out to the side, feeling crucified. I started feeling dark.

My world caved in front of me. I was unable to speak, unable to find words, holding my breath, unable to see straight (maybe because I wasn't breathing and was slowly going unconscious). I repeated endlessly, "This baby has to be okay." I kept asking, "Is the baby going to be okay?" and "Do what you need to make sure baby is okay." It didn't matter how you arrived, just that you did arrive. I remembered

Phillip's chilling words when I told him I was pregnant: "I won't believe it until the baby is alive in our arms."

My epidural was so good that they didn't have to put me under. I stared at the anaesthetist behind me, getting lost in his eyes. I think I even mouthed the words "I love you." With every tug I felt in my body, I thought the doctors had pulled you out, and I got nervous when I didn't hear a scream. Then your Daddy watched as the delivery team lifted you out. I breathed heavily, praying for your safety. You cried a brave, strong, triumphant cry as soon as your lungs felt the air. I was elated with that sound.

On top of your glorious screams, we heard Linda yelling, "Where is it? Where is it?" Right. We forgot to mention during the delivery that you had a double vessel cord. Daddy filled them in, and the team laughed. Linda rolled her eyes and said, "Really? You forgot to mention that?" Yeah, turns out, I was definitely not the easy patient she had bargained for.

Then we waited for the most exciting announcement. We stared at you (Mommy more than half-drugged and blitzed out), but no one said anything because we were so overjoyed and relieved. Your Daddy finally announced, "It's . . . It's a girl!" I knew you were a girl, even staring at you, but I just couldn't speak or see straight.

You were born at 2:51 p.m., weighed seven pounds, nine ounces, and measured twenty inches of pure beauty long. Mommy got to naturally use her dream name for you, secretly happy we didn't have to use plain Jack. Your name has finesse! You showed us that déjà-vu dreams really do come true. You are a little princess, as your name implies. Okay, everyone in the OR may have called you a little drama queen, but my theory is you were just getting it out of your system. Now you will never be dramatic from this point forwards, your majesty.

My high-risk obstetrician, who followed us with Kaia and Case (who wasn't following us for this pregnancy, as it was not deemed high risk), popped in and gave me a big hug. We both held huge tears in our eyes. We didn't have to say anything more; it was just so heartfelt. Three years ago, Phillip and I never would have imagined having a family, and now we had a beautiful one. We are definitely all on a cloud with you and your brother. And speaking of your brother, his initial sibling reaction when he met you was to throw a bear at you while holding an "It's a girl" balloon. It was actually sweet. He loved you right from the start.

Mommy got to spend her last night in hospital with Gramma, you, and sweet morphine, as Dad was dealing with strep throat and was home with Case. We were released on April 12, and as we got home, we noticed two robin's nests at our doorstep. The robins were still busily flying to and fro, building the nests up, a symbol of new life and spring. Being greeted and welcomed in this way could not have been more in alignment with our experience.

You are Miss. Mellow Maelie and a cuddle master. You love to eat, just like your parents. Your brother likes to feed you from Mommy's postdelivery (kinda clean) squirt bottles and compassionately suffocate you with blankets. Mommy, Daddy, and Case love you to the moon Miss. Maelie, forever and always!

April 15, 2019: One Week Postdelivery

At our one-week checkup, our family doctor said, "You just can't seem to have a regular, normal birth, can you? I read your birth report."

"Yep, I've had them all, eh?" I said.

Then she continued, "And the placental abruption . . . that must have been so crazy for you."

"What?" I exclaimed. "No one mentioned that to us."

No one had bothered to tell us. During the high stress of it all, that was okay, but after the fact, they should have told us. But in that moment, it also would not have made a difference. We had our healthy and alive baby girl in our arms.

My family doctor said, "It was good that you went in when you did. If you had waited one more day, your daughter would have likely been a stillbirth."

The thought of this still sends shivers up my spine. To have made it that far . . . I cannot even begin to imagine and never wish to. I am so glad I trusted my gut after that bright red blood at 2:00 a.m., knowing full well that it is a sign of early labour for so many people. It was a sign that had only ever signaled alarm in our history, and I couldn't shake it. Even Phillip had said, "We may as well get checked out." He never ever doubted me.

Our baby girl is here in our ever-loving arms.

A Tribute to Baby Maelie

May 11, 2019: One Month Young

The easiest baby ever.
Only cries when hungry. You've got your priorities straight.
Scrunches up face, and it shows your sweet cheeky jowls.
Sucks thumb, like all babies do, and I love it.
When cuddling, always puts hands up around our necks.
Poopy McGoo (because of your Mommy's laxatives).
Makes little chirps, snorts, and snores.
Belly goes in and out as you breathe on and in rhythm
with Mommy's belly.
Receiver of so many kisses and strangulating hugs from your brother.
Suffers with goopy eyes, but when they are open . . .
we can clearly see the purest soul.

May 12, 2019: Messing Around

Think about what kids do to an adult life already in motion—to your romance, your couch, your car, your house, your time, your creativity, your money, and most of all your art. They are a work of art; they make you love more, and everything you need is on one couch, in one place, and they fit perfectly. Fingerprints and snotty noses on the windows make me happy, as I know my kids are here. Kids are the best time spent and raising them is the greatest form of creativity. What's the point of working our whole life anyways?

If you had asked me four years ago, I would never have imagined this moment right now. Sitting in our messy, chaotic house that used to be meticulous—we're talking fixing chipped baseboards with white-out—I have both arms completely full and am unable to move, clean, or do anything but just be with them. I would take all that pain and heartbreak all over again if it meant my current amazing life.

Our children leave handprints all over the windows everywhere we go. Oma said that when we were young, Opa always wanted to wash off the handprints on the van and the house windows that we left behind after visiting them, but Oma liked to keep them up, as then, to Oma, it was like we were still with them.

Leave the messy handprints up and keep them in our hearts. Never wash them away, so they may be lasting handprints and forever with us.

May 16, 2019: Dreams Really Do Come True

Hi Janice,

I just wanted to send all of my tremendous love to you from my jackpot family. If only three years ago I could know I would be blessed with a boy, Case, and girl, Maelie, my endless loves! Dreams lost and dreams had are what kept us going. My life couldn't be fuller, and I just want to thank you for sticking with me and getting me to the other side of the rainbow.

Janice responded:

> With enough time, healing is revealed, and people are able to move forwards with the memories of their babies tucked inside, as they embrace the future with hope.

June 13, 2019: Second Annual Butterfly Release

*We must continue to look for messages from our loved ones,
and when we listen carefully and remain mindful of what is going
on around us, we will hear them.*

Whether it's a butterfly, a bird, a smell, or a warm embrace, we are connected for a moment to something bigger. Together is my favourite thing to be, and on this day, with Case, Maelie, and their siblings surrounding us, we are complete. As we take time to really listen, see, and open up to now, we can receive and feel the love that they send us. As Case giggled, chasing the butterflies and trying to catch them, and Maelie fully observed their bright colours soaring overhead, together we were all playing with our angels.

Babe # 7
Miscarriage

A butterfly lights beside us, like a sunbeam,
and for a brief moment its beauty and glory belong to our world,
but then it flies on again,
and although we wish it could have stayed,
we are so thankful to have seen it at all.
—Author Unknown

July 14, 2019: Intuition

I am one week overdue for a period. And I already feel pregnant. I took a pregnancy test, and it was positive. This means your due date is on Maelie's first birthday! This is absolutely nuts; we should have used protection. Isn't it always when you don't try? I am breastfeeding, and I thought it would lessen my chances of ovulation. Literally, the one and only time (I swear) we had intercourse, and I got pregnant. Still, I welcome the thought of you with open arms.

July 19, 2019: Butterflies

Since the day I found out I was pregnant, I have seen a butterfly every day.

July 25, 2019: Angels

I kept seeing 333 today. As in, angels are telling me that our plans are going well, and our prayers answered.

August 2, 2019: Together

I spotted a butterfly in the sky while I was in the lake with Case. I threw him up in the air to try and touch it, and for a brief moment, we were all together again.

August 4, 2019: Not Alone

Today, we stopped behind a car with a butterfly bumper sticker that read "Those who are gone are not gone but walk among us." I think that this babe not only sent me this image today but wanted to remind me that we are not alone.

August 14, 2019: Babes in Canyon Land

A man with his elderly mom of eighty years spoke to me while we were touring the Grand Canyon. He saw my two babies and said, "How lucky you are." This made me stop. I am so busy chasing dreams, adventure seeking, ticking the accomplishments off the bucket list, making up for lost time, and wanting my children to experience and have the whole wide world in their hands. I forget to stop and really appreciate how lucky I seriously am.

Yes, I am lucky (although lucky has meant many different things to us with our history). I couldn't agree more. Not only do I have two healthy babies, but I also have two superstar sisters (who are on summer break), who help me in ways I can't even describe. Our trip would not have been possible without them. We lived out of a Dodge Grand Caravan, with Maelie sleeping between the seats while Case and I shared the back. We washed in sprinklers and camped in Walmart parking lots before hitting up the next national park, with no agenda, doing whatever we pleased along the way and making memories that will last a lifetime.

That man told me I'm lucky, not even knowing what it took for me to get to this point in life. But it doesn't really matter because in every moment, I am lucky. Together in this moment of luckiness, with my family and the old man and his mom, we recognized there may have been bumps and bends along the way that none of us could have known. But no matter the bumps and bends, either way, we all got there. Oddly, travelling in this way, with this timeline, was perfect. We were living on the edge. In the words of Oma, "If you are not dreaming, you are dying." We are forever dreaming big with our babies.

August 17, 2019: Stormy

It hailed and thundered today. Case and Maelie gave me the best snuggles in the comfort of the Caravan, all cozied up together and safe. "You're just a period. You are just a period," I kept repeating, unable to even convince myself, as I held my belly and felt the cramping. I knew I had to say goodbye. The snuggles from the kids helped me to feel better as I lost you. They subconsciously knew I needed them a little extra today.

I called Phillip, who actually said, "What a relief." I felt bad that he confirmed what I was already thinking in that moment while I also grieved the loss.

August 18, 2019: Presence

For a moment so brief you connected me to something greater than myself, and in your presence, we enjoyed our big-dreaming United States mountain road trip. Somehow the time was even more precious knowing I was pregnant. I saw things more vividly knowing you were with us—the trip with my babies.

August 21, 2019: Investigating

Sometimes, I wish I hadn't tested for the pregnancy and that I would not have grown so attached. Of course, I was attached. When I arrived home, I couldn't stop myself from doing a little more research, as to me, you were not just a period. I learned that our pregnancy was probably not a chemical pregnancy but a miscarriage. I had been closer to seven or eight weeks pregnant.

September 8, 2019: Even Still You Are Near

The other night, on a Sunday, Phillip and I made the poor grandparents watch our kids until 10:00 p.m. even though they both had to work the next day. We felt extremely guilty yet liberated when we went to the hundred-year-old local theatre where we had some of our first high school dates. We watched *The Art of Racing in the Rain*. The lesson of the whole movie is that our soul in this life comes to learn what we need to learn and teach what we need to teach, and then it moves on to a new version of ourselves to continue the journey.

My husband left the movie saying, "That was rough. It had all things I love in a movie: cars, dogs, family, oh, and my wife. For me, it was all things I love. Soulfulness." My husband, who never ever cries, had obviously been crying, as I saw a wet stream flow out from his left eye. This touched me in more ways than I could have imagined. We've been through a lot together and he has always hidden his emotions.

As we drove home, it was a cloudy night. The bright full moon shone through when there was a break in the sky for a moment. We both looked up at the exact time to relish in the light of the moon and in unison blurted out, "It's a footprint"—a perfectly formed footprint, clear as day (or should I say night), that we both undeniably saw for a matter of seconds.

I believe our souls synced up, as we remembered our babies as well as our daughter and her tiny footprints that continue to make a mark on our lives in these soulful moments of togetherness. That is how I interpreted her message and believe that is what she was brought here to do. She reminds us to make a mark that is as pure and beautiful as her name Kaia Belle represents.

September 12, 2019: Gifts of My Children

From all the things we cannot explain, we learn to reflect and to love fully. My children are my biggest fortune and were gifted to me for deeper discovery of myself. Every day, they help me and teach me and remind me that I love all that I have.

September 14, 2019: Letting Go

I never carry a fifty-dollar bill, but it is what I had so I brought it to the fair. The whole time I kept thinking, *What if I lose this?* Lo and behold, that is exactly what happened. In complete despair and tears, I thought about how I needed the money for daycare and how I work hard for the money each month. My mom had given me the fifty dollars in cash. I wish she hadn't, as it was her hard-earned money I lost. How could I be so stupid? I ruminated about the money, which made it worse.

I mentioned it to the lady at the entrance to the fair, and she said, "I am sorry, but the quicker you forget about it the quicker you will get over it." I thought about that. This may be true in the case of fifty dollars, but not when it comes to pregnancy loss.

This also reminded me of how I ruminated over the loss of our children. As I tried to make sense of it, my thoughts spiralled out of control. Why can't we be like this with the good things, like ruminating over Maelie's laughter or Case grabbing my finger and guiding me everywhere? Let it go. Hopefully we brought fortune to another kid who had fun at the fair and was more in need of the money than us.

While cuddling that night, Maelie hit my phone on the slow record button, slowing me down and reminding me to let go of the racing thoughts in my brain. Even the video in slow motion seemed like eternity, but it's only sixteen seconds—sixteen seconds of pure love, and that makes all the difference. Just like the few seconds I had with my babies who died. Every second of those precious, pure moments will last my lifetime, and that was all I needed to go on living fully engulfed in timeless love.

September 18, 2019: Girl Days

While Case is in daycare, I get to enjoy every Tuesday with my girls, Maelie Lynn and Kaia Belle. Although they happen to follow the same timeline, and both share the same due date month, I try not to get too caught up in the "could-have-beens." I am grateful for what I do have and the "get-to-bes" with my girls.

September 22, 2019: A Series of Unfortunate Events

After my wallet was stolen, which contained many gift cards to buy toys and clothes for the kids, cash, coupons to buy formula, and the children's health cards—what felt like everything—I struggled in finding the good.

This event was actually a trigger for me, making me fully aware of what I have lost in life. Although I appreciate what I have, it doesn't hide or take away what I have lost. Grief doesn't pass, and time doesn't heal; it just makes you less numb. These hands have nothing, yet they hold everything. These hands and heart have held and carried many memories of lost children, and it affects me every day.

I know that my children are all I need.

I am still angry.

September 25, 2019: Connect the Dots

As I was in the Service Canada replacing our stolen essential cards, there sat a lady, one who would later teach meditation in the yoga studio where I also taught. I would later find myself in her meditation class when my yoga class times had swapped with hers and we connected the dots. In sharing with the group my upsetting wallet experience, she remembered me from Service Canada. I hadn't even seen her in that moment, just a figure sitting in the back corner. I found her when my grief was bringing up long-term and deep-rooted anger that I had buried, which I thought I should be over. She taught me to feel my anger and turn it into power. The wallet event was the straw that broke the camel's back (and mine) and fuelled me.

September 29, 2019: The One Where I Bit My Husband

Our wounds are often the openings into the
best and most beautiful part of us.
—David Richo

Dear Janice,

I hope this email finds you absolutely wonderful! I think of you often as I enjoy most moments with my littles and the journey that brought them to me.

I am so sorry to bug you, but you were the first person I thought of to help me. I was wondering if you maybe had any suggestions for a therapist who specializes in postpartum depression. Lately, I've been struggling emotionally, and I know a lot of it is hormones and being tired watching two kids. But I do trust in my gut that there is more going on.

I have talked to my doctor about it, and she says it's just motherhood. I never lash out on my kiddies, and they do bring me endless joy, but I find the littlest things do get me really upset lately, which scares me and is not fair to my hubby who I usually take it out on. I can't thank you enough for all your love and support always.

Carmen

September 30, 2019: Traumatic Birth

Janice's response reminded me that a C-section (an emergency one at that) is still a trauma to the body, even if it is for a positive outcome, and I needed to remember that sometimes our mind doesn't process the trauma until much later when we start to heal physically. Although I am grateful for my daughter, I am hurting. What no one has told me is how long it will really hurt. I haven't healed quickly, since I continue to run after and pick up my babies.

After cracking myself open to reveal what lies deep under the surface, I have found a profound anger. I've begun noticing how things like dog hair, carrots on the ceiling, coffee spilling, or things falling out of cupboards will completely set me off. I find it easier to get mad at a mess or at Phillip than to confront my anger, accept it, understand it, and turn it into something else.

What I didn't include in the email was that prior to sending it, I bit Phillip on the arm. Feeling psychotic and primal-like, reverting back to a pissed off, frightened, protective mama animal, it all started by him saying I had that look in my eye. I now feel so embarrassed, but it was the breaking moment when I knew I needed help. I broke down crying immediately after, apologizing, and feeling completely horrible. Where did this moment of madness even come from? It scared me. Maybe I really am completely mad. There were bite marks to prove it.

Janice trusted my mother's instinct that I needed more emotional help, an instinct that will hopefully continue to help me down the line.

October 10, 2019: Being

If our kids haven't made you laugh a bunch of times a day,
there is something very wrong with you.
—Phillip Grover

Today, we indulged in the day. Being on maternity leave, you would think this is what I do every day, but it has been the opposite. As the days pass by, I'm often in my own brain with the constant "should have" list. For example, Wednesdays we should go to story time because kids need the interaction with others, and it's the only way they will learn how to read; Thursdays, we should see a special friend, and Fridays we should do groceries. The weekend is the time we should do the cleaning up and be with Daddy. The constant should haves pile on top of me.

So, today we left the house in total shambles, and we did not go to the library as planned. Nope. I started by getting a pumpkin spice latte. Then I let my toddler lead the way in and out of stores. We found ourselves heading into the pet store and picked out his first fish. Later we headed to the beach, both kids fast asleep in the car as we arrived. I rolled down the windows, sat on a rock next to the car, stuck my toes in the sand, and wrote in my journal. I simply needed to be with my own thoughts.

The kids woke up vibrant and excited to leap into the sand. Next, we visited an animal park, and I enjoyed watching Case, who baaed back at the sheep. He laughed hysterically at this, as if he had discovered a new language and cracked the code to life—the pure joy of being just like the sheep. This was so simple, and it was what my soul craved, and I did it. How rare that was.

I could have stayed at home, drudging through the normal day of dishes, laundry, and sweeping floors, thinking I had too many chores, heavily spiced with mom guilt. We are given the freedom each day to do as we wish to some degree, but how quickly we can get caught up in daily routines as life passes us by. The days can blend together. I would have missed the contagious laughter of my son enthralled with the sheep and also the sleeping cuddles of my daughter on my chest as we walked through the park. We are often shaped by society with respect to what we should do, and we so rarely ask ourselves, "What would make a good day for me?" I must remember to do what brings me joy. Today, being with my true joys reminded me of why we do all this in the first place.

October 12, 2019: Six-Month-Old Maelie

Dear Maelie,

Today, you are six-months old, and, oh, does mama ever see your sweet, spunky little personality. You have definitely kept your drama queenie-ness from birth. You are starting to find your voice. You relish being loud and boisterous just for fun. You smile at everyone you meet and then stick out your little tongue (such a little tease). You love being held, my snuggle bug. When we sleep, you always place one hand on

Mommy's chest, grounding me. I can get lost in your soft, juicy cheeks and kiss them for days. Your eyes always keep us guessing; one minute, they are blue-green, and the next they show a hint of brown. I can tell by your spirit you are driven and ambitious, strong and mighty. We love you for that.

October 12, 2019: Twenty-One-Month-Old Case

Dear Case,

You are your own little man, and you are such a kind soul. You call me Mommy and grab my index finger everywhere you go. You love telling me to sit or stop, to just be with you. You give the biggest hugs when you don't want to do something, and I can't break out of them. You dance in circles on your tippy toes. You laugh when you toot, saying "poop." You scream and so does Mommy, letting everything go, and we laugh about it. When we scream together, the force of the vibrations is undeniably moving. Every mom should try this; it is so invigorating.

You eat apples, which you refer to as "nanas," and nicely spit out the skins all over the house, leaving little trails of where you have been.

You name every animal sound as you hear it. When you see Mommy jumping up into the tree, you say "ooh, ooh, aah, aah" like I am a monkey. You say "book" before bedtime, and you say "baby" when you look for your sister. You love everyone.

My favourite thing is that you still cuddle up with your bottle and twirl your sweet golden hair, doing the one thing that has always brought you comfort, not needing to explain yourself. I love that about you. An example I wish to follow. You are more than I ever could have imagined. Every day, you make me laugh, and every day, you comfort me with your all-encompassing snuggles.

October 15, 2019: Pregnancy and Infant Loss Remembrance Day

As I look at my two children, I recall that I, in fact, have seven children. A woman should be able to say these words, not for sympathy but for awareness. It takes courage for mothers to feel comfortable in saying these words out loud on Pregnancy and Infant Loss Remembrance Day. This day is about honouring those souls that were here briefly but live on in our hearts forever.

October 20, 2019: Glimmers of Light Leading Us Home

Today, during our Maelie Day and while Case was away at daycare, I meditated at the beach. *What is it I need to know?* As I opened my eyes, I saw five seagulls, signifying to me the five pregnancies I have lost. As the sun rose, the birds shimmered like white twinkling lights. In that moment, I was reminded of the many souls or lights guiding us on our path. We must have faith that we are surrounded by forces much greater than ourselves. I was almost blinded by the light of the seagulls, but it was only in really looking that I saw them. I tried to capture the moment on my phone, but it quickly faded away.

Pictures try to remember for us. I think that's why I couldn't capture the twinkling wings. I needed to capture them in my heart, for myself, and not in a picture. The light from the souls/seagulls was guiding me home, to exactly where I needed to be, with my loved ones and with the ones I cannot see but can feel.

November 12, 2019: Twenty-Two-Month-Old Case

Case Emerson Grover,

I adore your spunky attitude in the morning, when you tell me, "No, I don't want to wake up." Neither do I, son. When I say, "I love you big much," you laugh and say, "No, little much!" Thank you for the laughs, kisses, nighttime cuddles in your firetruck bed, and elbow handshakes. Thanks, too, for never forgetting that Mommy's every body part is big. There is no place bigger or fuller than my heart for my kids. Love you so much, my boy.

November 12, 2019: Seven-Month-Old Maelie

Maelie Lynn Grover,

You are my sunshine, my smiling cheeky monkey girl. You have a good sense of humour and a virtuous approach to life. I can tell. You have been powerful from the day you were born. You speak your mind. You are beautiful and brighten every single moment with your light by just being. You are wise beyond your years. I can tell you are an old soul. I love you so much, my shining girl.

November 15, 2019: Our Silly Monkey Brains

Motherhood is beautiful. Yet we are all imperfect humans trying our best. We all love our kids unconditionally but don't want to admit or show when things are tough, out of shame, fear of judgment, or lack of support. It is the same with pregnancy loss—we hide our feelings for fear of making others uncomfortable. Why do we only share the good things? Is there something in us that wants to prove or pretend there is never a bad moment? Does admitting this mean we don't love our children?

That is absolutely not true; motherhood is hard. Of course we know our kids are blessings, and we are grateful for them, but that doesn't mean there aren't moments we feel like we could shatter. It is easy to feel that we are never enough, especially when we compare ourselves to the perfect-mother posts on social media.

Life hit me hard and fast, as I went from trying to have babies for two years with four pregnancy losses to having two kids in sixteen months. The transition from only having to care for myself to responding to the constant needs of a baby was huge. Then, suddenly, my easy baby was not an easy baby anymore but an independent toddler. I don't feel able to fully tune into his every need as I have another kiddo to attend to who is also dependent on me for survival. As I said, becoming a mother hits many women hard and fast.

After a day out with the two kiddos, I often come home feeling judged. I realize now that it is probably in my head. We ask ourselves, "Why does my kid lash out and my friend's child doesn't? Why can't my kid share like my friend's kid?" Somehow, it always feels like people think it is the mom's fault. If she wasn't so selfish, or if she followed more of a routine, or if she disciplined more. We are all trying our best, but somehow, it's not enough.

If only we could speak our truth and support one another. Yes, we chose to have kids, but that doesn't mean we are not entitled to complain that it is hard work. Our complaining is not out of lack of love or support from other moms but out of needing connection. We are seeking to feel like we are not alone and that we need to speak of our struggles with mothering to help validate them. We've all been there—deep in guilt and ashamed of ourselves. We have all been vulnerable, sleep deprived, and, oh, so hormonal. I wish we could be more real and open with one another without fear of judgment from other moms.

Our brains are always on overdrive, judging ourselves with the "shoulda, woulda, couldas." I call this the "silly monkey brain." I sometimes ask myself why I am sad when my life seems perfect. Who am I to complain when I've wanted this for so long? I feel a deep guilt that I, of all people, sometimes feel like complaining. But I also feel different because I suffered a loss that no one could possibly understand. They would think I am ungrateful. Here I am being too hard on myself, assuming others will judge me, yet I am the one judging myself. NO! My monkey mind is my worst critic. This needs to stop. Sometimes, and we may not know why, we should still be allowed to feel and be sad with no explanation required.

There is a lot of loss that comes with motherhood—loss of independence, self, body confidence, time, sleep, energy, cleanliness, dreams, and aspirations. But motherhood also brings tremendous gains. Like anything, though, it's an adjustment and takes time. Change is good, but the process still needs to happen over time, and that is when we need support most. A child becomes frustrated learning to crawl or when unable to express what he or she wants. Like us, our kids have to adjust and go through changes. We do not frown on our children's struggles, nor should we frown at a mother doing her best and learning along the way.

We should all work together and not shame or judge others. By growing in this journey together, and knowing that we don't have it all together, maybe we can share our stressors and our losses, and we can start to feel less isolated. With understanding, support, and serious listening instead of unsolicited advice, maybe we can learn to be kinder to ourselves and to quiet our monkey minds. We must erase our unhealthy standards and rewrite healthy ones—ones of self-love and compassion towards other mothers.

Motherhood is an adventure. A roller coaster ride where the parents are the guards, and the children do what we all do when we go on the ride of our lives: Test the guards. With lots of happy and scared screaming (mostly me into pillows), I wouldn't have this wild ride any other way. Hang on but also let go; it is thrilling.

My biggest discoveries have come with my children. I haven't even figured out this adulting thing, so how can I be responsible for these kids that are in my grocery cart? My little ones have taught me the most about being an adult. I know for them I am enough, and this rids me of any harsh expectations I hold. They bring me so much patience and love beyond measure, and they help to ease this mama's monkey mind.

November 26, 2019: Until We Meet Again

As Phillip and I boarded the cruise ship after exploring the island of Kauai in Hawaii, we both were talking about our babies at home and how we missed them and about our dreams for them and us. As we did, a single monarch butterfly in the middle of the Pacific danced around our heads. I love moments like these when they happen with Phillip, as he usually laughs at my "woo-woo-ness," teasing me and reminding me he doesn't believe in that kind of thing. But it was undeniably beautiful and shocking to see. I said to the butterfly "a hui hou"—until we meet again.

December 2, 2019: The Lost Find Us

Today, this message whispered itself to me as my heart hurt while I sat in meditation. Holidays can be painful when we remember those who are no longer with us—playing songs, hanging ornaments, and having special dinners. We hold on to traditions for the sake of the lost, or of not wanting to let go, and in doing so, we are reminded again and again of what we are missing. We can always find comfort in knowing that the lost find us, and we find them in our own way. For me, I know that this is through meditation. When I am with myself, sitting quietly, I am with those that I have lost, who are still with me forever deep in my hard but beating heart.

December 21, 2019: S-top, T-ake a Breath, O-bserve, and P-roceed with Love

When things seem too much, or I am too much in my own head, Case and Maelie say, "Mommy, stop." This is the greatest teaching they could ever offer. I am deeply thankful. I will do my best to always stop, be present, and hug. There is always time for that.

December 30, 2019: Seeking

I lost a kid's mitt again. Instantly, I was convinced it was gone forever this time. But it keeps being found. This is just like the loved ones we have lost; they turn up in our thoughts and in our hearts when we least expect it, when we think they are gone for good but when we need them most to keep us warm. To comfort us. We never stop looking.

January 1, 2020: Onwards

Crazy morbid thought: As I reflected on the past year, looking for hope in the new year ahead, I thought to myself, *We have no idea what lies ahead of us.* We should live the year as though we will be dead by the end of it. We should think about how we want to be remembered, how we want our stories to develop, how we make others feel, how we practice kindness, and how we enjoy the little things, like our little ones.

January 2, 2020: You're Going to Be Okay

No matter how big or small, our losses are not weaknesses. There is no greater strength than honouring all those we love; it is how we survive. Happy third heavenly birthday Kaia Belle. My life goal is to honour you by remembering you and to never feel bad about sharing you with the world or the sadness I feel that you are not with us. Whether we grieve with tears, smiles, laughter, or silence, speaking of you helps us heal.

Yet know that you are in the beautiful moments we experience together as a family. This morning your siblings, Case and Maelie, without prompting, started patting your memorial picture (that I had taken out especially for this day) and laughing, and it was just so sweet to take in that natural moment with joyful tears in my eyes.

Today, Gramma and I saw a musical called *Come from Away*. In the musical, the actor said to the mother bonobo that he was sorry she lost her baby. Gramma and I looked at each other tearfully. Then the primate's caretaker told her she was going to be okay.

We sat in Row K.

I reflected and prayed to you tonight. I realize I can do this any moment of any day but today felt right. I often keep thoughts of you buried, as they are still just too painful. But at times, I relish in the beauty of you. You grace our days so frequently. I know just how strong you are as you continue to fight to be with us.

February 17, 2020: Family Day in the Bahamas

Today, instead of spending Family Day with my family, I spent the day with the woman who gave me family. For my whole adult life, once I had discovered cruises, I told my mom how one day I wanted to take her on a cruise. As I started having my own family, I thought about how it was going to get harder and harder to coordinate. But I have seen this all played out before. There is never enough time, or the timing is not right, until there is no time at all and never a right time. So I said one, two, three, go... and made a pact to never stop journeying. I coordinated with Phillip and my in-laws to watch the kids while we embarked on a five-day cruise to the Bahamas.

We essentially celebrated being mamas without kids (even though I'm her kid). We were the "Bahama Mamas" and being able to say that brought joy to my soul. In a moment of guilt, when we hopped into the taxi that would take us to our ship, the taxi driver asked us about our mother-daughter expedition, and I faltered. Maybe he could sense the tone in my voice when I did share that I had children at home because he said, "You love your husband? Yes. You love your kids? Yes. Of course you do, but your mom has loved you your entire life. You are blessed. This is good that you do this together. You have to."

What a blessing motherhood really is, and I got to explore it in the Bahamas with the one who brought me life.

April 4, 2020: Twenty-Nine

Once again, I have that knowing feeling that I am not alone. I can't confirm it or deny it.

April 5, 2020: The Grief Walk

As I walked through our mucky, muddy road, taking the lightest most cautious steps, I looked ahead seeing the dry and flat clay road and green grass ahead. As I walked through the dirt, grime, and bumpiness, it got easier, and I enjoyed the walk more. I realized I didn't have to tip toe anymore.

With each step, I trusted a little more, my steps becoming stronger, deeper, and fiercer. Finally, my steps were triumphant when I made it to the dry road. As I reached the grass, my muddy shoes had dried up, and the mud had fallen off. I laid myself down and surrendered to the grass. I let my newfound strength sink into my body, my mind, and my soul. I watched a bird land on some very tall quack grass. This bird trusted that the blade of grass would support its weight, and the grass almost neared the ground and sprang back up again. Birds still pursue their love of flying and sing their songs while eating and gathering food and building their homes. They do not worry about what's going to kill them.

April 13, 2020: My Spot

The Tree

That spot that you go
Where you are met as you are.
Where worries and to-dos are not.
Where getting to is not always easy.
Where you are alone yet so comforted and loved.
Where you are spoken to with compassion from your own heart.
Where there is such nothingness that is everything-ness.
Where no one can touch you, but you are still connected with all things.
Where the birds know your name.

Where the grass cushions you,
the tree supports you,
the wind nourishes you,
the sky grounds you to your limitedness,
the sun calls you,
and the ants bite you, just a nibble,
To remind you that you are alive.

The kiss and taste of the place
That can always hold you,
That always is.
That saves our history's stories for us to hear
whispered through the breeze, buzzes, chirps, bristles,
and the language of the rickety, old wise branches.

This Spot is our place.
This place that gives us the answers that we and ourselves
before us always knew.

Take time to be at your Spot.
The Spot where all is lost, and everything is found.
Listen with your heart.
There you find heaven on earth.
Hold on to it tightly.
Don't let it get away from your daily grasps.
Nature, and what we gain from its wisdom, never changes.

April 19, 2020: Connected

Dearest Kaia,

You would think that sadness would flood over me when I think of you. But it is now the very opposite. My most beautiful moments are when I feel you with me. When I lay on my yoga mat, hands to my heart, my fingers tingled as I recalled feeling your strong beating heart on my index finger. You were warm and your beating heart connected us. My lifeline.

You continued to be with me when I was greeted by Oma with potato soup. Case and I jumped on the bed, and then Maelie and I rocked in the swinging loveseat. The sun beamed brightly above us. I breathed you in. Thank you, Kaia. You are the sun shining brightly over us, bringing warmth into our life, into each other, and into our hearts.

Part 4
Falling

We tried to navigate our pain, waiting for it to lift,
feeling like we should be over it by now,

but the pain is always there; it just shifts from struggle to light.

The pain caused us to rise the most,
even when we felt like we had fallen so far.

We still persevered and got through something
we thought we could never get up from.

Babe #8
Jude Simba Joy Grover

Take nothing for granted yet take in all you've been granted.
—The Grovers

April 21, 2020: Confirmed

I found out I was pregnant on April 9, confirming that deep knowing feeling that I am not alone. The pregnancy was Mommy's gift and another sibling was Maelie's first birthday present. I simply told Daddy that we have more than just Maelie's birthday to celebrate, as we both expected me to be pregnant. We had been trying for you.

May 13, 2020: One Baby, You Are Here

The first ultrasound—nine weeks young. The ultrasound tech said three times that there was just one baby. "Here is your one baby." "You can see there is the head on your one baby." "Looks like a good one baby." I never even asked if there was more than one. I thought this was entertainingly funny.

May 14, 2020: Life

It sounds so obvious when you say it out loud, but this hit me hard. You never really know the last time you will see someone until that person is gone. That's the thing about life: No one knows when their last day is going to be; it's just one of those things you can never predict. It really makes you value the time you have together more than anything.

June 6, 2020: Day at the Park

Sweet Kaia,

Every once in a while, there is "that" day. The one day that is perfect in every way, where the butterflies dance beside you while you bike and play. Those days you live fully, love completely, and fervently pray.

Kaia, you and your spirit siblings are all spiritual beings on a human journey. That is what you are to us, along for the ride, giving us butterfly kisses all the way.

June 21, 2020: Facebook Announcement—COVID-19 Baby

Our circus is growing,
Tiebreaker coming on Case's birthday!
There's no place we'd rather be
(during a pandemic)
than at home with our family and growing baby #3!
Although this isolation is the pits,
we are about to be a family of six
(counting Nola, our dog, of course).

July 4, 2020: Help

Today, I walked to the tree. The tree that has always been my spot. I walked there as the moon shone bright. As I lay under it, I said, "Please help me." I could not name exactly what it was I needed help with. I started to sob uncontrollably, my eyes red, completely sore and swollen. Deep inside, I was aware I needed tremendous help.

July 10, 2020: Innocence Lost

Phillip came home to let me know that a girl from work had just miscarried at twelve weeks. She shared this news specifically with Phillip. He believes it was because she knew of our losses and felt he would be a good support. I can deeply empathize with her, and I reflect on Amity, our first loss at almost twelve weeks. The first blissful baby we knew before loss hijacked everything: hope, imagination, anticipation, eagerness, dreams, and tremendous joy. I didn't know then that I would forever be chasing the feelings that a first pregnancy held. I didn't know then that Amity would be the first and last time I would feel such naïve elation during pregnancy.

I have not experienced that in a pregnancy again. I simply never knew a loss of that kind existed prior to my first loss. Now I constantly wish to feel that naïve excitement while pregnant, and I feel shame when I pretend that I'm so overjoyed by this baby when really I'm scared. I know I'll never get that back, and it doesn't make me want it any less. I've been stripped.

July 19, 2020: Life Back at Children's Hospital

In working a set as a paediatric nurse, which consists of two twelve-hour day shifts followed by two twelve-hour night shifts, I can see unbelievable things in just the course of four days. I had left the paediatric ICU after having my own children as I found it triggering. Yet no matter where you work as a nurse, you are always dealing with unimaginable situations.

A boy about Case's age (three years old) turned his head up to marvel at the stars, lost his balance, and fell into a bonfire. He was the family's only child. One split moment in time, and he was forever scarred, but he was alive and healing fast. When I changed his dressings, he screamed for his mama and dad, wanting to go home. I completely lost it. I had to change my tear-stained masks way more than the allotted amount I was supposed to use.

I went home after my shift and squeezed the living starlight out of Case, who was still awake. Later that week, when we watched the fireflies under the bright moon, and as we slept together in our backyard tent looking up at the stars, I bawled. I bawled for the beautiful, blink-of-an-eye moments. I will spend my whole life trying to understand these heartbreaks.

Last night, in our backyard tent, both my kids were lying with me, their heads on my shoulders. I touched my hand to my belly and mentally took a bird's eye photo. Then, just like that, Maelie fell off the mattress. I found myself yelling at her about how awful she was that she couldn't just sleep in peace and stay still.

In a split moment, I moved from feeling blissful awe for my sweet children to desperate anger. This is another phenomenon I wish I could understand—how my emotions can change so quickly, like in grief, when I'm okay and then suddenly I'm not. I was once more reminded how my world could change in an instant. As I reflected on the families of the children I had seen at work, grief stricken and angry, I suddenly realized that my daughter falling off the bed did not seem so bad. It could be worse; she could have suffered a brain bleed.

July 20, 2020: Foreseeing

I am desperately looking for answers and trying to find comfort, so today I went to a psychic so that we can absolutely know our future. Athough they say this predictability is not certain, I am constantly trying to test and prove this theory wrong. What an easy life to know what is coming! I was told that we were going to have a baby boy—one of the babies my granny had miscarried, apparently.

July 21, 2020: Self=Love

Today I got the mail, went to my appointment, and picked up some groceries. I did the things I was supposed to do. I had Aunty Holly watch the kids so I could do these errands, and on the way home, I took one extra side road.

I took one hour: I crocheted and listened to the waves for fifteen minutes. I did yoga with other children's happy screams as my background music for ten minutes. I read for fifteen minutes, wrote for ten minutes, and watched children jumping in the water, dogs walking, and teenagers snapping photos. I meditated for ten minutes. One whole hour, and at the end, yes, I felt some guilt. But for a brief moment, I went back to the me before I became a mother.

I needed the time to go back to me with no regrets. It was unbelievably amazing what just one hour could do. I drove back happily and energetically refuelled. I embraced my kids with all of me there, completely content and present. Thank you, Aunty Holly, for this hour of power but also no thanks required.

July 22, 2020: Trauma

A broken heart still beats. Just like a sad face still smiles.
—SA Jones

Here we go again.

I sat in lucky room number seven for our eighteen-week anatomy ultrasound, the same room that each and every one of my previous ultrasounds had taken place. The same yellow tree decal stared at me from the pale white walls of that windowless room.

I was thinking about how I needed to get my deposit back for the parking transponder and that I had to pick up prenatal vitamins and snacks for our mama's group beach day outing the next day. I ruminated that I would have three kids under age three before I was thirty. Maybe I could even have one more in my thirtieth year. What?! I hadn't even had this baby yet but freely assumed that I would.

I lay there thinking that after the ultrasound I had to go to my family doctor appointment, then visit Oma, then work on my yoga class for the next day, and lastly get my teeth cleaned. Then I would head home and spend the evening with my beautiful kids and hubby.

The technician interrupted my thoughts and said, "We can't find everything we need. I am going to get another tech. Can you lie on your side? Hopefully, the baby will move."

The ultrasound tech came back with the radiologist, who said, "I was told you work here." Pleasant and light conversation before the big blow. But then he said, "It appears that you don't have any amniotic fluid, and your baby does not have kidneys or a bladder. For the baby's lungs to develop, the baby needs amniotic fluid. I'm sorry."

I remember my first thought being, *What does that mean?* But I knew full well what it meant. Yet I needed to hear the words spoken: Your baby will not survive. There is no surgery that can be done that will save it.

He left. I stared up at that yellow tree in total shock and disbelief. This was supposed to be a casual eighteen-week ultrasound checkup. This couldn't be real life. Why did I ever trust that everything would be fine? But I truly, wholeheartedly did this time because Case and Maelie were fine. I thought that the third time was a charm. We were past our worst days.

After a few minutes, I processed what I had heard: The baby was not viable, and I was going to have to say goodbye to yet another baby. I didn't even know what I needed when they asked me what they could do for me. I was alone, with no hand to hold, no one by my side, nothing. They asked me if I still wanted to see the baby. I glanced up and had to look away. How quickly it changed from wanting to see my babies on the screen at any chance I could get to being unable to look because it made the pain even worse. I didn't resent the baby, but right then, I needed to not see it. The baby was my entire world gone.

Did the baby somehow feel that I did not want them? I was so distracted, with my mind racing to everything else besides the baby. Did they feel this? Could it be why this was happening? I felt this fear, and I felt the burning sensation of the blame I was placing on myself.

The tears welled up as I said, "I just need a minute." The ultrasound tech who had concealed what she knew all along said, "I'm going to cry with you."

My real life thought: What the fuck?

How could this actually be happening again? This couldn't be happening. Why me? Why us? This was so unfair. And it felt so crazy because I wasn't expecting it at all.

But I was in fact expecting this.

Here's the play-by-play replay:

Strike one: Amity, our first loss.

Strike two: Will, the baby whose heartbeat they never found.

Strike three: Kaia Belle, lost at twenty-four weeks, our first birthed baby.

Strike four: A chemical pregnancy.

Save one: The Case man, he is an absolute miracle.

Save two: Miss. Maelieboo, our delightful surprise who gave us a scare.

(Case and Maelie are the two most beautiful saves that allow me to write this piece.)

Strike five: A pregnancy lasting almost two months that ended in miscarriage.

Strike six: Being told our baby has Potter's syndrome—no kidneys, no bladder, and no amniotic fluid.

Although this was even worse than with Kaia, it was actually better than Kaia's situation in that there were no decisions to be made. This baby would simply not survive for absolute certain. The baby might only live a matter of minutes after birth. You never know how many minutes you will have, but those minutes are everything.

In a time like this, you don't just lose your baby, but you also lose all the hopes and dreams you had for that baby. And there is such a stigma attached to the termination of a pregnancy. Trust us. We don't want to terminate this pregnancy. We are crushed. It is a selfless decision broken-hearted parents have to make. Sometimes in these situations, where the decision has been made for you, death is a better fate.

Am I selfish to believe that after having two beautifully healthy babies that I deserve another? Who am I to think this way? I haven't felt sick with this pregnancy. In fact, it is the best I've ever felt during a pregnancy, blissful under the summer sun.

Our integrated prenatal screening (IPS) with this pregnancy came back positive for Down's syndrome. During my pregnancy with Maelie, the IPS also came back positive for Down's syndrome, and we vowed never to do another IPS. Yet we did. Our Harmony prenatal test, an invasive blood test that screens for many syndromes, including DiGeorge syndrome, had come back negative. We deeply trusted that we were in the clear.

With the testing we had been offered this time around, I felt confident that maybe this was one baby I wouldn't have to worry about, and maybe I could be spared the dreaded wait of the anatomy scan results. Maybe I could just actually enjoy my pregnancy, and I did for once, which was something I never got the chance to do with Case or Maelie because I was always on high alert, in denial, and in protective mode. This was yet another robbery from pregnancy loss.

After our losses, I should have known that I can't plan shit. I was thinking we were all good, yet here I am dumbfounded again, in total shock and disbelief. Why can I not have every chance at happiness or plan anything? You know, like everybody else can?

The truth is life has been going better than ever. I am in a job I have dreamed of since I was a little girl; my summer yoga classes have really taken off, and I spend my days playing with my kids with only a few yelling matches. I'm learning to do what I please. When things are going well, why must I always feel like I am due for a strike? Sadly, this is how I think. Why can't I just have it all?

I smile all the time, and I feel it's important to leave my crap in the glove compartment. As a nurse, I need to be fully present, happy, and compassionate for others as they go through their darkest days. But I have to say, it is getting harder for me to smile.

After receiving and somewhat processing the news, I drove to Oma's and witnessed my daughter spinning in circles; it was her discovery of the day. She was happy as a spinning top. My son was in the flower garden, digging in the dirt and laughing hysterically in joyous delight. Oma's eyes spoke nothing but wholehearted compassion. I was unable to bring myself to smile at my innocently playing children, and she understood when I said, "It's not good Oma."

I walked up to the step, putting on a brave face as both kids grabbed hold of each leg. I tried to stand tall, almost collapsing by the weight of them (and all of it), and my hunnies gave me the biggest bear hugs of sticky love. Oma shed tears and poured us tea. The simple act was caring. I held the cup, feeling its warmth, although I couldn't bring myself to sip from the cup of compassion it offered. In that moment, I appreciated anew the absolute wonder and miracle that is life.

I am beyond devastated. As I prepare to take time off from my new position, I understand I will go through horrendous physical and emotional pain yet again. It is a pain I never thought I would have to go through again. Just the same, subconsciously, I think I prepared for it every day. When one goes through the worst, it seems one prepares for the worst.

July 23, 2020: The Calm Before the Storm

On July 21, I took myself to the beach to read, write, and do yoga. For no reason, I started making a rainbow blanket. I had an urge that I wanted to. My soul somehow knew I needed this. As I prepared to leave the beach, I saw a bald eagle. Every time that I have seen a bald eagle, either immediately before or immediately following, someone has died, or we were pregnant. I think I already knew what was coming my way. I have looked up what eagles symbolize many times, and often it means that change is coming, bestowing the freedom and the courage to look ahead. Recently, I found out that eagles are associated with death and the journey of souls. Welsh legend tells of how the souls of brave warriors flew to heaven in the form of eagles. Oddly, right now, this fits, although I find little comfort in it.

This year, I dove deep into meditation. I asked for help and to be shown how I can serve others. Was this my answer? Is sharing our story my purpose? I have such rage at parents who can have kids without the constant fear of loss. I am saying this now with full knowledge that I will immediately take it back.

This is grief. First there is the disbelief, not even hearing correctly, if at all.

Next comes the anger. Unfortunately because of the COVID-19

pandemic, I had to go to the ultrasound alone. I was angry at Phillip that I had to hear the news alone and that he did not pick up his phone for an hour and a half, even though his phone battery was dead. I knew that it was, and that morning, I thought about it briefly but then never asked him to charge his phone. I believed all would be well. I let my guard down, trusting that this time might be different and jinxing it.

After hearing the news, and in a panic, I hurriedly messaged my best friends and instantly jumped to cancelling appointments and mom group visits. I called my doctor in hysterics to cancel my appointment. The receptionist asked, "Are you sure you want to do this?"

In my rashness, I replied, "Yes I don't need an OB appointment for a baby that isn't going to live."

I called the geneticist, who told me to keep the appointment for a doctor's note. I cancelled shifts at work and spoke to my coordinator, who suggested that maybe I could go in to work on the weekend to cuddle other babies. I briefly thought this was a good idea; maybe the distraction would help. But at the same time, did nobody get it?! All I wanted to do was cuddle my own babies and the baby within me. Later, someone from the occupational health department called my coordinator to let her know that after hearing this news, I would in fact be a liability issue.

In our culture, why do we say "I'm good" when someone asks how we are? Even after I had been handed a shit explosion of shit piled on top of the shittiest worst news, I still said I was good. Or is it just me that does this? I found it easier to go to my dental appointment than to reschedule it. I just acted like I wasn't even pregnant, saying I would get the x-rays before they even asked. I found it easier to say I would work my Saturday and Sunday shifts so as not to disappoint anyone, knowing in my heart that I will need them off. At Starbucks, it was easier to give an extra big smile than say it was one of my worst days ever. I didn't want to burden anyone or bring anyone down. Over the years, I thought I had become better at not doing this, but instead I smiled even wider. I am now even more nervous to show any hurt whatsoever, armouring up even more. This all brings me back to losing our daughter. I remember smiling in the conference room, going into autopilot, and comforting others when we were given the worst news of our lives.

My greatest anger of all was Phillip, when immediately after I called him with the news, he said, "Yup, this is the end. Just the two kids. No more of this shit."

Can you believe I was still pregnant with a dying child, and I was already thinking of the next chance for a baby? My mind jumped to a conversation I had with Phillip, when we had previously discussed having a third child. He said, "I'm happy with our little family. We have two healthy babies already. I don't want to risk anything."

Who could have known that, again, he was right?

May I say that my dear husband was in the instant pit of grief and understandably so. You know how they say that hardship makes you stronger? There is a large and lengthy comatose space to endure before that door opens.

July 24, 2020: Why? Why? Why?

Why did I randomly pick up that pregnancy book on grief for five dollars at the grocery store one month ago? I thought I could give it to a friend one day.

Why did I go for a walk two weeks back, randomly asking the universe to help me, with tears in my eyes for something I didn't know, but maybe I did?

Why did I feel so confident and not go to the repeat ultrasound for a small bleed detected a month back, electing instead to see if it resolved in one month?

Why did I have a fall at Jess's gender reveal party, which really awakened me to the fear of losing this baby and still carrying on?

Why did I believe this time would be different?

Why was I shocked when told the expected truth?

Why was I mad at the ultrasound tech for talking to me through the entirety of the ultrasound when all along she knew full well the baby's prognosis?

Why did this have to happen to us again? What am I doing so wrong in this life?

Why does the universe think I can live through these scenarios that aren't supposed to happen?

Why do I not understand that you can't control anything at all in this life?

Why was it not clear enough the first time?

Why did our marriage really need this test again when parenting two little ones is test enough?

Why did my body need more physical pain and emotional turmoil?

Why did this happen this year, when I especially have felt good about myself for supporting more locally, trying to be more authentic, and holding free yoga for all who wanted to join for a mental health break?

Why did I put myself through this again when I could have taken more time off on Maelie's maternity leave and not rush back to work in a pandemic because I was pregnant?

Why, when my son finally understands that there is a baby in Mommy's belly and says it to me every day, does the knife twist just a little deeper?

Why?

Are we not meant to have a third child?

We definitely deserve to be parents, and I say that unapologetically. We know that we would be more than complete with our two beautiful children and would give them a life of adventure, but we, too, are allowed to have our number.

Upon my arrival at home after picking up the kids from Oma's, I threw my shoe at the door. Hard. I brought stuff in from the car. I spoke not a single word to Phillip. Later, we embraced hard, with no words, and that was enough.

I went back to the same bedroom where I had wept when we lost Amity and then Kaia. At that time, I believed life was over. Not knowing how to cope with it all, I wanted and did take a bunch of alcohol to black out. All those hard, dark-day feelings and memories flooded back to me. But I also thought of the midnight cookies in bed, breastfeeding, and morning snuggles with my whole family that had also happened in that bed, the same bed where Case and Maelie laid their heads on my pregnant belly.

A tiny and sweet voice broke my despair. "Case likes Mommy," he told me, as he kissed my hand and proceeded to cup my face with his hands. As he patted my arm, Case asked, "Feel nice, Mommy?"

Maelie entered the room and walked around the bed proudly, playing peekaboo and saying "Mama."

I need to remember that I do all of this for them, to hopefully give them the gift of each other. That is my purpose, and, yes, I'm lucky to be able to do that for them, even if this pain is something I need to endure. Yet something is different in me. I feel awful playing the blame-why game. Phillip does not want to go through any of this again. I recall that for two years after Kaia, I was messed up—like, properly messed up. He doesn't want that again, for me, for him, or for the kids. I understand that he doesn't want to see me suffer. He is scared. Nonetheless, that suffering has changed me.

I know I won't make a whole shrine book for this babe like I did for Kaia. I won't write about the little comforts that we experienced together. For this babe, I see little pollination fluffs that float overhead, and I realize this baby has given me the gift of grounding in nature. As I am writing this, crushed, I lovingly and cruelly feel the baby move for the first time. And for the first time in this pregnancy, I feel sick.

July 25, 2020: Something Greater

I weep for the lost time and for not having three kids under three before I'm thirty. I weep for my body not bouncing back. I weep for what our life would have looked like next year.

At the same time, I relish in the absolute gifts that we have right before us. I still get angry at those lucky, baby-having parents, yet I recognize they have their own setbacks every day. I am grateful for my setbacks (said through grinding teeth) since I always collect myself, and when I think I can't appreciate it anymore, I do.

This is still very raw. I know the next few weeks will come with even more emotions—anger, rage, and unbearable pain. But in writing this right now, I know that the age gap between Maelie and the next child is such a minuscule thing to worry about. I have my living children and the babies that get to walk beside me in life. I can honestly say that in the last five years, I have never, ever been alone. And in all this hurt, I have never felt more loved by the universe. How bizarre is that?

Call me woo-woo, but there are exact moments I'm talking about. That dove that reminded me of Opa, when I happened to just be thinking of a thing he always said. The song that came on the radio while I was reminiscing on my cousin's incredible zest for life. The randomly found gift card from Granny for McDonald's coffee when I started my new job. The image of Grampa holding a baby, which gradually appeared in the wall design after his death. The wind-up singing nun trinkets that have not been touched in the cabinet in ten years that randomly started to sing on the ten-year anniversary of Phillip's grandma's death for both him and his mom to hear as they came walking up the steps together. The bald eagle that appeared on the telephone wires (we called each other every two weeks) just before I was told Granny had a stroke. The bald eagle our whole family spotted standing in the field as we drove to Grampa's funeral. (He died working his land.)

There is something greater than us, loving, comforting, and guiding us, which I am reminded of frequently. It is always in the depth of grief that I feel the most spiritual and see the beauty and feel the love. The most beautiful memories I have are of holding the babies I lost. It is the only gift that comes out of these times.

On another crazy turn, Phillip doesn't want me to go through delivering a nonviable baby. (Is that not still a real baby?) He thinks it would be easier for me to be knocked out and the baby removed (disposed of in medical waste), never seen or held, and for us to carry on like nothing happened, with no physical or emotional pain. Not possible. I can't think of our baby being treated like some discarded tissue. Phillip doesn't want us to feel deep pain again. He doesn't want to make this harder than it already is. Yet I crave to feel the same love I felt that day we delivered Kaia in the pale-pink-tree-decal private room. It would be a chance to hold and fully be with my baby. There was such hurt but even more love in that place.

I will forever cherish the professional family photos we had done two days before hearing the news. What prompted me to have them done at that time I will never know. Our family was so full of truth, joy, love, innocence, and happiness. It would not be possible to recreate that joy after we heard the sad news. That day I was pregnant; that day was a gift. Tomorrow, I may not be pregnant, but that cannot take away that I was pregnant that day.

If there is anything I can convey it is this: When planning for future moments, just stop and know you can't. Although we are allowed to dream, it is the planning and the expectations that leave you hurt.

We're going to be okay. Love gets us through all things and comes to us most in our darkest days. Namaste.

July 26, 2020: Stupor

Why did I even post anything on Facebook? How could I be so stupid? Now I have to argue with my husband about how I posted to let people know of our hardship, an outcry about our tragedy that he thinks we should have kept private. All of this when I do not want to be arguing at all. I wouldn't have had to do this if I hadn't announced our pregnancy in the first place. We went down this same road with Kaia and said we would never announce a pregnancy on social media again. Have I not learned anything? I so badly wanted to write, "Well, another one bites the dust." In my spite and anger, those were the first words out of my mouth.

Second Entry: Here We Go Again

> *Children—yours, mine—they don't necessarily live.*
> —*Once More We Saw Stars,* Jayson Greene

Hi Janice,

I hope you are keeping so well in the beautiful weather we've been having. I'm not sure what counselling looks like for you right now, but I just wanted to let you know that Phillip and I are pregnant again, and upon the awful twenty-week ultrasound, they found that our baby has no kidneys, no bladder, and no amniotic fluid, so lungs can't develop, and the babe will not be viable.

I am completely heartbroken that this is happening again, but I am in a different place. I know we have two beautiful, healthy kids, and at the present time, if I'm being honest, I just don't want to go through all the formalities of it all, if that makes sense?

This is me just speaking right now, but of course our geneticist said to reach out to you, and I couldn't agree more. I know I will for sure need to talk about it, but I also just want to skip over the grief and pity party. I know you and I both know that is impossible, but that's where my head is at the moment.

Sorry that whenever I reach out to you it is with sadness, but at the same time, I am happy to always have you to turn to.

Kindly and warmly,

Carmen xo

July 27, 2020: Through Hell and Back

I grew up in a family with two sisters and two brothers. Our father has bipolar disorder, which meant things could get chaotic, and our mother was often the victim of his moods. Although life was far from perfect, it was perfect in many ways. Having lots of playmates was one of those ways.

We grew up on a farm, caring for animals, sledding down barn rooftops, jumping on old cars, chasing caterpillars, biking to the creek, falling in fox holes, playing in grain bins, and smashing golf carts into barns and dikes. We were reckless hellions, but we were always together. When Dad had his fits, we hid in sheds and basements together. Sometimes, we all lined up in a row and biked to Oma and Opa's place. Somehow, we always knew what to do together.

When our farm business folded, and we almost ended up living on the street, it didn't change our love for one another. Somehow, with very little, we held together even stronger. Farm accidents and loss made us love even deeper.

My husband grew up an only child, always feeling lonely. He loved spending time at the trailer park where he could play with other children. He looked forward to going to Scouts. He also lived a full life, but it was very different from mine. I was surrounded by built-in playmates.

Growing up, I knew a family who lost a daughter in a motorcycle accident and a son who fell asleep at the wheel. Phillip knows of a family where the daughter died of flesh-eating disease, the brother died in a motorcycle accident, and the last remaining brother had nine close calls, including falling from a silo. My granny, who had seven kids among several miscarriages, lost her daughter Brenda at two years old to leukemia and her twenty-year-old son, Darren, in a car accident involving a transport truck. My own brother survived many close calls himself. He was struck by a truck while driving a combine on the road. The nineteen-year-old driver of the truck died.

It goes on and on.

I believe in my heart that Maelie deserves a younger sibling and that Case deserves a brother. It is getting exhausting though; I have been pregnant eight times in five years. I was pregnant for seventy-nine weeks total with my two living babies and seventy-nine weeks with the six babies I have lost. At what point do I cut my losses? My body, mind, and heart have been through hell and back. I know it is time to accept it. But how do I let go of the hope? To keep trying is so nerve racking, but I am just so desperate. Why is that?

It is also exhausting in the sense that there are so many dates and anniversaries to keep track of. There's hardly a month that we haven't been pregnant, lost a pregnancy, were announcing a pregnancy, or announcing a loss—years of constantly remembering the good, the bad, all of it. Some years I felt the loss and hurt more, and sometimes I celebrated the memories of our babies.

July 28, 2020: Punishment

Should I have been there more with Case and Maelie? Phillip says they feel it when I keep going through all the pregnancy trauma. Phillip also says that this baby is not a baby until it is delivered alive. Our perspectives have changed so much. But like every single family that goes through heartbreak, we are always left asking why. So we continue to self-sabotage. Is there some reason this is happening to us? There must be a diagnosis of some sort that explains this.

The world will tell you many things about pregnancy loss. I have been told: you keep miscarrying because you never sit still (which I believed); it's where you work and related to radiology and chemo drugs; it's because you were on birth control; you haven't given your body a break; it's your cell phone; you do not appreciate what you have. Yada, yada, yada.

Today, Phillip and I had to go for our repeat ultrasound to confirm the diagnosis of what we both already knew. Before I went in alone for the ultrasound, Phillip said, "Do you think maybe the kidneys were just too small to see?"

I just looked down until they called my number. After the door closed to the ultrasound room, the ultrasound tech handed me a Kleenex and said that I didn't have to be strong. This small act of honesty and compassion meant everything (the first I had ever received from an ultrasound tech), and we both said nothing as I let myself completely and safely fall apart in that room. Following the ultrasound we met with the team, something I did not get to do on the day I received the horrible news, when the radiologist left, and I was sent home.

We sat at the round table, and I asked about carrying the baby full term for possible organ donation, needing something good to come from all of this but knowing full well it could not be done, since there were too many of the baby's organs affected. I then broke down, saying I was too selfish in wanting three kids. The obstetrician stopped me and said, "Some families are complete at one, and others are complete at five. You are allowed to want what you want."

The team went over our options and promised to get us in as soon as possible. Unlike with Kaia, this time we knew what was coming, and we couldn't bear the wait.

July 29, 2020: The Dark Days

I am trying my hardest to put grief on hold, and, trust me, it's not possible. I know I have to move through grief, and I know I will have to revisit my daughter's death. I try to look away, to be able to get on with my days, but it just hurts too much. Why have none of my closest friends gone through this kind of loss? It always has to be me.

July 30, 2020: My Body

Selfishly, in losing this pregnancy, I feel I have ruined my body for no reason. Last November, I ran a marathon to prove to myself I still could. Although I did, I nearly killed myself, crawling to the finish line. After going through numerous pregnancies and the emotional component that goes with them, I have not bounced back the way I would like. I do not feel healthy.

I want to feel happy in my own skin. I would be lying if I said I didn't want to be back to my in-shape, skinny, prepregnancy self. I often find myself saying it was worth it for the living children. Nonetheless, it is hard to know you suffered through the exhaustion, the nausea, the vomiting, and the headaches all for nothing. That is the dark truth.

Today, I cried hard at my body, the same one I hated when I was younger. With hard work and the wisdom of years, I have learned to love my body and appreciate its ability to birth and nurture children. But the appreciation is fleeting. The self-hate creeps up behind me and knocks me flat. Did the self-hatred of my own cells, engrained so strongly in my body, destroy the cells of my babies? Some days it feels like I am emotionally seventeen again.

July 31, 2020: Disturbed Revelation

Case ran into our room this morning with his flashlight and told us, "A ghost is coming!" How do I explain death to a two-year-old? Do I even have to? The answer is that there is no answer; there is no right way to do grief. I took his flashlight and together we looked for the ghost—woo-woo-ing all the while.

August 1, 2020: Preparing

Each and every day since the diagnosis, I find myself crying off and on. My dear Case keeps saying on repeat all day every day, "No, Mommy is not sad. Mommy is happy Mommy." Yes, dear son, Mommy is sad, but Case makes Mommy happy and thank you.

I think back to a moment etched so clearly in my mind. Maelie held her pink dolly with such care, grace, and love, for what was essentially a fake baby. Case chimed in, "Case wants a blue dolly." Oh, how something so innocent packed such a deep punch to my crying heart. I could have given my children a real blue baby doll.

Things have not been easy. Work messaged me asking if I was going to be in tomorrow (the day of induction), as they didn't see me on the sick list. Are you freaking kidding me? No, I will not be in tomorrow. I mean, yes, I will be there in the hospital but not for what you need me for. Except I gave them a response in the most polite way possible, something along the lines of "Nope, I am still off sick. Thank you for checking." And as an aside: I will be a little busy, incapable, and hella emotional tomorrow. I then thought to myself, almost as if coaching myself for what lies ahead, *I'm not doing well, and I am having a really hard time, but I will get through this.*

Last weekend, the weekend prior to our induction date, Phillip and I went boating with some friends. The water was choppy and the wind fierce. We wanted to be powerful and spontaneous, just like the water. Instead, I felt like I was breaking apart inside, just like the waves breaking against our boat, the waves of grief. I quieted myself afterwards, walking to a willow tree. I drank a beer with my husband. He offered. I accepted. No further words were spoken as I drank in silence with my thoughts, and the tears stained my face. My children found me there. They cheered me up when together they ran under the willow tree, letting it tickle them, with laughing fits and the sun sneaking through the branches.

Today (the day before induction day) was such a blur. The thought of taking the medication that induces labour makes me feel very scared. It also makes the next stage very real. I have been through an induction before, but taking the induction pill a day prior in order to kick-start labour before my hospital admission is new to us. Even so, how do I prepare for the pain that is coming? I've made a mental note to make sure to ask for the pill that suppresses milk production after "it" happens.

Tonight, dear sweet Phillip tenderly held my hand as if I would break and shatter beside him. He said, "We're going to get through this."

I then laughingly offered him my breast, saying, "Here squeeze my boobs. That is the only good thing that has come out of this."

Being a member of the itty bitty titty committee, I must say that actually having boobs has made me extra proud of myself. Finally having a B cup has been a monumental moment for me. A moment I need to gloat in. A moment I need to feel lighter in and to enjoy finding humour in. Being pregnant brought me some cleavage!

Lying on my side, I joked that it was the first time both boobs had enough weight that they would both touch my hand when I put my hand between them. For once, Phillip needed two hands to squeeze my breasts. Normally, his one hand squeezed them both simultaneously.

Then Phillip said, "You'll have them again."

It is like we walk a tightrope, both testing each other yet not wanting to say we are done with the baby thing. You can hear it in the undertones.

I said, "Well, I'm just going to finally get super fit."

After Maelie was born, I didn't. Why get fit if you're going to get pregnant again, right? Please don't quote me on this. Of course, it is still good to be active and maintain a healthy lifestyle for your own general wellbeing.

Phillip said, "Don't get super fit yet, in case we want another one."

And there it was again, slapping me in the face. We both suck at this game. If he could just say "no more," and I could say "no more," it would make this much easier. But a heart knows what a heart wants, and we just want our baby, our family, each other.

Although I have pretended like I've had no time to make a blanket for this baby, I started working on what looked like a rainbow dish-cloth. "What are you making that for?" asked Phillip. He knew full well what it was and who it was for. In his grief, he couldn't find the words to say it; it was easier to pretend he was ignorant.

Yes, I am in fact working on a tiny blanket for our tiny, soon-to-be dead baby. I am running out of time. I really wanted to make a blanket, like I did for Kaia, even though I said I wouldn't this time. I need to know that I'm not brushing this baby aside; that I also put time and thought into their being. I have tried doing a different pattern and failed. If the blanket was different the experience would be different too, right? Very quickly I stopped trying to do something different and just did what I knew. The same pattern but for a different baby.

I want this baby to know that deep down I care for them, even though I pretend I just want to get this over with. I have fantasized about the dilation and curettage (D&C) option, yet I know that is not by any means an easier option. We all have to do what we feel is best for us to cope. Phillip wants the least memory-producing option and I desperately want to hold our baby. This is definitely not easy and has added strain to our already strained selves. We are being stretched thin. What if this time our marriage doesn't bounce back?

I remember how I held our daughter before she died in her blanket. Did she feel the love? I was so afraid for our baby to be born dead and not feel the love, convincing myself of Phillip's words it was only a real baby if it was born alive, almost wanting to prove a point.

Tonight, Phillip said he does not wish to hold our baby, as it will be "just a thing, a nothing, a bundle of cells." Although this sounds harsh, I know this is his grief brain talking. It is what we do to blanket ourselves, only now those words have come up again. Those words that have been buried so deep below the surface and the years and years of Phillip suppressing his feelings and holding it all in. Phillip told me he will be haunted forever by holding Kaia Belle while she was dying in his arms. He has spoken her name only four or five times since the day we lost her.

I changed the topic, talking about the new van we purchased on the same day as our repeat ultrasound, the one that confirmed the bad news with this baby.

"Hey," Phillip said, "You're doing pretty good. I'd be curled up in a ball in a hole somewhere if I was you."

I chuckled and somehow found comfort for a brief moment by that little bit of encouragement. I almost said it was better than "you're really killing it" when Case was born. But now was not the time. Not funny, Carmen.

Phillip, who pretends he doesn't care, was up all week with night sweats. Both he and I have not been sleeping. This "thing" that we have to deal with may in fact be affecting us whether we like to believe it or not. I ruminate and ruminate again, spending the night searching for answers into the wee hours. We had a one in four thousand chance of having a baby with a syndrome the first time, and now it has happened twice. I've searched to see if there is any association between DiGeorge syndrome and Potter's syndrome. Nope. Was it the one drink I had? The hot bath? Maelie jumping on my belly that one time? That dandelion tea I drank? Doing and teaching yoga?

As I spilled out these concerns one more time, Phillip humbly said, "Those are not things that cause kidneys not to be present."

I knew he was right. Everyone keeps saying it's not my fault. Over and over again, I find more things to be sorry for, more promises to make, more statistics, and more lost hope. I know full well that Google can't help me or offer me any do-overs.

Saying goodbye to the kids tonight as we dropped them off to sleep over at Gramma's nearly killed me. They are supposed to be doing this in December while eagerly awaiting the birth of their sibling. I wanted to see their surprised faces as we shared our baby with them. They cling to me all day. Each day they feel my belly with hands, feet, heads, and each day, I am checking if the baby inside me moves. It all feels so cruel. Baby does not deserve this, yet baby knows no other life. Baby does not know that the end of life is near.

Tonight we had sex, and I cried every tear that was within.

August 3, 2020: Hey Jude

I think back and reminisce about the bright summer day when we told our family of your existence, with Maelie dancing freely and banging wildly on the steering wheel to the song "Hey Jude" by The Beatles. That is how I want to remember that moment of joy.

As I sat there in the delivery room, I had a déjà vu moment. Phillip and I were dumbfounded that our worst nightmare was actually happening again. It is devastating. Having experienced this before definitely does not make it any easier. Being in that delivery room brought back a lot of old emotions for both of us. This time, we know we have two beautiful and healthy babies for whom we are very grateful. But here we are, with our two healthy babies, asking ourselves why that wasn't enough.

We sat there, and I thought of us as that fluky couple that had a terrible baby loss happen twice. Yet I also think of us as the lucky ones, and Case and Maelie the lucky flukes we get to keep. Does this make us luckily unlucky or unluckily lucky? I start to see clearly that it is time to let go of the hardships and drama because in this moment, nothing else truly matters.

My mind is full of replays. I recall the ultrasound, that blurry, unimaginable, and highly forgettable day. The baby was moving his or her mouth. I watched it. The baby was wiggling around trying to get away from the ultrasound probe. The ultrasound tech told me that the baby's heartbeat was positive. I am still haunted by those words. Then the radiologist delivered the news. In that moment, it occurred to me to be kind to everyone, as you never know what somebody else is going through. I learned that lesson the hard way by being the person going through hell, the one on the other side of that big smile.

My Response to My Counsellor's Email

Thanks so much for checking in. On August 2, we welcomed Jude Simba Joy into the world. Our cute-as-a-button boy was born at 9:49 p.m. He had no deformities and was the purest perfection. He came fast and was born with a heartbeat. The delivery could not have been smoother; placenta and baby both came out in one little push. I am sorry for the picture, but I couldn't help but share him with my favourite counsellor to honour his sweetness. I will never forget, just prior to delivery, Phillip and I observed two helium balloons, pink and blue, float together past our window into the clouds and beyond. I know our angel babies are looking out for us.

Love always,

Carmen, Phillip, Kaia, Case, Maelie, and Jude xxxx

August 4, 2020: Postdelivery

Instead of waking to a baby crying (Case and Maelie both sleep through the night), Phillip woke to me crying as I looked at pictures of our son Jude. The nurses had kindly taken pictures at my request, but I wasn't prepared to see them printed in the memory box. I fell to the floor; the pictures were beautiful, but the shock was fresh. What had happened? It all happened so fast. Our entire world had changed in a single ultrasound reading. From dreams of a future to nightmares of a funeral.

If I was born to be a mother, why does this keep happening? Today. I got my dream, of mothering two boys and two girls, two million-dollar angels in our hearts and two million-dollar children who walk among us.

Jude was the only pregnancy I never felt sick with and actually enjoyed. I white knuckled it through each of my other pregnancies. I should have known. One would think this loss would be easier to get through, but I am depleted in other ways. I am up at night longing for the devoted and loving sleeplessness that would have accompanied Jude in my arms. The emotions, the hormones, the exhaustion, and the physical pain can be drowned by the delightful distraction of a new baby and the automatic amnesia that ensues.

Parting Thoughts

I must remember I don't have cancer or anything that is going to end my life.

This pregnancy was a problem I brought on myself in some ways.

Life is precious; if I haven't seen or known this already, it's time to slow down.

How many spirit guides are we lucky enough to get in this life? We don't need anymore.

We were never promised or guaranteed anything.

In some spiritual beliefs, I chose this life. I have to remember that I knew these things were coming; therefore, subconsciously, I knew I could handle them.

My body needs to heal. Jude, you showed me that in many ways; in mind and spirit, I am healed or getting healed. Thank you.

Each time I make it to the halfway point in pregnancy, I shudder.

Second Entry: My First Panic Attack

A letter I received from Gramma.

To our sweet, perfect grandson Jude,

I didn't get to know you for too long, nor did I get to know how the pregnancy was going for your Mommy because we had just found out that you were due to come in December. Then shortly after we heard that great news, we heard the very sad news. I wish I could have held you in my arms, as I did with Kaia, to tell you how much I love you and how special you are. Your Mommy and Daddy were so happy and so excited, as were all of us.

You and your sister Kaia are together now. You are the guardian angels to your brother and sister on Earth, and for your Mommy and Daddy and for all of us who love you endlessly.

I love you so very much Jude and thank you for the love you brought us all. We will meet again someday.

Love forever,

Gramma

I read this letter today and started breathing heavy, my head going dizzy, and I was unable to see straight. I felt bad that because of COVID-19, my family could never see or hold Jude. I thought about how Oma confided in my sisters, saying she wished she could have baptized Jude as she had Kaia, and how it was the closure she needed. Everyone is hurting.

I wanted to pass out and let my tears carry me out to sea. Instead, I meditated, taking several deep, boxed breaths, and what came were these words: We... will... receive.

A Tribute to Baby Jude

Love is like a balloon, easy to blow up and fun to see grow.
But hard to let go and watch fly away.
—Author Unknown

Jude: Praised, a delight.

Simba: powerful lion

Joy: denotes great happiness and is derived from the old French "joie."

August 5, 2020: My Lion Cub's Birth Story

To my sweetest love Jude,

Daddy is watching your siblings as I sit outside under my tree (our spot) to write to you. Already, as I think of you, my thoughts are only filled with love and joy. Oddly, there is no anger. Undeniable heartbreak, yes.

I still try and picture you as a boy, a brother to be born on your brother's birthday, a companion, a mister fixer, and mischief maker. I still see in you a little brother for Maelie's motherly and sisterly instincts to nurture.

You were the best pregnancy that I ever had. I was that annoying pregnant person who never had pain or nausea; in fact, with you, I found a new level of energy I never knew I had. I was able to be fully present with my family, to dream bigger, to let things go, to simplify, and to offer yoga classes to others in the hard days of COVID-19. We shared our first pandemic together.

This year, we really appreciated time spent with our family. You were always with us as we hiked, biked, swam, stretched, laughed, bounced, rode in our classic cars, and danced in twirly circles. The days we had were perfect; our gratitude is great.

Life seems so unbelievably unfair. It is not for us to know why these things happen or to figure out a reason. There have been families who go through far worse, and others who have had it far better.

On July 28, 2020, the day when the sad news that you had no kidneys was confirmed, your dear Daddy and I rashly bought a van. We both seem to cope with stress by going on wild spending sprees. We bought the van with the hope to fill it in the future. Sadly, Daddy couldn't convince me on a Jeep for the same price.

"All summer long, I can keep a floaty in the back for the beach," I said. Sold!

You brought us our van and our hope, as we drove home under the rainbow skies. Who after hearing the worst news imaginable in life (again) buys a van the same day?! Us nutbars! That was our grief cycle at work.

We can only make sense of it all when it is our own time. I do feel that in life we are dealt only what we can handle, although it never seems that way at the time. On a subconscious level, we already knew what life had in store for us, and we picked it just the same. Despite all the hardships, I did get to hold all my birthed babies and surround them in such love as they passed. I so hope I gave your soul exactly what it needed and more.

The night before induction day, I woke up at 3:00 a.m., as I had every morning since hearing the unbearable news. I went to my meditation spot, and I listened to the silence of the house. I spoke to you. I felt your every move. I told you I loved you, and every time this would set you into a flurry of somersaults. I prayed to God, the universe, and anyone who might be listening that you would be born with a heartbeat so you could feel our love (even though the odds were against it given your gestational age of twenty weeks). I held on to this hope, and you did in fact have a heartbeat.

I prayed for a speedy, uncomplicated delivery, and as soon as the epidural was in, you were out. The delivery was filled with a certain symbolism and comfort; the same nurse who delivered your sister Kaia happened to deliver you while she was covering our nurse's break. You were my most normal delivery, but not in the way of welcoming a screaming, healthy baby into the world. You were a peaceful boy just like I had imagined. You had a lightning bolt birthmark on the back of your head, which to me symbolized your exceptional power and how we were struck by calm love for you.

As grateful as we are for technology, it does detect things sooner than in the days of our parents. In the past, parents would go through the entire pregnancy and discover different tragedies at birth. How awful does it sound to say we are grateful to have known ahead of time? But knowing about it is also horrible. No one ever wants to know a baby is not going to live.

The blanket I made you was the perfect length with the perfect colour change row by row, making a beautiful rainbow. The Ken doll clothes I picked for your body fit so perfectly, as if they were tailor made for you. The nurse asked, "How did you know?"

Acting all cool, I told her I had an idea of the size because of my twenty-four-week-old daughter. In reality, though, it surprised me too. It was another sign that I needed.

At one point, in my grief, I said to your Daddy, "He has your one foot."

Daddy jumped up. "What? My deformed foot?"

It was the wrong thing to say. We all say and do crazy things in grief. Your Daddy already worried that he had caused the syndrome and that it had been his fault. He was usually the one who said crazy grief things to me. This was me doing it to him. It laid bare our fears to each other.

By the way, dear Jude, your feet were absolutely perfect. It was just the way your one toe was stuck and crinkled to the side of your adjacent toe that made me think of it. Besides, how cute would it have been if you had your Daddy's foot? You did have your brother's chin and lips, which I now see every time I watch him sleep. So small yet so developed.

Following the delivery, when you were taken away to be examined in the quiet room, I mind numbingly scrolled Instagram. The first thing I saw was an old friend who now had a family of four in the order of girl, boy, girl, boy. I was jealous... that could have been us.

Your dad and I were the only ones who got to be with you and experience all that you were. We took in every moment as we went in the quiet room to say our last goodbyes. I kissed your cold, handsome head. I told you I loved you and that I was sorry. I watched huge drops of tears flood your blanket. I patted you with just one hand. I could hold all of you in my one hand; now I hold all of you in my heart. Your Daddy spoke few words during all of this, so when he said, "Poor little guy," the words took me off guard and made my knees buckle. We didn't want this for you, dear Jude, or for our family. Please always know that.

When we left the hospital, we heard the birds' songs as they greeted the morning sun. And we followed rainbows all the way home. I wanted to hold you and never let you go. In my heart, I will do just that. But I so wish I could choose to physically hold you whenever I want. It was so hard knowing that one hold was all that I got and all that I would get. The hold that would leave my heart strained, from holding on to the hope of you. It was so immediate and so final. That hold is all I will have to sustain me for a lifetime.

The morning was crisp and foggy. There was not a word spoken as Phillip and I stared off into that purple-hazed pink sky, both hypnotized and dazed, but we held hands the whole way home, loving each other with our purple and pink strangled hearts on the outside.

I called the funeral home that following morning after you died, and the director at the small-town funeral home told us to take our time and that the cremation costs would be covered. We went to the funeral home that same day, and we agreed to get an urn for both you and your sister, deciding you will always be together with the picture of the beach wrapped around you. It was there where I always felt both of you the most.

It rained August 2, 3, and 4, three days in a row, after we lost you. It rained more than it rained all summer. The world collectively felt our sadness. At the same time, rainbows lit up our social media feed. Like Simba in *The Lion King,* when they showed him off on Pride Rock, you touched so many of us, and it rippled outwards. You brought such joy to our days. You gave us light in the current darkness of this world.

Today, as I meditated, again I heard myself speak the words: You will receive.

August 6, 2020: With Great Learning Comes Great Understanding

Dear Jude,

Today, I woke up angry at your brother for testing me. I said, "Please, not today." I was angry with your sister for screaming so loud, and I yelled back at her "That's enough" and "Stop it!" I remember thinking, *I just want my sweet Jude.* I knew full well that even though I so craved my perfect innocent baby, that it was only an image, a fantasy to busy my mind with. You, too, would cry, hit, get angry, and throw fits one day, as your siblings and as all children do.

Auntie Kerrie demanded we visit the sunflowers today. Although I felt so down and couldn't pretend to be happy, the sunflowers waved at me and told us we would be okay. Case said he had work to do as he ran through the field. Maelie spun around laughing and giggling as the sunflowers tickled her. She pretended to hide and got completely lost in them. The moment was a bright one, and with you by our sides, I am glad you gave me the oomph to go.

Today was a hard day. Thoughts of you floored me. It seemed that nobody got it, and everyone said sorry and moved on. Am I to continue showing up and pretending I am okay? Today, this time, I was just not okay.

I just needed to be alone. I returned to the same tree, my spot, where a short time ago, I lay bawling and asking the universe to help me. As I sat there, I received a text message from Chelsea: "My daughter and I have been exploring our garden this morning. A butterfly joined us; I immediately thought of Jude."

Her family has always believed that if a cardinal comes to greet you, it is a loved one who has passed that is making a visit. She had begun to see butterflies in the same way.

Today also marks the day of my darling cousin Janelle's death in a motor vehicle accident at age sixteen. Today was also Grandpa's birthday. So many emotions come with this day. No one could replace you or my cousin. You are not to be replaced but honoured by the living. I sincerely hope that is the least I can do, dear Jude.

May I also mention here that I distractedly learned an amateur version of The Beatles tune "Hey Jude" on the ukulele? Case and Maelie laughed tremendously at my pitchy singing rendition, with them strumming along. That in itself was worth it.

Grief can be such a bitch. I feel so lost. I feel bad when I can't find energy, yet time flies by, and I wonder what I did with my time. I am tired of being sad, yet I don't know how else to be. I realize this must be the reality for everyone experiencing grief, and I wish I had some answers. It seems like I had more guidance before with Kaia. Now I am more attuned to every little bug, wind, and song. It hasn't worked, but I will continue to listen. Perhaps another tattoo is what I need. Sometimes even I can't believe this is our life. I can't believe it's our life when it's awful, and I can't believe it's our life when it's beautiful.

I want you so bad. Kaia has been gone three-and-a-half years now. Thoughts of her have lessened and no longer hurt as much. The thoughts and memories are still there, but they no longer bring pain like the current thoughts of you do. I know that the same will happen to thoughts of you. Somehow, I don't want that to happen, as it will mean I've moved on. Well, not really. It means I will have moved through the pain, and it will start to get better.

Pregnancy loss is such a shock; one minute you're pregnant, and the next you're not. It is something so incomprehensible, something too many women are ashamed to share for fear of constant judgment. Nothing can prepare you for this kind of trauma.

When we lost Kaia, I did a thing that many people would hide. I posted a picture of me holding my dead daughter. I later learned how this photo would haunt Phillip. "We just do such different things," he said. "Things that I would never do, you do, and vice-versa."

In the loss of my daughter, I was so focused on my own feelings that I never once asked my husband what was okay with him. I was too absorbed in my own grief, and it was all I had energy for. I will spend my whole life being sorry about that. At the time of Kaia's death, posting that photo just made such sense. I wanted to commemorate and honour her in some way. Looking back, I see more clearly the horror that I may have caused to so many. I didn't see it. I saw nothing but love and the purest beauty.

Phillip never talked about it, and that is okay. This time around I will think of him and his feelings, but I did put my foot down after he said I couldn't take photos of the experience. Photos can always be deleted. These would be the final and only photos I would ever have of my baby. So I took them. I now cringe at the photos I have, smiling with Jude, completely unaware of how to feel in the moment. But they are photos I get to keep. I sometimes feel like I should be crying in them, but maybe one day, I will find different meaning in them.

Now, as I sit next to my tree, my tummy aches with phantom movements, a gentle reminder of the baby that is no longer. Not long ago, every tummy cramp was a happy reminder of a growing baby. I hugged my dear tree, and as I did, a fluff flew by my face, and I felt the warmth of the sun on my shoulder. I know the fluffs are everywhere this time of year, yet they especially seem to be everywhere when I am with my thoughts of Jude. Or is it because I just think of Jude all the time?

I sometimes wish you had just been a miscarriage. At this point in our journey, it just seems like it would have been the easier hardship to deal with. Seeing you sucking your thumb in my womb, living happily—it now makes no sense to me at all. Why didn't you die earlier? How do we say goodbye to someone who never lived? How do we remember someone who never took a breath, but took our breath away and is now in our every breath? Is that why we never buried you? The funeral director asked the question everyone wondered: Was it harder this time around, as we now knew what we lost? In some ways, yes it was harder. With Kaia, we had no living children. With you, Jude, we knew and were humbled by having Case and Maelie. Their faces light us up, but they make us long for you.

When we discussed the urn for our children, I thought about my own granny and how she would always talk about the loss of her son Darren at twenty years old, her daughter Brenda at age two from cancer, and her many miscarriages. She would talk about this to people in restaurants, grocery stores, and even brought it up the first time she met Phillip. I was so embarrassed, even thinking less of her for it, and thought it was a cry for attention. For that I am deeply sorry, dear Granny.

Being a mom and losing babies now myself, I cannot even begin to know how to cope with the loss of an older child, but it makes more sense to me now. She was not looking for sympathy but for understanding, repeating the trauma for reassurance that she had honoured her babies in the best way she knew how. Granny used to say to my aunt that she still felt pregnant even at an old age. She thought this was because she never forgot the feelings of the pregnancies she lost. She never forgot them. She never grieved them properly either.

Back then, men did not talk about the loss of their children, although I know through my mom that Grampa would wake up screaming in the night from nightmares of his dead children. Granny held her daughter as she died, and Grampa had to identify his son's body, and together they buried these babies, including the one they lost at twenty weeks.

Burying doesn't mean the end, and that is what Granny needed to know and understand in order to go on living in this world. Although I never knew them, her babies' names and their stories were always so engrained in my life. That is how I know it's not in the act of burying but in speaking our babies' names that they live on in our lives. This knowledge has helped me. I realized I am getting an urn because I'm not ready to bury my babies; that act seems too final.

I sometimes look at old photos of Phillip and me. The pictures that came before the miscarriages, our daughter Kaia, and you, Jude, are a testament to our happiness. I notice the innocence in our faces. These photos hold no hint of the forthcoming loss. But that is how it has to be in life; if we knew what was coming, we wouldn't enjoy life properly.

We have had grief before children and loss after children. People say compassionately, "At least, you have your kids." Although I don't love this comment, they are not entirely wrong. Without them, I would probably still be in bed. But it still hurts. Grief is forever because love is forever.

August 7, 2020: A New Journey

Today, we went to pick up the van—the van we got for our family of three babies. It was such a beautiful day, but something was missing. When I drove home with our children in the back, I cried the whole way home, hydroplaning in my own tears.

Later, we ate out on the deck, and for dinner we had a free salmon meal—free because dear Daddy didn't have his debit card on him, so the teller said it is on the house. Case and I spotted three little kittens from our adopted cat. You bet this mama took it as a sign. We had a bonfire and watched the kittens play and share in some of our salmon. It was pure magic.

As we wound down the day, talking about life and our most exceptionally good day all things considered, Maelie puked up salmon chunks everywhere. Case screamed, "Maelie pukes chunks all in her hair!"

It was a bit of comic relief with a side of truth that imperfect endings can be alright for us. I know we will continue to be greeted by such days.

August 8, 2020: Our Family Photo

A mother is not defined by the number of children you can see,
but by the love she holds in her heart.
—Franchesca Cox

Today, we were sent a file from the photographer with our family portraits. I looked at the photos with blurred eyes. We were then a family of five but would be a family of ten if every pregnancy had come to be. Yet our family portrait would not feature ten members. We would not have had other children had those babies survived, and our timelines would have changed.

If our first baby Amity Lynn had lived, we would not have gone through our second miscarriage, the trauma of losing Kaia, and the chemical pregnancy that followed. We also may not have gone on our trip out east or the several trips it took me to heal and to start finding myself and to grow closer with Phillip after the loss of Kaia.

My dear friend Kristen, who had experienced her own losses, said to me that even after so many years, the only thing that she could say for sure was that their losses gave her a different family than the one she would have had. This didn't mean better or worse, just different. Had Kaia lived, we definitely wouldn't have had Case and maybe no other children, as our life would have been spent in hospital, or we may have re-evaluated the scary unbearableness of parenthood.

Had our baby after Maelie lived, we would have had so much chaos in our lives. Then again, we may have never even been trying, not that we had been during that time anyways. If that pregnancy came to be, there would have been no Jude.

It goes on and on. This is hard to grasp, but it is something I notice as I stare at that family portrait. This is our family, the one I know and the one I love, as we continue to grow together. We are everything and more, our family of ten, and we will always count them all. I can see them.

August 9, 2020: Facebook Announcement Take Two

Within the same year, Phillip and I posted "It is with broken hearts we announce..." and "Our hearts are full to announce...."

If Phillip and I have learned anything, it is that there is always love no matter what. Even in our saddest and hardest days, our babies' souls were brought into the world by love. By being with them for the briefest moments, the love I felt from and for our babies is like none I've experienced before. It is hard to explain that in the depths of undeniable grief and the darkest days, love endured and nurtured us onwards.

Rest in peace, Jude Simba Joy. We will forever remember our time with you and will continue to feel your love. We owe it to ourselves and everyone around us to spread love, light, and joy, and it is okay if that can't be right now. May Case and Maelie be blessed to know they have a brother to guide them and hold their hands as they walk through their glorious lives.

Phillip and I vowed to support each other through sickness and health; we never imagined this could mean the sickness and health of our babies or our mental states. We also vowed we would never again have to share such devastating news on social media. For that, we are sorry, but we let our guard down. We shared our pregnancy as we truly believed it would be perfect in every way. Know that I am not that strong. I still collapse in utter grief and wake Phillip up at night.

It's a wonderful life. Yet it is sad that it takes these dark moments to snap us out of our own heads and the hustle of daily life. I am always chasing perfection and never feel good enough. There is no such thing as perfect. Our babies were perfect to us even though they were medically labelled otherwise. How I wish we could always live in the state of enlightened gratitude that grief brings, but I do fall away from it naturally and sadly until the next wake-up call. Each morning, I get to look at my babies and for a brief moment, I remember I am alive. I am here. I am love. I give, and I receive love. Nothing else matters. It's a bad day, not a bad life.

August 10, 2020: Forgetting

*Forgive yourself for not knowing what you didn't
know before you learned it.*
—Maya Angelou

After losing Kaia, I got a tattoo. During the process, I felt no pain; I was my own numbing agent. It wasn't until I got another one (after being told by the tattoo artist that I was a pro to have one on my ribs—one of the most painful spots apparently), which packed some sweet merciful words, that I realized I had begun to feel again. I made a whole book devoted to Kaia, writing what we did each day of the pregnancy. Then I blacked out about ever doing it. Too distraught to think properly or even know what it was I was doing and why.

I think I need to be over it. An agitating and eerie recalled response from our earlier losses frequently pesters me. *At least you can get pregnant, just have another one* replays in my mind. I wear a locket of my dead babies and look at them each morning. I did get through grief with my girl and know I will with Jude. But I don't want to. I'm not ready to give him up or get over it.

I glance at a date on my calendar. On July 22, 2020, I wrote in my agenda: ultrasound, appointment, organize videos of the kids, work on yoga, lunch at Oma's, teeth cleaning, new beginnings, and sleep in trailer with kids. Looking ahead to July 23, 2020, my agenda listed beach day, yoga, and freedom. I had also filled in all the days in the calendar that I was scheduled to work until December. Little did I know how many of those planned dates I would have to scratch out.

August 11, 2020: Decisions

In making the decision to end our daughter's life, we weren't that strong. We worried about the pain our daughter would feel in her life and didn't want her in a group home or at home with constant care. We could not bear the journey of her being in and out of hospitals her whole young life. My new job would be nursing her. There was no guarantee she would make it from one surgery to the next. The fear of growing attached to this little being under the daily threat of losing her was too much for us to handle.

Many parents of children with chronic illnesses know their time is limited. Although we would have cherished our time with her, we would have always wanted more time. Although people say they will help you through it, in the end, it would have been Phillip and I who would need to cope as her parents. We essentially got to choose the life we wanted, yet it wasn't at all the life we wanted. I felt both selfless and selfish.

Today, a pair of bees landed on me as I was floating in the pool. Out of reflex, I instinctively swatted them away. After they landed in the water, I felt bad. I instantly wanted to save them, and I scooped them up. I was delighted and relieved to see them fly away. Later, I was greeted by a hummingbird, the symbol of love. These were small moments of comfort today. I saw a couple pass by with a baby in a stroller. Again, the sight of them no longer swamped me with dread and anger. It again brought me hope.

As I shared my grief on social media, other moms opened up about the grief they never got to express, and it became clear to me how we all need to talk about it. I began to wonder if I could create a platform for people to start openly speaking about it—to create a safe space for sharing the unspeakable grief of losing a child.

I realized again today that I love my husband a great deal; I couldn't love him more. Perhaps the silver lining in all this grief is to show me I am grateful for him. But did we really need this test or lesson to prove our love and gratitude? I sincerely have worried we might not survive this time around, with more stressors on our plate, more loss, more trauma.

Tonight, my dear sister Kerrie gifted me a night to myself in her tent while she watched the kids overnight. As I chose to listen to the saddest music, a meteor shower played in the sky. I saw three shooting stars, and they coincided with the lyrics about being okay and holding someone dear in your heart. Two stars really stood out, one flickering and the other shining bright. Am I starting to pay more attention? Noticing more in grief? Is this the gift or am I being shown the answers? Or am I completely losing it? Most times it feels like the latter. I am lost. Somebody find me, please.

August 12, 2020: You Were

My dearest, sweet son Jude,

I cannot believe that I am saying this. At this current moment, and it changes by the minute, I am at peace. I feel comforted knowing you have a sister and other siblings with you, embracing, hugging, holding, and loving you.

You always seemed too good to be true, and you were. How does one even begin to explain it? I wanted you so much. I know when I go back to work in December around your due date, it is going to bring me excruciating pain. I know that you're okay. I just don't know that I am. I know that you felt love. I know you will always be with me until I hold you again.

Oma, bless her, said, "It must have felt different this pregnancy?" Yes, it did. For once, I felt good. That's why it all went so wrong. I had the same dreams for you that I have for your siblings. I wish them to be undeniably themselves. You were exactly that, dear Jude. You simply were.

It is time to change the self-dialogue in my head:

I am.
I am enough.
I am love.
Just as you were.

It is important that I take the "sick leave" time I have been granted with my little ones. Time that I know I am fortunate to have. Time that I sometimes feel in the wrong for having. But I need this time to be able to do the kind of work that is my passion. I literally have nothing to worry about. Living, trying to survive, that is all I have to do. Somehow, even that seems hard. I know December is going to be a difficult month, yet I look forward to it in some ways. December will bring thoughts of you, and those are always cherished and welcomed, even with the flow of tears running down my face. I love you forever and always. Thanks for choosing me to be your mama, choosing to be in our lives and choosing me to hold you when you had to go.

Part 5
Floating

Together we will touch the sky,
Floating all the way to the stars.
I'm letting go to see if you will hold on to me,
releasing you and finding where we land together.

Unknown Territory

The hummingbird symbolizes the enjoyment
of life and lightness of being.
—Elena Harris

August 13, 2020: Applause

Today, we enjoyed the day. I called Phillip to tell him how proud I was of my mothering. Honestly, I was wishing he was there to applaud me. I took my kids to a blueberry activity farm for a day of fun. Both my kids wore their pandemic masks when they needed to. There was no hitting; they waited their turn in line, and they baaed at the sheep in good fashion. In a moment of generosity, Case even wanted Maelie to drive on his tractor with him. Later, they sat on and steered an excavator–together. They even followed me in the store without prodding or grabbing everything in sight. It was some form of sorcery, let me tell you, but I was lucky to bear witness to it and tell the tale. We had a picnic and shared ice cream, and we watched a hummingbird that danced for us.

August 15, 2020: Honouring

Dearest Jude,

Today, I put your things together in a memorabilia picture frame. I reminisced and marvelled at your perfect, angelic picture. As a young child, I was fascinated by angels. I wrote physical letters to angels hoping they would answer my prayers. I placed them on the windowsill before heading to bed, believing fully that they would be picked up in the morning. It was my way of finding proof that angels existed. I never faltered doing it each night, just like I waited for the tooth fairy to gather my tooth and leave a reward. I desperately wanted my prayers to be answered, and at such a young age, I earnestly trusted they would be. Now I understand that although the angels could never physically pick up my letters, I was never disappointed, and I always held on to the hope of one day. Instead, I've been able to experience angels physically. And, yes, they did finally answer my prayers.

August 17, 2020: Stuck in the Dirt

Today, I took my shoes off and felt the soft yet gritty sand below my feet. As I walked the path towards the tree, I recalled that it was sometimes dry and sometimes messy and sticky. Today, I found a puddle. Not knowing its depth or how cold it might be, I knew for sure that it would clean my feet. If I kept walking, more dirt would gather on my bare soles. I stepped into the puddle and discovered that it was lined with clay at the bottom. I worked hard, pressing deeper into the clay in my effort to get back up. My feet felt heavy with the burden of the wet clay. As I continued to walk, the clay dried and fell away from my skin. Finally, all that remained were my brown, dirty soles.

I realized that this walk is a lot like my experience with grief. I never know how deep the pit of grief is going to be. Will I sink far inside and fall to my knees? Or will the water tickle my toes? Will the water be warm and comforting? Or will it be cold and unbearable? How messy and raw will I be as I walk through the puddle?

I kept walking through the muck and the mire, and in time, the puddle became shallower, cleansing my feet, but they still always held on to the colour of the dirt. That part had not faded; that part was an honorary tattoo.

As I walked on the path, I thought about feeling lost and how when I go through grief, I feel there has to be a gift through it all or something to guide me in my life's purpose. My spirit guides must be working on overdrive because daily they bring me many messages. I saw a yellow butterfly. What could it mean? Well, it is the signal of transformation.

I thought of how some children are here on this earth for the right time to complete their mission. For some people, it takes a whole lifetime to find their purpose. I recalled a story in a book on grief called *Permission to Mourn: A New Way to Do Grief* by Tom Zuba about the author who lost his eighteen-month-old child, his wife, and then his thirteen-year-old son. There was so much loss in one life. Each time, he must have believed there would be no more loss sent to him because he had received his quota. Horribly, he was proven wrong again and again. How does one deal with this? What was his grief walk like? We are all always searching for meaning, no matter our stories.

I feel that I have already had my quota, and I am scared to even think of it in those terms. What if this loss is preparing me to go through a greater loss? After all, "God only hands us what we can handle," the words I despise the most. I already feel like I can't handle what we've been dealt. I have started to feel a bit fanatical, with my questions spiralling out of control. Grounding myself, I remember that all I can do right now is to let the dirt settle and to love my family hard.

I feel sad for that man, the author, who in his grief wrote a book to help other families. How did he muster up the strength? In grief, positive things can happen, and they often unwillingly do. He does not realize how much he has touched my life. If only we could see the butterfly effect of our own lives on others. If only we understood in a deep way that we touch many others simply by being. I realize how lucky I am to have kids who have touched my life and to have lost babies who brought me into all the lives of those who sympathized or shared stories of similar loss.

As a newlywed many years ago, I said to my mom on a walk, "I feel like Phillip and I are going to have problems with having babies."

Why did I say that? Where did that even come from? Did I know this deep down? We hadn't even started trying yet. While I was pregnant with Kaia, I worried that I could never cope with living with a child with special needs. Did my baby hear that? Did she think to herself: *This poor girl can't handle and love herself properly, how can she handle and love me?* Although I know this is crazy talk, this is the real life talk of my grief.

In a moment, I can be swept and submerged into self-sabotage, and in the next moment, I can be looking for meaning and beauty. Sometimes being overly positive and optimistic is all I can do to find ways to fill up my days and distract me from my pain. Other days, exhaustion takes over, and I'm stuck, unable to pull out of it all. No one knows the cruel stories we tell ourselves in the darkness.

I've noticed how in some of my journal entries I talk a lot about how beautiful life is and how grateful I am. Life is beautiful, and I am grateful. But I realize that this is also my way of convincing myself to see the beauty and to hold on to hope, constantly writing it to prove it to myself, almost like a mantra to motivate myself to keep going through my grief. But I have to remember that it's also okay to say things aren't always rosy.

Grief can do insane things. My coordinator at work called ,and I immediately jumped into defensive mode. Why am I off? When will I be back? It never occurred to me that she might be calling because she cared about how I was doing. Sadly though, that was my first and only call from work. I have noticed that people hide and turn away from phoning during these times. I, too, ran from answering the call.

I don't feel like I can go to work and handle the two children. I need to work on my screaming daughter and unpotty-trained, unsharing son. I need to invest in them rather than jumping to or chasing the next dream. I tell myself to enjoy what I've got. Slow down, Carmen. Let me be stuck for a while, not forcing anything and finding the pause. This may just allow me to find a way out of it

August 18, 2020: A Social Media Post: Holding On

Home has a way of letting the most beautiful
people hold your hand.
—Wilder Poetry

Loss becomes part of our story, and we should not be afraid to tell it. My hope is that I can honour Kaia and Jude by breaking the silence surrounding infant loss whenever I can. Speaking their names and sharing their tiny hands holding mine is how I do that.

The topic is uncomfortable in many ways. Babies should not die. As a society, we turn our heads, as it's too dark to look there. It is easier to pretend we don't see it. In my university bereavement class, I was taught to not shy away from saying the word "dead." When children hear "lost," they may think that the baby is hiding somewhere. I need to get used to saying it for myself and for my children to hear it, even if death doesn't feel like a soft word.

Through talking, I am beginning to understand and to heal. I hope I can be an avenue for other people to crack open their silence. I don't need to talk about it all the time, but sometimes when it feels right, I do.

Today, I posted something on social media to commemorate my babies. Why is it okay to post our living babies holding our hands but not our dead ones? My husband is hurting, as he has no one he can talk to about it. For some, talking is uncomfortable. My husband does not agree with sharing our grief, as he feels it is personal. He says, "Our babies were our babies, no one else's."

He is absolutely right. That is what is hard. When someone you love dies and they are an adult (still horrible), people can share in their grief collectively. I think that is what makes pregnancy and infant loss lonely. No one can share in my grief collectively because no one knew my baby like I did. This kind of grief can keep couples together or tear them apart. Posts of my dead children holding my fingers sincerely upset him, whereas posts of my much alive children holding my fingers are fine. I don't understand. It is hard, and it is personal, but as a mom, I can't let my dead babies, and the grip their fingerprints hold on me, disappear. At least not right now.

I messaged my friend Christen who couldn't have babies of her own. Thinking of her journey, I asked her how she was doing. Later, she wrote this in our email correspondence:

Hey lady! This week we had a big old negative after our last embryo was transferred a few weeks ago. That's the book closed. Grieving not only the transfer cycle but the possibility of a second child. Feeling all the feels. Sadness, anger, bitterness, and then some. But during a bitter day I had to tell myself, "You are lucky and have a blessed life," which really did help. I still have moments. But those always pop up at the strangest times, don't they?

I replied:

I sit here with the two babies you dreamed to have, and yet I am grieving the two that I lost. It's unbelievably unfair. Even in knowing there are others who have it better and others who have it worse, we can still say a big "This Fackalackin sucks!" You and I are not fine, and we are not okay. Here I am, not fine, with you for all the not fine moments.

Christen wrote:

It has been unfair to us both in different ways for sure (yet similar in some). Fackalackin sucks for sure!! We are lucky in many ways. The waves get less ferocious. Who knew we knew how to surf well? At times, it feels like the darn wave is a tsunami. But they get less frequent, thank goodness! Yes, no regrets at all! Even for feeling the sadness. You have to, I think. Let the rawness be felt. It's a part of it. We may not have exactly the same stories or know exactly what it's like to be in the other's shoes, but I find great solace in knowing you are sincerely with me for the not fine moments. As I am with you in yours.

Deep down, I know that our stories are part of us and shape us in ways we could never even begin to imagine, and we don't have to know or see that right now. I am feeling grateful yet messy.

August 19, 2020: Splashing

Today I wanted to work on my yoga class and write in my diary. Instead, I went to the splash pad with my children who jumped, leaped, and giggled happily. Again, butterflies came to remind us to enjoy being rather than doing.

August 20, 2020: A Story about Hats

A rainbow is a promise
of sunshine after rain, of calm after storms,
of joy after sadness, of peace after pain,
of love after loss.
—Author Unknown

It all started as a dream I had. Then it became a dream that is even bigger than me. I began to crochet hats as a distraction to keep my head out of the darkness of our own recent loss. Then I launched a campaign encouraging people to wear colourful hats in the month of October to bring awareness to Pregnancy and Infant Loss Month. We have all met or know someone who has lost a babe. It is a dark topic that society tends to keep covered up, and it's hard to know what to do. But we can all wear colourful hats and speak the names of the babies that couldn't stay. In honouring their spirits, the world becomes a brighter, more colourful place.

For the month, we can show support for each other by sharing on social media. As the weather gets colder, we can wear rainbow hats in solidarity with one another. We can let others know we are willing to listen. Together we stand stronger by sharing our stories of loss. We will make this world a brighter place. Love is forever.

August 21, 2020: The Lost Locket

Today, I took my sweeties to a tractor show, and they loved the rumbling and popping sounds of the machines, and it was after visiting my aunt that I discovered that my locket holding Kaia and Jude's photo was missing. It must have come off when I removed my sweater. After our visit, I drove back to the fairgrounds, desperate to find it but with no luck. In need of a distraction, the kids and I played at the park. That evening, when Phillip came home from work, I left and found myself at the fairgrounds again, even though I knew it was a lost cause.

I feel like everything that matters to me I lose. After building the strength to buy a locket to hold my children's beauty close to me, I lost it. Here it is again: the not giving up, the holding desperately on to the hope that I will find it. I never wanted to give up on my children. I retraced my steps, turning on my high beams and looking for a flicker, and forming an intention to email the fair committee. If I do replace the locket, will it seem like I've replaced you? Please know that you are irreplaceable. I sit here in my car knowing that in three and a half more months I could have held you, Jude. Please help me to find my way back to you always. In doing so, I hope to find the pieces of me that have been lost, broken, and battered along the way.

I have lost you. That is the honest truth. I am not ready to move on.

I sat and crocheted, thinking of you. I thought of all the other families who have lost and never found. As I stitched, I patched up the broken pieces in my heart. The hat was not perfect. But neither is grief nor life. Some days, my hats are dimmer shades of grey, and other days they are bright.

August 22, 2020: Lonely

Somehow, I got myself out of bed to do sunrise yoga. I crocheted some more hats. I then found myself making posters to encourage other people to make hats. I sat down to continue writing our stories of loss with a sense of ease. Not once have I checked in with Phillip about what his thoughts have been while I am grieving. Sometimes, I am completely consumed with my own predicament, in a trance, not even realizing it.

Phillip once told me, "It must be nice being able to talk to your friends about losing a child and to be able to talk about it more than once." He feels he can only tell other men such news once, and even then, the opportunity to talk about it rarely presents itself. Phillip thinks they definitely don't want to hear about it again, and they usually crack some joke to get it over with and move on.

I offered to talk with him about it or to set up a counsellor for him. He never wanted to and told me to never mind. I feel helpless about how to support him. How do I change this script for my Case? Do men really feel this way, or is it just all that they know?

Second Entry: Delayed

Today, the real tears came. I am feeling more alone our second time around. It is definitely the tactile things that get me; I remember the warmth of my daughter on my chest. As she turned cold, I placed my hand below my collar bone. I also recall the cold taste on my lips as I kissed my son's sweet, tiny head goodbye. These memories stay with me like muscle memory, only conserved as tactile memory.

Prior to today, I would say to Phillip, "I think if I could just be drunk all the time, I would be pretty happy."

Phillip replied, "Words to live by."

During this time, it has seemed easier to numb the pain and all the emotions with alcohol, just like I used to drink to pass out in the dark days after having Kaia. With time, I've been able to admit this fact and say it out loud.

During "round two," I find more people wanting to know what causes us to have these problems. The geneticist did say with our one-out-of-four track record—one healthy baby to two miscarriages and one lost after twenty weeks—that we do fit the statistic of a 25 per cent recurrence rate. Yet we are not carriers, and neither of us have chromosomal abnormalities. In losing both a girl and a boy to different syndromes, it does not point to X-or Y-linked abnormalities or certain deletions in genetics. In not knowing what caused my children's syndromes, how do I move forward?

Trying to convince myself, I repeat to myself every day, "I'm done trying for another child." There are many people who have two children and are happy and content. This can be our happily ever after. Yet in some ways, I do feel it would be easier if I was pregnant or drunk. Perhaps with December approaching, I want confirmation that there is a life where a life should be.

August 23, 2020: Death by Cats

This morning the children and I woke up eager to see our COVID-19 cat, her kittens, and the bunnies in the bunny cage. We have fed and nurtured these orphan kitties for the entire pandemic. Well, we found our bunnies dead. The COVID-19 cats had killed them. They strangled them, removed their heads, and placed them side by side, like a horror movie. Watching my husband carry the two lifeless bunnies with no heads was a bit traumatic. Honestly though, rather than being utterly distraught, I kind of had to chuckle. Our life seems full of ridiculous, sick, twisted, and unbelievable events.

The shock and disbelief I felt in that moment brought me right back to our loss of Jude. Like the two bunnies, I nurtured two babies, and at times, I do feel like I killed them. I then think of the bunnies and how they represent Kaia and Jude's untimely, unfair, and unfortunate deaths. Grief is exhausting. I drown the feelings with drinking tea (mostly spiked) and making hats.

It broke my heart to have to explain to my two-and-a half-year-old son that the bunnies were gone, the same bunnies we had cuddled the night before as we watched them explore our living room, the bunnies that he named Belly and Toonie.

Phillip was shaken up by the event and said, "Wow. That kind of put a damper on my day."

We ordered Chinese food for dinner to lighten things up a bit. His fortune cookie said, "A grand adventure awaits!"

August 24, 2020: Shocked

We were told that our in-law's neighbours were away on holiday, and the pool was ours. My plan for each night they were away was to selfishly ask my mom or Phillip to watch the kids so I could swim. Today was a good day. I made soup, knitted more rainbow hats, and let the kids play with the neighbour's non-murderous cats. Case didn't have any potty-training accidents in the house, and we all enjoyed a big dose of vitamin sunshine. There was also a downpour after we finished swimming, and we all cozied up together, wrapped in towels.

Later that evening, as I swam in the pool, I recalled a terrifying event from the previous week that stopped me cold. It happened when we were visiting Oma. My girl was playing behind the side table, and I thought she might have had an electrical shock because she started screaming and then stopped breathing. I picked her up and yelled her name. I flicked her toes, slammed her on her back, and watched her turn from yellow to white to grey. I felt like vomiting. The incident was likely not even a minute long, but it felt like an eternity. I watched her finally take a breath as the blue corners of her lips turned back to normal. I'm not sure what had just happened, but I was relieved she was okay.

I sobbed, as I knew this could have been my worst day ever. Imagine the agony if my daughter had never taken another breath. Worse, what if she had an underlying heart condition that had gone undetected? I thought of my Kaia and Jude. They had lived briefly without ever taking a breath. Their heartbeats were enough to sustain them

As I write this, a caterpillar is dancing and doing backflips on my computer screen, and it playfully tickles my tingling fingers on the keyboard. We are electrifyingly alive.

August 25, 2020: Blaming

Today, I spoke to Bonnie, Jess's mom, who had nine miscarriages prior to having her daughter and then another nine prior to giving birth to her son. She said, "It all takes time. Sometimes, it takes nine years, and that is okay."

Bonnie recalled that she and a friend were both pregnant at the same time. She herself had ended up miscarrying and found it hard to watch as the other pregnancy continued on, similar to what Jess and I had both gone through together. Like me, she conjured up many ways to blame herself, from the foods she ate to the razor blades she used. How absurd it sounded to me as she recounted the things for which she blamed herself. Yet she assured me that no matter what I blamed myself for, it was really out of my control. I was able to summon compassion for her self-blame but not for my own.

I wish I could put the grieving on pause or skip through it all. I must be gentle with myself. There are days now when I can't believe I am not overwhelmed. Other days, the grief surprises me. Some days, it comes in waves. The waves no longer knock me off my board. That is what I say today; tomorrow, I may just drown.

August 26, 2020: Now

Today, I feel exhausted. After talking to Janice last night, I realized just how tiring grief is. I recalled all of the bad things that have happened recently. I mentioned how I am getting annoyed at myself because I constantly imagine how my life could be worse while simultaneously thinking of the unlucky flukes I see at work. She pointed out that I was really expressing my gratitude. True.

My hubby says, "Why don't we get you healthy?" like I am something to be fixed. That is the difference between Phillip and me. He sees a problem and wants to fix it. But I could have been at my healthiest, and this still would have happened.

Janice pointed out how recent studies have shown an increase in posttraumatic stress disorder (PTSD) related to induction births. Thirty-plus years ago stillborn babies were whisked away after birth. Parents were not able to hold the babe, know the sex, or where the child went. How did they grieve a child they didn't get to hold or even know? Now we take pictures, have moulds done, and hold the babe for as long as we need, but it turns out that doing so causes trauma in other ways.

That is the problem with research studies: We try new things, time passes, and new studies tell us it wasn't ideal. There is no right way when it comes to navigating pregnancy loss, and there is no right way to grieve.

Today, we got the call that Kaia and Jude's urn was ready for pick up, bringing me right back and reminding me of the grief I had been avoiding. I also yelled at my kids today. It was a hard day with the children in the normal day way: messy house, lack of sharing, and constant screaming. I couldn't do it. I wanted to crawl into a cavern somewhere.

Tonight, I am hosting my last yoga class for the season, on a rainy, dreary kind of day. I do not feel I can do it, and, of course, no one is making me but myself. I am aware of how grief changes by the day and sometimes by the minute. I have embraced it and let my true colours shine. While I was deciding on if I should cancel the class, a yogi messaged me saying how we can be one with nature. She wrote, "I will be there no matter what to get wet and wild" and that "happiness is in the now."

This is true. As I write this, I see the sun.

August 27, 2020: Yes

I signed up to speak to a psychic via telephone again. I need confirmation that the coincidences and answers presenting themselves to me are the right ones.

August 28, 2020: Spinning Wisdom

I am no one special. I know there are much sadder stories than my own. My mind spins thinking of my friend who had three miscarriages, my friend with infertility issues, my friend with her last embryo, my friend who never got married. It is said that people who have miscarriages are the ones granted a spiritual awakening. I believe it and I am grateful for what I have learned, but also wish I didn't have to go through pain to gain these lessons.

Daddy longlegs are everywhere tonight. According to an old French peasant legend, seeing a daddy longlegs in the evening is a good thing, foretelling good fortune, happiness, and hope. I'll go with that one, as it sounds better than the seriously venomous spider myth. The sufferer becomes the master.

August 30, 2020: Lost Child's Pose

Prior to partaking in a sunrise yoga class, a woman asked me how many kids I had. I replied that I had two children. She said, "It is good you are doing yoga because after the third baby you never bounce back."

Those words stung hard. With her pleasant ignorance, she unlocked my core. I wanted my third baby, and I still had the third (actually fourth delivered) baby body to prove it; my belly is a constant reminder.

I hear much judgment. A friend told me that her mother asked, "Why would they ever have tried again with all their problems? They already have two kids." I think this served as a way for my friend to ask the question through her mom to settle her own curiosity without putting herself at risk. Nothing good could possibly come from mentioning this to me.

"Look at this family. They have eleven children, and they never lost any," my friend's mother had said.

To that I replied, "You don't know that."

A flurry of recollections flooded my head space. It was okay that another lady tried having children again after losing her two kids in a car crash. That was totally fair (yet unimaginable). But why not me? And so it goes. This is exactly why we don't talk about pregnancy loss. I was upset with my friend for sharing her mother's statement, and it affected me the whole week. I know full well that no one ever knows what to say. But sometimes, just say nothing.

Today was my first run since November. I felt recharged and alive. The tears flowed. I have been holding on to you for a long time, dear Jude. Today, I felt the tiniest release.

August 31, 2020: Health

This morning, I woke up mid-sleep crying for my boy. I wanted my boy. Instinctively, I sensed this was to fill up the emptiness inside me. It is amazing how much an innocent run can unleash, and I started to think about my health.

Both with Kaia and Jude, I was told that my thyroid levels were high, and both those pregnancies involved severe chromosomal anomalies. Thyroid imbalance is a taboo topic in some circles. Often one is told their imbalances or exhaustion is anxiety or that the tiredness comes from being pregnant and having children. I HAVE HAD IT! I do not need a diagnosis to give me a reason for my hormonal imbalances, mood swings, head fog, constant fatigue, and memory loss. But I am also tired of feeling like I'm crazy even though I do agree that I am tired and anxious. Each time my thyroid levels were checked post pregnancy, they were normal. The doctor tells me we can re-evaluate the levels every year.

What if the thyroid levels were the problem? How can I know what to do about a future pregnancy? I was told today my wait time for an appointment would be four months because I am not pregnant, so I do not take priority. Medical investigations are rarely done on people whose bloodwork comes back normal. Once more, I am punished for my lack of pregnancy.

Today, I passed what I believe was another placenta after the birth of Jude. Another thing I cannot know for certain. This tissue had a cord. We did see two balloons cross our window. Could it have signalled another babe? This knowledge would change my course of grief yet again, even though when I called, I was told by my OB that it was probably just leftover fibrous material and perhaps a big clot I had passed. No. I know the difference between a clot and a stringy, dangling thing the size of a grapefruit that falls out of my body.

The nurses, delivery doctor, and residents believed and charted that I had passed the whole placenta. As I think back, there were moments when I did think I was pregnant with twins. There had been bleeding through the early stages. The ultrasound tech did remind me three times of my one baby inside me after all.

That is all for now. Oh, things they are releasing.

Second Entry: Needing Direction

Last night, Phillip talked about a summer bike trip to Ireland for next year, and it choked me up. Yes, I want to think of a bike trip, but this is where it is difficult for a woman. By then, a) I wish to be pregnant, b) I could be pregnant, c) I may have delivered a baby, or d) I may be grieving the loss of another baby (or lack thereof).

I could wait the year, but there is no guarantee I will get pregnant after that. There is no guarantee the pregnancy will last. If I wait a year, it will mean another year and nine months before our next child arrives. It is hard to know what to say or do. We are no longer able to make travel plans on the spur of the moment, something we would not have had to think about if we had Jude and our completed family.

September 1, 2020: Fading

Today, I had Jude's footprints tattooed under those of my daughter. Seeing the freshly inked footprints against Kaia's faded ones exposed the truth that time does fade things. I wasn't sure that I liked this realization in this moment. As I looked at and studied my fresh, dark tattoo, it was as though the tattooist could read my thoughts. He said, "Don't worry. It will fade like the other one."

Afterwards, I went for a walk, and, you bet, a butterfly crossed my path. It made me smile. A welcome, approving friend on my journey.

I made public on social media the dreams I had for my rainbow-hat campaign. How sad it was that I got more likes for announcing the loss of Jude than for this new project. Even sadder was that I found myself comparing these things. The frank remarks came, and they always seem to find a way to make me oversensitive: "Is that what you are doing with your time, making hats?" or "Shouldn't you be enjoying your children while you have this time off?"

I crochet at bedtime or when the children are actually playing with each other, which is oddly happening more and more. I crochet to keep my hands busy; it is a distraction, and I find it healing. This was truth slapping me in the face. People say they are there for me, yet when they have a chance to support me, they run and cower.

It amazes me how when I try to bring awareness to pregnancy loss, most people slam their doors on me. It makes me feel more alone, and I never thought it would be this hard. There are three women who have reached out to me wanting hats for their own rainbow babies. They told me they like the project. I have to remember it is for them that I do this. Hopefully, we four can hold space for one another and have a conversation, with compassion and love for one another while the world carries on. We and our children will wear our hats proudly.

September 2, 2020: One Month after Losing Jude

Tonight, was my first ever online support group meeting with the Pregnancy and Infant Loss (PAIL) Network. The meeting leader greeted me by saying, "You are fresh in your grief." Really? I feel as though I am aged in it.

After hearing of my loss, a woman grieving the loss of her thirteen-week-old baby said to me: "We are both healthy, both believe in God, and both have no chromosomal abnormalities." She then asked, "Why does this happen? What can I do to prevent it in the future?" I recognized her desire for answers, but sadly there are no answers. Only one month after losing our twenty-week-old baby and I find myself here and comforting others in the group. It showed me really how far I had come.

There are days I forget why I'm off work. I am not on maternity leave. I have lost a baby, and now it is termed sick leave. Other days, I'm sideswiped with deep and penetrating grief. As I imagine another pregnancy, I know I will be asking the same questions as that grieving woman every day.

September 3, 2020: Power

I went to the beach. I played with my kids rather than bringing a book or untangling yarn. I admired the power of the waves and their receptive and fluid nature as I splashed in the water and enjoyed being with the kids. There are days when I feel like I am pawning my kids off on others just to get this, that, and the other thing done or to even get through the day. Today, I sit here feeling lucky to be with my children.

Later in the day, while doing yoga in the backyard, with the kids playing beside me, I did my om chant and my son joined in. We were in perfect unison. As my chant got louder and changed octaves, he matched himself to me. It was powerful and moving, and it allowed us to feel the true vibration between us and the souls of each other.

I thought of a woman who reached out to me. After four years of infertility and many infertility treatments, she was finally pregnant with a baby boy. At the thirty-six-week checkup, they discovered that the cord was wrapped around the baby's neck, and she had to deliver a "sleeping baby." I wondered what she was doing to keep her head out of the darkness and the heartbreak.

I watched my kids chase their replacement bunny, Mustachio (yes, I caved and bought another one), and I rejoiced in their efforts to catch laser beams from Daddy's flashlight. They stomped their feet on the ground in happiness. They came to me and wanted to be held as we sat under the turning night sky. I listened to the humming calm of crickets. We were all there, together as a family, but without our sibling /child. It was not fair and beyond our power. Yet it was everything.

September 4, 2020: Defeat

This morning was horrible. I had to cancel on my best friend Celina's phone call when I probably needed it the most. The kids were screaming, and I was screaming for no reason. We couldn't get ourselves fed (no, I don't want that) or dressed (not those pants) without throwing fits. As their mama, I would have loved to not wake up, eat, or get dressed, but I had to show up. I was in my most ugly form, and the kids sensed it.

I don't know how I ever thought I could handle three kids. I am tired, angry, and want so desperately to be happy. Perhaps that is what I was hoping for with the phone call. I knew my friend's voice and the adult conversation would cheer me up and help me snap out of this dark mood.

I feel defeated in my job, motherhood, body, and mind. Being a mom puts a lot of things on hold. That is okay when you have a baby to show for it. Now I am wallowing in self-pity. I still feel I am not enough of a mother, friend, colleague, or person. I yelled at my kids and cried on the bathroom floor afterwards for being such a bad mom. I want to yell freely as they do. I don't want to do this or that either.

Shit, the waves of defeat are intense on this grief journey. I didn't want to talk to my friend because I knew I would have bawled uncontrollably, unable to form words, and I wanted to conceal that part of me. We never announce triumphantly to the world what we want or need, as children do. I find this ability in them both beautiful and inspiring.

September 5, 2020: Believing

Today, I realized we are each given two guardian angels for life. A book I was reading, one about talking to your angels, explained it. The angels change as your seasons of life change, and what you are striving for changes. Luckily, I got to birth my two guardian angels. I feel like I am back on track again and moving closer to enlightenment. After all, that is the goal of life, right?

September 6, 2020: Rising

Today, was another day where I felt horrible about myself, my body, my career, and my forgetfulness. Phillip said, "You forget because you have a million thoughts racing through your mind."

He was absolutely right. I stopped everything, and I went outside in nature where I can always clear my head. I started with wanting to read, write, do yoga, go for a run, meditate, and work on a hat. Instead, I ended up in tears. I tried to watch my thoughts as they came and went, from feeling ready to drop everything and run, to wanting to get really silent, to wanting to play, to wanting to sleep, to wanting to be super productive again, to wanting to, wanting to, wanting. I started doing yoga. I played in the grass, chasing happiness, like an animal jumping and leaping and bending. I pretended to be a gymnast. In the end, I realized that I wanted all the wanting to fall away. I wanted to feel, to create, and to do what intuitively felt right for me in my body.

I cracked out of my primal play and looked up with engaged eyes. I saw a single sunflower emerging from my garden. I was a sunflower; I had forgotten. There it was, a single flower, bright as ever, boldly standing tall and alone. The joy was not in another child; the joy was in right now. What I have right now, right here. Sometimes, even with decreased sunlight and compromised nourishment, a sunflower survives.

I jumped up from meditation and tried to do a playful flip, the kind I did as a kid. I tried to kick up three times with no success. I kicked the other way and surprisingly shot up just like the sunflower. Maybe sometimes we are meant to go in another direction.

September 8, 2020: All's Well That Ends Well

A friend posted her ultrasound at the eleven-week mark. She wrote, "All is well. Baby is moving."

I thought, *We don't know that all is well.* I also thought about how nice it must be to feel confidently that all is well.

September 10, 2020: Path to Healing

My friend Sara said, "I hope this week at the cottage, you are enjoying special time with your little ones." Having this time off has been special, although I would much rather be off with a baby come December. I find this special time is strictly for healing.

I left the kids with Oma as I drove to the reiki master lady in the community, the one that Sara had told me about. I took the road along the lake all the way there so I could stare at the calm clarity of the water, hoping to gain some clarity myself.

Before the treatment took place, we talked about energy healing and how sometimes the reiki therapist sees visions during the treatment. If I wanted, she would share her visions with me after the treatment. The moment the reiki therapist touched my feet, the footprints of my babies flashed through my mind. Little steps appeared and vanished across my vision. Next, my mind wandered to the chubby feet of Case and Maelie and how lucky I am to tickle those feet. An image of Case's footprints at the beach came to calm me.

I then thought of how both my children and I all rub our feet together for comfort before going to bed and how Kaia and Jude may have done the same. As the healer held my hand, I thought of holding my granny's hand as she lay in the hospital bed after her stroke. I knew she was gone, yet it still seemed her toes wiggled as if responding to me.

I thought of my own mortality and how lucky I am to be here and how I cannot imagine a moment without my children. I thought of Phillip, holding my hand as he did after I delivered all of my babies. I thought about how my granny's only wish was to hold my grampa's hand to say goodbye, and how this simple wish never came to be for her, as he passed away in a farming accident. Granny's hands still hold my babies on the other side, and Grampa's hands still hold mine, comforting me each step of the way.

At the end of the session, the healer shared the visions that had come to her. She saw my grampa holding a baby boy. I found that so eerie, and it brought to my mind the image that appeared in the wall after he died. It all made sense now. Now I understood. The healer also thought we had three babies, as she saw a recent blue blanket. Somehow, she knew that "the birth had changed me."

And so it had. Jude continues to be with us, guiding us through the loss.

September 11, 2020: All We Want Is Answers

The questions: Why did this happen to me? What other wake-up call do I need, since I've already gone through this twice? Can I make it through this again? Why did this happen when it did? What is my life work? Where are the souls of the babies I lost? Will their souls come back to me?

Today, I had a reading with a psychic via phone chat. She said that everyone has two archangels and that the ones she was seeing for me were Archangel Michael and Archangel Gabriel. After the session, I googled Archangel Michael, who is referred to in the *Epistle of Jude,* and the Archangel Gabriel, who guides me in intelligence. "Gabriel was the archangel who announced to the Virgin Mary that she had been chosen to bear the Son of God." (Luke 1:35)

The conclusion I drew from this is that Jude is my son of God.

During the phone chat, the psychic also assured me that the souls of our lost babies were just not ready, that their timing wasn't right, and they were a bit premature. And that the time they spent in the womb was testing the waters, so to speak, getting their souls ready for a ful-filled birth one day. She said it was invaluable teaching for them. How great it was to hear the pain was not for nothing. She went on to say that when these souls are ready they will join me in my life, whether through friendship, acquaintance, or birth. We have souls that travel together through each lifetime and are always with us in some way.

Okay, I'm aware and sure that psychics everywhere say such things to make people feel better, but I have to admit it darn well did make me feel better. I was vulnerable, hurting, and holding on tightly to any shred of a fortune-told future.

September 12, 2020: Head in the Clouds

I took my kids to a friend's cottage with Oma. This was Oma's sneaky attempt to cheer me up, and I thought, why not, I am off work anyway.

For a whole week, we lived and found healing at the cottage. I watched the same Oma who cared for me and raised me do the same for my children, all the while still caring for me and raising me up.

I sat at the beach from sunrise to sunset and watched my kids slide down the sand dunes, laughing and snorting sand out of their noses. They loved being tickled by the cool water running along the shore. They kicked up the water from the waves toppling over their little legs. They flirted with going deeper, giggling and holding on to my hand for dear life, slightly fearful, slightly enthralled. Every day, the bathtub and their ears were filled with sand. How it should be.

One night, my hubby came over to visit us at the cottage, and we biked just the two of us, exploring the enchanted forest, getting lost, and navigating our way back together. I took the kids for a day trip to the closest town, where we walked on the boardwalk, jumped in puddles, threw stones into the water, and watched the boats come and go. We found a fort-style playground with stick huts hidden in the woods; it was ours alone, our secret garden.

We sat on the deck listening to the birdsong. As the acorns fell, my son scooped them with his bulldozer and my daughter collected them for him. The trees snapped like gunshots from the squirrels leaping in the branches and my kids screamed gleefully. We played cards and had drinks with family as they came to visit. Life suddenly felt lively again, with such meaning and purpose.

September 13, 2020: Spirit Babies

Let the healing begin. Today, I read a book called *Spirit Babies: How to Communicate with the Child You're Meant to Have* by Walter Makichen. I am no longer searching in the self-help book section. Now, I need spiritual answers.

What did I need to learn? I read a sentence that suggested things were not my fault. Goosebumps rose up on my arm. At the same time, a leaf hit me with quite epic force. I jumped and instantly began to cry. It is not my fault.

As I am writing this entry, I just looked at the clock casually and saw 3:33. Is it all in my head? Am I becoming crazier on this grief journey? Probably. Or am I merely noticing more? I began noticing the angel number 333 after the loss of Kaia. Then Case was born at 3:33 a.m. Now, the same is happening with Jude. I need to remember that this number can be seen as a sign of comfort and encouragement not to give up.

Second Entry: Not My Fault

I took off my sweater and went for a walk. As I walked and talked to whoever it is I talk to about missing my son and wanting answers, a fluff passed by. Suddenly, I realized my locket was gone. The locket I had bought to replace the previous lost locket. The locket I looked at for motivation before setting off on my walk.

My hands started to sweat. I felt like I had the air knocked out of me as my heart stopped. I frantically reached at my chest again and again for my locket. I recalled what I had read in the book *Spirit Babies* and said to myself, "It is not your fault." I struggled with retracing my steps to search for the locket. I then realized I could take my time, I could focus on breathing, on unsinking my heart, and staying in the now. Nothing would change if I rushed back to look.

I didn't freak out. I realized that having the same experience twice in life does not necessarily mean I must have the same response. Sure, I held out hope I would find the locket. I hoped it had not come off in the tall grass because you have to dig deep in the tall grasses to find what you are looking for. The grief walk is not easy.

With each step of my return, I said, "I forgive. I forgive. I forgive." Tears fell. I wanted to transform the loss of the locket into something positive. I wanted to stop blaming myself.

The mantra continued: "I forgive. I do not always lose. I gain." I stumbled along the way and my heart continued to skip beats. I realized that I do not need to wear my locket heart to know that I am guided by my babies. I wear them inside me and around me.

These moments are ours alone on the path of grief. We spend countless hours searching but not finding what is right in front of us. My husband, who loves me fiercely, came to help me search for the locket. Finding the locket wasn't the point. The point was that we had found each other.

Instead of lashing out in anger and hating myself, like I had with the first locket I lost at the fairgrounds, this time I was kinder and gentler with myself. I realized it was not my fault and not all was lost. I had set out on that walk not faltering and feeling intrinsically good, and that feeling is beginning to happen more and more. The journey of self-healing on this grief walk is endless.

September 14, 2020: I Just Felt Like Running

I decided I would go for a run tonight. Phillip came home from work, and without a word, I slipped on my sneakers and ran out the door. As I started running, everything seemed to hurt: my lungs, my legs, my arms, and my heart. As my anger rose, I ran faster and faster until I fell into a familiar running rhythm. I recognized the feeling from running during my childhood days. I realized that I have spent the last couple of years running around for others or away from something. It was now time to start running for myself.

Running was freeing. When I wanted to push harder, I could. When I needed to catch my breath, I could slow down to a jog and take in the scenery. As I stopped, I crouched over to catch my breath, and I began to cry. The rush of fresh air in my lungs and the feeling of freedom woke me up to myself and to life. I decided today that I would continue to run but in a productive way. I wouldn't run to get everything on the to-do list done. Instead, running would now become a priority task on the to-do list.

Moving forwards, I decided and told my husband I was going to run for twenty minutes a day for thirty days. If my body couldn't run one day, I would still get outside for twenty minutes and walk, skip, or be. This would be my "me time" that I was prioritizing for myself. We discussed that this could become a game of tag. When Phillip came home from work, I would put my shoes on and head outside. When I returned, I would say, "Tag, you're it," and Phillip could go out for his own "him time," a twenty-minute bike ride.

As we took on this challenge together, endless things started to shift. I became happy to greet the day and I wasn't burdened by my daily tasks because I knew I would get me time that evening. By getting outside in nature, I received the many benefits of fresh air and meditation—the release of the day's anger, stress, and guilt. And this challenge finally brought us closer. We began to run towards each other.

I used to run to exercise, for vanity, to lose weight, and to prove my self-worth to others. Now, I run to feel alive, to reflect, to let go, and to feel good. Each day, I run with hope that I'll be a little better for myself, my kids, and my support system. I have learned that in doing this for me, I am benefitting others. I have been able to turn off the autopilot mode, be present with those around me, and be the best version of myself. Running is my time to connect to myself and come back to the me I know and love.

September 15, 2020: High-Risk Doctor Appointment

I think there is pressure on people to turn every negative into a positive, but we should be allowed to say, "I went through something really strange and awful and it has altered me forever."
—Marian Keyes

I sat in the obstetrician's office. I asked about my thyroid levels, which I am trying to improve with diet. I asked about the hormone levels for which I am using healing oils. I asked about my questionably delivered placenta. I asked about the pain in my right side. I asked about the bleed. I asked about future pregnancies. Could my previous abruption have impacted all of my future pregnancies, risking bleeds and the ability to have more babies?

After losing Jude, I experienced severe pain in my right side, which manifested similar to what felt like a string near my C-section scar. I had vivid dreams of Phillip holding my hand as I prepared to die. This was worst-case-scenario thinking. I wondered if I had an underlying terminal illness, not yet diagnosed, that led to the loss of so many pregnancies.

It may have been psychosomatic pain, compartmentalized emotional pain, or shock pain that my brain stuffed neatly into a box which presented itself as physical pain. Either way, the pain was real, and I did not pretend to hide it. Although I couldn't say the words, I was sad, and my body felt it. How freely and easily our children tell us they are hurt or have an owie. Why can't we keep that freedom and ease as adults to confidently say, "I hurt."

The doctor explained that the tissue I had passed could have been extra fibrinogen that had hardened and that any little webbing that hung off of the tissue could resemble a cord. The pain in my right side could be ovulation. I was told to keep an eye on it. If we had pregnancies in the future, an extensive twelve-week ultrasound would be done to monitor the situation. Other than the absent kidneys and ureters, testing showed Jude was normal. Genetic testing for both Phillip and I was normal. Once again, I received no concrete reason to help me understand why my last pregnancy went wrong. I think that has been the hardest part—the not knowing and trying to heal all the things and fix all the pieces but being unable to. Nothing gained but expensive healing treatments, tests, and herbals. Someone is profiting on my vulnerability.

September 18, 2020: Coming Together and Belonging

Today, I cried as I sat in an advanced asana yoga course. The course was all about being vulnerable and attempting bigger poses. By embracing vulnerability we would empower ourselves and others. I felt lucky to be here. I needed this courage, this ability to let go and self-reflect towards a brighter future. I needed this the most when my mind was constantly thinking about a future pregnancy.

I read in the class outline that many of the big poses in this course are contraindicated in pregnancy. That got me. The reason I couldn't and didn't sign up for this course previously was staring me right in the face. I never thought I would be here and wouldn't be pregnant.

September 21, 2020: Leaving

We went on our first family get away in a long time. On our drive up to the camp, we heard of a fatal accident close to my parents' house. The man's name was Dave, and we know a Dave who lives close to their home. He is our age and has two children. The news shattered both Phillip and me. We thought of those children without a parent. We were reminded of the unexpected finality of sudden death. It made us absolutely sick.

It turned out it was a different Dave, but we still grieved together, unable to imagine it.

September 22, 2020: Warmth

I realized that the silver lining of grief is that I have been given the gift of not taking anything for granted. As a result, I enjoy being with my children more than I could have imagined possible.

Once we arrived at the camp and I rolled my yoga mat out on the deck, Maelie gave me cozy hugs and lay on my yoga mat next to me. Case brought me a handpicked flower. I watched the children gaze intently at their father as he cast his glowing fishing line into the water. These are the beautiful moments of our lives.

I felt the warmth of the sunset like I had felt the warmth of my babies' bodies on my skin. As the sun fell into the water, how quickly it became cold and dark like it did with our babies as their hearts stopped beating. Yet there was great comfort knowing that in the darkness, we also experienced that light, and as our eyes adjusted, we could see more clearly and more brightly: the stars, the moon, the magic of the night.

I still feel hurt and pain when I see someone with three or more kids on the beach or on our hikes, and I'm always on high alert of this. Yup, I'm selfish. I still want that too.

September 23, 2020: We Need More Time

We need more time to...

Sing our rock n' roll road trippin' songs in vibrato as a unit.
Play the game "Where's Maelie?"
Watch Case do yoga like Mommy.
Eat at picnic tables.
Hear Maelie say, "Uuumm uuummm yummy yummy!"
Watch chipmunks eat this community's world-famous apple fritters.
Witness my daughter chirp at chipmunks.
Destroy a cabin that wasn't ours by playing fiercely together.
Hear Case say that he does not like commercials.
Laugh and love.

We need more time to...

Bike and hike to scenic views.
Watch the waterfall and see how it meanders many ways to reach its end.
Marvel at Maelie jumping into the small stream of the waterfall without hesitation.
Drink the purity of the stream and experience its cleansing abilities.
Observe Case navigating through the waters in a canoe with Daddy.
See the loons swim across the water.
Watch the sunset in front of us with the moon simultaneously beside us.
See our stunned children's faces as they ask how they can exist at the same time?

We need more time to...

Be with each other on our enlightened journey.
Let go of the fear of bears.
Imagine this life.
Trust in this time, with playful curiosity, and be completely in this experience.
Admire Case for hugging Maelie and looking out for her by holding her hand.
Unite to create more peace, strength, balance, and grace.
Continue to move forwards on our path.

Share and spill ice cream.
Breathe this in.

We need more time...

September 24, 2020: The Extra Link

Is it easier to be told, dear Jude, that your birth problems were hereditary?

As we headed home from our family time away, my phone rang. It was the geneticist. The results of Jude's DNA testing were in, which showed that he had an extra piece on his X chromosome. Jude, it turns out that you carried a gene associated with an intellectual disability and that the extra X chromosome could have been caused by a lineage of genes before me. Or it could simply have been a duplication that happened by fluke in my development that left me unaffected physically, unlike the catastrophic events of the duplication/deletion that happened and affected both yours and Kaia's development.

I learned that the learning disability was something that I could pass down and that would only affect my boy pregnancies, since I, too, carry this extra X chromosome in my DNA. So that is, if I ever have a son, he could have a learning disability.

The fact is that I do have a son, and if anything (as every parent says), he seems advanced in his development. The option is there to investigate if Case does have this extra X chromosome, but I have elected not to have him tested at the present time. Down the line, if we have concerns, we can have him tested. But it doesn't change him. A learning disability is something we can definitely live with.

So much testing and so little found. The absent kidneys were our biggest concern. I wanted to know if they were genetic so that maybe I could make it easier on my sisters who share the same lineage. If the absence of kidneys is genetic, perhaps my sisters could get tested before starting families and be spared the agony their big sister had. Something helpful has to come out of all of this, right? What if I learn that it skips a generation? Maybe it won't show up in my kids but in their kids? And, again, I will feel like I am to blame.

Still we sit here with no answers, still with no baby, still feeling at fault no matter what we are told. Even the geneticist, in an empathetic way, finds it comical that they are banging their heads against the wall looking for answers for us, answers that are just not there. Thankfully, it is easy loving our babies and being grateful for each of them. Some of them we lost and do not know why. And some were born healthy, and still we do not know why.

September 25, 2020: Coincidence

Yesterday, I spoke with a sweet lady from our church that had made a care package for the children. After hearing of our loss and not knowing our baby's diagnosis, she told me she lost her third baby at nine months to something rare called Potter's syndrome. I was not able to hold back the tears. Of course, her baby would randomly have the same syndrome as our Jude. Potter's syndrome is rare, but now we have the technology to identify it before the full term of the pregnancy. Sadly, forty years ago, this poor woman had to carry her baby, Christopher Charles, the whole time not knowing that something wasn't right. He would have been thirty-three this March. She knew the baby was much smaller, and she felt the baby move much more because of the low level of amniotic fluid, but that was all that had felt different. I will always remember his name.

September 26, 2020: Cloud Nine

Continuing on our holiday fever, yesterday Phillip and I missed our booked hot air balloon ride, an adventure we booked long before the pandemic. An adventure we needed to feel and be weightless together, heads in the clouds again, like we were on our Machu Picchu hike. We embarked on our own adventure—getting breakfast, going gun shopping, doing natural food shopping for a cleanse (I want to try and be healthier), and retrieving hats from friends for our cause—and missed our balloon ride. Later, we discovered that we can use our vouchers for the hot air balloon ride next year. Nothing lost and only more time gained.

September 28, 2020: Never Forgotten

The power of others is incredible.

Through the PAIL Hat campaign, I started hearing more people share their stories of loss who had never spoken out before. I made connections in the midst of my grief and realized that I am not alone in my isolation. They became my own small community support network.

A man recounted that his child was stillborn ten years and sixteen days ago. Others wanted to buy rainbow hats as Christmas gifts for their girlfriends to honour their babies' memories. In hearing their reasons, I experienced firsthand the warmth of others. As it turns out, we all have many friends who have been affected by this cause.

More and more people began to wear the rainbow PAIL hats in support of other families who have experienced pregnancy loss. Many opened up, saying they had kept silent so as not to trigger another person's pain. Others admitted feeling ashamed that their bodies did not sustain the pregnancy.

The PAIL campaign allowed the rainbows to shine through and onto the loss. Honouring and bringing awareness to the painful and dark stories was important because each one packed such tremendous beauty and strength.

September 30, 2020: Inspired Poetry from PAIL Stories

The rapid journey in silence had recovered her breath,
sitting among the ashes,
into the fire,
out of breath...
slowly struggled hours,
getting far better help...
clear
he could hear her,
see her.
Dreaming of fighting enough,
Fearing none.
In the skies that die
Dreaming of...

October 1, 2020: Another Language

I went to school for nursing, and we touched on X chromosomes (female) and Y chromosomes (male), reproduction, and recessive and dominant genes. We learned that some traits are passed down in family bloodlines, like hemophilia, which became known as the "royal disease" since it affected royal families in England, Germany, and Russia. Many of these royals carried X-linked recessive disorders. I always found this fascinating and, frankly, unfortunate.

The world of genetics seems like a foreign language to me (like robotics), one I do not think I will ever understand. We have had a team of geneticists desperately looking for answers for us as well as for themselves. They were looking to see if our situation was a new event for our family, meaning unrelated to anything inherited and where the DNA simply did not duplicate how it was supposed to during development. Kaia was a new event, aka. an unlucky fluke. We wanted to know if something genetic could be found, as these fluky things simply couldn't keep happening to the same family.

Here is the information that was provided. They had seen three uncertain changes in these three genes:

FREM1: involving the skull, nose, renal, and rectal functions

GLI2 : involving brain findings

ROBO2: involving functional problems of the kidneys and urine reflux

They confirmed that there was no diagnosis or genetic cause for why these changes happened. "Basically," the geneticist said, "I am calling to tell you that these are the answers we have found that give us no answers."

Talking about the genetics results has been hard. Phillip and I are closer now than before (no more bite marks), but he still wishes I could talk with him like I do with my counsellor. I find sharing my pain with him hard, mostly for his sake. I would rather pay someone to listen to my pain than spark unnecessary suffering for my husband. I have not let go of my need to protect him and myself. It is a work in progress.

October 2, 2020: Scared

In the darkest night, on a stroll to my tree, the clouds packed such knowledge. As I walked along the path, my mind swirled with thoughts. I thought about what Phillip and I had talked about regarding next steps. If there was a genetic issue, perhaps we would try in vitro fertilization. If it was a hereditary problem, we thought of our kids being carriers and worried for my siblings and the children they might have. On occasion, we considered that perhaps the best path was to stop rolling the dice.

Next to the moon, as it peeked through the pink clouds, I saw one bright star emerge. I was protected under the tree, my spot, and the wind pushed me forwards. I felt the tree branch tickling my side, knocking me over. Again I was in the dark; grief shadows scared me and made me extra jumpy.

I remembered how women who couldn't speak their truth started to come out of the dark shadows. I met a woman at the local art store where I was delivering hats to sell. After I explained the cause, she told me how it had been thirty years ago that she lost her daughter, Jessica, at eighteen months old. She still thinks of her.

As it started to rain, I headed back, quickening my pace. I felt as though a coyote was running alongside me, rustling in the corn field. I was scared. I looked back up at the bright star that now appeared like it was moving fast. I kept speed walking on the path with the confident hope of finding the glimmer of my lost locket in the grass under the moonlight.

October 3, 2020: My Post for October, Pregnancy, and Infant Loss Month

Pregnancy loss affects so many. We have lost six babies, some very early and some much later; some we never held, and some we held and couldn't let go of. I wear my colourful rainbow (chakra) hat to shine light on the darkness of pregnancy loss, which understandably we all want to hide from. Each of us knows a woman who has gone through this pain.

Pregnancy loss is so hard to comprehend. You are grieving a life that never got to live and a life you knew you had the opportunity to give. May we all support, love, and share our stories in order to heal together. Although for each of us the pregnancy journey is unique, we are not alone and stand united.

October 4, 2020: Not Yet

Today, I have the time to write. Writing allows me to reflect, to tell my raw truth, even though it hurts. This is my reality in this moment, of how I experienced the last five years and where I am with it. Grief changes. I am searching for answers, and I may never gain a conclusion.

Yesterday, I delivered our baby swing, chair, and exersaucer to Jess, who is due around the time that we were. Why not let them use something that while it sits here makes me sad? I am releasing. When Jude passed away, I instantly wanted to get rid of the baby bottles, something that felt both productive and destructive. Phillip stopped me. "Not yet," he said. Then he pondered, "Well, I guess we can always buy more."

October 5, 2020: Helium Balloons

Hope is a helium balloon.
It is a wish lantern set out into the dark sky of night.
—Sharon Weil

And there it was, just for me to see. A single blue helium balloon lifted up over a hill right next to the highway, floating, hovering there, and rising in slow motion. I had to stop and pull over. It was so peaceful and so surreal.

While driving home after a university friend reunion, I was daydreaming about the wonderful things happening with my hats and my writing. Thanks to Jude, all of this positive momentum was happening. My university friends and I talked all through the night, sharing and agreeing that our psychic moments were always present, and we just had to stop and allow ourselves to see them, slow motion in the moment.

I have a hate relationship with a specific highway, where there is a long-standing theme of me getting lost or repeatedly missing exits and seeing the same restaurants. There have been times when an hour has been added to my journey because of this, yet this was exactly where I found myself. After missing another exit, I turned off the audiobook so I could focus and not miss more exits. And there he was, my son, trying to reach me. He had picked me to be his mama. I knew it right there and then. Before this moment, I was too blind to see or believe it. I thought I wasn't meant to be his mama. I believed he took one look at me and said, "Nope, not for me."

He did in fact love me as his mother, or he wouldn't have gone through all the effort of making himself be seen in my distressed state, literally lost in endless thoughts of him. I found him in the single blue floating balloon on the side of the highway. He planted it just for me to find him again.

Just then a fluff floated by. I could watch its whole flight across my windshield because I had pulled over and stopped. There we were again, together in that single, simple, slow motion moment. The comfort I found in that one single balloon spoke volumes for the rest of my life. I can let the locket go.

October 6, 2020: Trying

Phillip told me how he just loves the stage Maelie is in right now. He laments that she is changing so quickly. In my sad place, I said I wanted another one so that we could experience these moments again. I realized that with this logic we would keep having babies forever. The truth is that the time to enjoy the special moments will diminish when life with more children becomes increasingly chaotic.

Phillip said, "I would, but we just have too many issues. We've got to get more answers first." He was right, and he was trying to protect me. Why can't I just be happy with what I have? Aren't all the issues proof enough that it is time to stop trying?

My groggy head thinks of the *19 Kids and Counting* show, where Arkansas couple Jim Bob and Michelle Duggar have nineteen children. Each child's name begins with the letter J. Why do they get to keep having babies and keep coming up with J names? Oma grew up in a family of twelve, and Opa grew up in a family of thirteen. I always thought it was their religion that resulted in so many births. Oma finally told me the truth: "My mom was so healthy that every time she had sex there was a baby." I thought that was such a crazy thing to say, but she meant it. She said, "Men didn't have much respect for women and their bodies. I never knew my mom. I knew who my mom was, and I loved her, but I never played with her or did anything with her as it was my sisters who raised me. Then I was taken to boarding school from the age of twelve to eighteen. We also had a maid."

The light bulbs went off. Thank you, Oma. I was beginning to think I was even crazier than the average mama bear. Of course she couldn't do it alone; it takes a village. Of course the kids were wanted. How ironic that I am sitting here wanting more kids, and Great Oma was trying her best to have fewer kids, changing the cycle. I do notice, though, that all of Oma's and Opa's siblings went on to have five or fewer children, as they wanted to know and consciously raise their children.

October 7, 2020: Messages in the Clouds

Today, I ordered blue and pink helium balloons for the grief balloon release that I was planning for Case and Maelie's baptism day. It somehow felt fitting, and the idea sprang from that blue helium balloon. The clerk asked me if the balloons were for a gender reveal party, and I laughed it off. What I wanted to say was "It is actually for a letter reveal to our babies in heaven. They are for our angels to receive our heartfelt messages as we baptize our children."

Grief is not sun and rainbows; it comes with many clouds and rain. In honour of my babies, Kaia and Jude, and all lost infants everywhere, may we let their spirits soar around all of us. I cannot wait for all of our babies to greet us again one day, but for now, we feel them and meet them in these special moments.

Part 6
Soaring

Descend to rise and meet the future.

Finding Meaning

October 8, 2020: Alone

Today, I think of all the mothers who twenty years ago did not have mom groups, let alone grief groups. When a miscarriage happened it was kept within the family. Most times not even the grandparents knew. I think of the young mother, who likely had all the same feelings I do, completely alone without resources available to her. How isolated she must have felt.

October 10, 2020: Duck

Just as ripples spread out when a single pebble is dropped into water, the actions of individuals can have far-reaching effects.
—Dalai Lama

We've taken our kiddos to Algonquin Provincial Park, as life is one big adventure, and I deemed the theme for this year to be YOLO—you only live once. I know, an old saying but with new meaning.

As I meditated next to the river this morning, with my eyes turned over, I heard the wings of a bird flapping. Might she be flying to new terrain to nurture herself for a moment? Suddenly, the bird landed right in front of me. Maelie ran to me yelling, "Ducky! Ducky! Ducky!" My son was not far behind and leapt on my back.

Case has a favourite book, *Little Blue Truck,* in which a dump truck proclaims loudly that he has important things to do, and he can't spend his time with every duck he passes during his day. My own story has progressed in a similar fashion. But unlike several years ago, I now take time to see and hear every duck and every feather. I feel and watch every splash and every ripple along the way. The duck is thought to offer lessons in protection or emotional comfort. I have noticed growth and transformation in my years, and I am on a spiritual journey of slowing down and improving my life and the lives of those I love. Right now, I am landed in this place.

October 11, 2020: Hello

Thanksgiving is a hard time of year because it was on this weekend that we announced our pregnancy with Kaia. Two months from now, we would have been thankful for Jude. The other night, Maelie slept on the couch with me as she was coming down with a cold. (The best part of colds is the snuggles.) I looked at her as she lay sleeping next to me and found myself whispering, "Hello, Kaia." Could it be? The flood gates opened. Later that night, I was thankful for Case finding me to cuddle up to me and be with me.

Things can look so dark and beautiful at the same time. When I look and feel with my whole heart, I feel the love of angels here on earth. They offer us their angel fingers to hold and lead the way, protecting us in every step. I am grateful for the angels who guide our lives and show us how to live in the heaven that is right here on earth. Nothing else really matters.

October 12, 2020: Coming Back

I felt my cousin Janelle strongly today and I had an urge to refer to her in my journal. As I quieted my ever-racing brain, I felt her in her entirety and in all her beauty. I said how sorry I was for what happened to her. That she had to die in a motor vehicle accident at such a young age of sixteen. That she never got to be a mother when here I was. When I posed the question to Janelle in my mind, "Should we try again?" I got my answer. She said she was coming back to me as our future third baby, a beautiful, curly haired, twirling blond girl. A daughter for us. I could suddenly see so brightly an image of me holding a little girl come fall. She will return and bring our families back together.

Phillip actually listened to my crazy antics and said, "Whoa. That's deep, with a side of you're nuts." I have to agree. The whole experience felt strange, yet I welcomed it.

I don't want another loss, but I do still want what I want (the baby we were meant to have) and do have hope that it will happen for us. I know Phillip holds on to this hope, too.

October 13, 2020: Cloud Gazing

With lots of time to reflect, I stopped and stared at the clouds, searching for an answer. Was it time to try again? As I waited for my answer, I pondered if I simply see what I want to see in my mind's eye? Maybe I do? Then right in front of me, a baby/blob womb appeared with Kaia and Jude's faces beside it. The faces that never clear away in my mind, always right there on the surface. I also saw several hearts and footprints float across the sky, appearing quickly and vanishing even faster. In an instant, the vision of my babies' faces and the one in the womb evaporated. I strained to look hard and couldn't find them again. I thought about how my heart aches when I think of Jude. It made me sad to know that one day thoughts of Jude would be less painful.

October 14, 2020: Time

I boldly explained to Phillip that I was ready for a third child. Everyone tells us that time is on our side, but if I have to go through more losses to have a third living child, then I don't have much time. I also wonder what impact working as a nurse is having on me. I see and hear so many awful stories. Still, I want to give my children the gift of each other. Sometimes, I wish the decision would be taken out of our hands. In some ways, the ability to make the decision is a curse.

Phillip said he's too old and that another pregnancy is too hard on my body. My thinking is to do it now while my body has already been under stress. Phillip believes if we had babies when we were eighteen things may have been easier. He's not wrong. I recall all those years trying not to get pregnant, fearing it, and wishing now that we had.

Phillip sent off his spit sample today, and although we laughed at the concept, I admired his spitting skills and the specimen he produced. We are still testing our genetics in an effort to find the cause of our loss of Jude. We can't try until we know answers for certain.

Second Entry: The Funky-Hat-Making Train

I sit here overwhelmed by tears of gratitude. A project that started out as a way for me to heal myself turned into a small dream of giving colourful, funky hats to the women and their families who helped us on our pregnancy loss journey. Would I have done this if I hadn't lost Jude? No. I would have been working, in the full swing of life, and trying to run the chaos of our lives with two little ones and a baby on the way. My healthy distraction turned into a therapeutic healing platform for myself. I heard the stories of others, and my heart busted for them. I formed my own support system and community, the one I desperately craved.

There is a movement happening; I can feel it. We don't have to feel or be ashamed anymore nor do we have to keep our vulnerabilities, helplessness, and losses slammed shut. We don't need to talk about it every day, but people are willing more than ever to listen and show support.

I'm so thankful to everyone who believed in the dream and jumped on the funky-hat-making train—to Oma who tied up the loose ends, to my mama who wrote out little tags, and to Phillip, the best delivery man ever.

Grief doesn't always need to be spun into something positive. I crocheted my sadness into every stitch, saying I am sad, but I am also proud—proud to be my babies' mama, proud to heal myself, and proud to nurse myself back to health. Proud to know I can.

October 15, 2020: Our Pain Can Bring Light

For Pregnancy and Infant Loss Remembrance Day, I bought a little candle holder that conveniently held two candles. In the shop, I hemmed and hawed over whether to purchase one or two single candle holders. When I found one holding two candles, I thought it was meant for Kaia and Jude. Although a baby may be gone from this world, their memory will endure, and their light will inspire and guide us all.

When I opened the door of the van, the first thing to fall out of the bag was the precious candle holder. Even though it was wrapped in newspaper, it snapped perfectly in two separate pieces. This symbolized to me my own weak spot—that these were two separate souls and two separate losses and grief experiences. But they remain together in my broken heart.

Or it could just have been an unfortunate moment; things break sometimes. I have had several mugs break. I've even purposefully thrown some on the floor to watch them shatter in times of astonishment or anger. There is a Japanese art called Kintsugi, the art of fixing pottery by using powdered gold to mend the breaks.

We all shatter and break sometimes. That shattering pain never goes away; it becomes part of us, helping us as we move along our journey. It becomes our story; it is who we are and shows that we can be mended and that eventually we can find beauty in the cracks and scars by flaunting them and showcasing our total broken selves.

Today as I lit my candles for Kaia and Jude, the tears came instantly. I looked at Kaia's dress, the dress I had put on a doll I played with as a kid. That day we couldn't bring ourselves to put Kaia in her funeral dress, the one my aunt had made using material from her own wedding dress. Instead we put her in a dress my doll wore, a doll that I always used to play with. That is how I wanted to remember her—full of life and giving me the imagination and innocence of when I was a kid and as babies should be.

I saw the ripped sleeve that Phillip, in grief stricken haste, had cut with his pocketknife so that we didn't have to fight with her little hand to get it through the sleeve. Dressing a dead baby is challenging. Just before we delivered Jude, Phillip asked, "You're not going to dress him, are you?"

Jude, I look at your pictures and the frame with your clothes, measuring tape, and mementos of fluffs and Chinese fortunes and think that even though the candles will change through the years, you never will. Our constant wish as parents is of never wanting our children to grow up. I have this cursed wish. I will look at these same pictures every year. New memories with you will never be made. The way you are in my memory now is how you will always remain—untouched, a steady constant, and never needing to face the many unknowns of life. My unchanging babies and their never forgotten faces will forever be in my heart and live as long as I live, where nothing can hurt them or take them away from me ever again.

With you, time stops, and it brings me right back to that one and only special moment every time, so unnatural and so natural, so horrifying and so beautiful. Every time I look at these pictures, I will draw in something different and access memories where the hurt is still there, but the suffering is gone: a smell, a touch, a word spoken, a look, or a hand held. I know that from you both, I will receive what I need to in each moment and ignite my flame within.

October 19, 2020: Awestruck

I was surprised how upset I was when my friend announced on social media that she was pregnant. I was not at all mad at my friend; I was excited and pitifully jealous of her and in awe of how she could announce that so freely with no worries. Going back to work has made me bitter and angry.

October 20, 2020: Broken and Holding On

I hold on to hope. I can't hold on to my dead baby, but I can hold on to hope for a baby that will one day be inside of me. I know that is dark, but I have been broken, cracked open, hardly breathing. The intention to have another child and the hope I hold to maybe announce another pregnancy give me a bit of peace and relief. I'm obsessed with holding on to hope while also being utterly pissed.

October 21, 2020: Surprise

When I took Maelie for her vaccinations, I was surprised the family doctor didn't acknowledge what we have been through. She sees many patients, and perhaps she forgot. At the same time, I was grateful I didn't have to talk about it. Oddly, though, I was longing for a little sympathy, although it has been more than two months, so she probably thought I didn't need to talk about it anymore.

When Janice said that we still get to hope if we want to try for another one, I was again surprised. I was surprised when my husband said our situation was self-inflicted. He was right. Had we chosen not to get pregnant, the loss of Jude would not have happened. We asked for this, so we deserved this. We played with fate too much.

I wish I could let go of wanting a third child. Phillip says it would make life so much easier if I just accepted that this was the end of making babies. For me, my problem remains that I have not been given a diagnosis or told, fortunately, that I can't have more children.

I am surprised that I don't believe I am done trying for another child. At some point, we will have to cut our losses, but it doesn't have to be today. I want what I want.

October 24, 2020: Buried

I think about my old university roommates who had their first babies in August, as they were supposed to. I think how they excitedly shared their birth stories with us as we eagerly asked for them to. Then I remembered how I also had my baby in August, just not in the same way. It was not how it was supposed to be. We were all supposed to be on maternity leave together. How quickly it is just forgotten that we, too, went through the birthing process, yet naturally no one wants to hear our birth story. Nobody talks or asks about this. Our birth experience felt as though it died, then and there, with Jude.

I weirdly think about how I wanted to share the birth of our son. People don't want to ask in fear they will remind you or make you uncomfortable, yet they, too, are uncomfortable. The only way we can become comfortable with the uncomfortable is to become comfortable talking about the uncomfortable and by asking the questions and giving rise to our babies' peace and light. We must change the script.

Oddly, Jude's birth story was beautiful in every way besides the obvious way. I still got to hold and love my baby. I still got to feel his fighting spirit. I still got to be on this journey with him as I had been all along. I still felt no pain and was in awe of this little human, but I did have to say goodbye, and then the pain came rushing in. There was such an ease and comforting light that was palpable in that place that was the birthing room, but that ease and light did not exist past those doors to the outside world. It can't exist, as even though Jude existed, he never existed past our birth story—that story never came to be. A story buried. It is not asked about and never shared, except on these pages.

October 26, 2020: Got My Thyroid Checked

Today was the big phone call from the endocrinologist. I felt like my body had failed us, and I wanted answers. Stress is known to cause hormones to go haywire.

Drum roll please. My diagnosis is gestational thyrotoxicosis, which means my body tends to have higher hCG hormones circulating when I'm pregnant. They mimic my thyroid stimulating hormone (TSH) levels, driving them to go high and give a false-positive reading of high TSH. So apparently, I am a high-wacky-hormone person. Phillip said he had already known this (how rude), but now I can blame it on the hormones. And PS—my thyroid is fine.

October 27, 2020: Babies

Case: You're going to have a baby boy.

Mommy: What?

Case: There's a boy baby in Mommy's tummy and a girl baby here (pointing to my chest). A boy baby for Case and a girl baby for Maelie.

Mommy: Wow!

Case: And there's a mommy in there.

Mommy: Really?

Case: Right there (pointing to my head).

Mommy: Are you happy about that?

Case: (Gasps)

Mommy: What are the babies' names?

Case: Jula Juuuu and Jack Hammer. It's a present.

October 28, 2020: Patience

Dear future one,

You are not here with us currently. I was so convinced you would be that present Case predicted yesterday. Your due date would have been July 7, 2021, which is Gramma's birthday. How perfect would that have been? But instead you are a period. I wasn't late or anything and wasn't even trying, but for a moment, this was a thought I could get lost in. What a high standard I set for myself. I am disappointed I am not pregnant. Also, who am I? Some people take months to years to get pregnant. I want to be pregnant so that I can once again look forward to the future.

I'm heartbroken, as I want you so badly. After the loss of Jude, saying goodbye to the possibility of having another baby, possibly forever, was a new kind of finality. I know it has only been three cycles since losing Jude. What if we can't have another? What if this was our last shot? This is a whole new terrifying territory, one where I have never had to let my head go before. In some ways, I'm relieved that my body can have the little break that it requires. Yet I also hope this break does not last forever.

I will hold on to hope that my son's prediction will be right. He believes so hard and completely. It is just not the right timing. Let it be. Now I just have no excuse for my emotions. Today I love, today I work, and today I think about my babies while trying to help other babies; my patients remind me to be patient.

October 31, 2020: Pain Persists

There are moments where everything works out. But they don't for everyone. It doesn't work out for the woman riddled with arthritis as a result of her IVF treatments, which leaves her with no baby and even more physical pain as a constant reminder. What do I tell this person? How do I tell my patients' parents that it gets easier? Does it? Does the pain ease or ever go away?

There are women, like my second cousin, who never have kids. She opened schools in the Global South, and the kids in those schools became the children she never had. But is this what she wanted? For some women, yes, and that is okay, but others have been robbed of the simple wish for a child. They have to adapt to their new situation, a new plan and life.

And the answer is no, it doesn't get easier. The pain is always going to be there, as it still is when I hear these stories and think of my own babies in their urn. The pain is there because they were real, and the experience was real. The physical pain, constant tears, feeling alone with no baby to hold—all this suffering does go away with love and support, but the emotional pain remains. It is the cost of love, and sometimes it can even help us to see what we have and what we have not.

November 1, 2020: Legacy

Well, Jude, we did it!

Although I thought we had no support in the beginning, a hopeless endeavour, something changed. Together, we raised $2,588 for the Pregnancy and Infant Loss Network. Even more important are the ripple effects that extend far beyond raising awareness. We have touched people in the process. I am so proud and so is Daddy. Your legacy lives on.

November 2, 2020: So Many Stories

Early this morning, before I headed into work, a colleague sent me a video about a mother who suffered a miscarriage and then became pregnant with a child with Down's syndrome. The baby was stillborn. My heart aches for this mother.

At work, I get the opportunity to speak to many moms as I care for their babies. I often reflect on their stories. Today, three months after Jude, there were many tragic stories. One mother whose baby had no heartbeat at six weeks, but the doctor found the heartbeat prior to her D&C procedure. The mother went on to have a terrifying delivery after rupturing, one where she almost lost her life. Her husband had found her lying on the floor. Luckily, both she and her daughter survived.

Another mother, whose pregnancy had progressed with no concerns, delivered her baby but he required IV nutrition at birth that bypassed the intestinal tract. The procedure went badly, and the healthy baby boy now only has 10 per cent of his intestines left to work with.

Another mom stayed strong for her eight-week-old baby who came into the hospital with a fever. She thought she would get her baby checked out in the ER, and they would be given Tylenol or Advil and then sent home. The baby had meningitis. The mother is my age, with a seven-year-old at home, trying to balance it all. She told me, "I never expected any of this." I hear this statement from many mothers. But she was happy that she trusted her gut to get her kiddo looked after by a doctor. Her instinct saved her child's life.

I came home, as I always do, longing for my children. One day away from them at work, and I had forgotten the sound of their voices. I revelled at Case as he put together his Lego and played hide and seek. After Case was in bed, Phillip asked me about my day. I recounted the stories of all the mamas and their babies. Today, I also had my first patient with DiGeorge syndrome. Other nurses asked what it was, and I hid the fact that I knew exactly and completely what it was. On a deep level, this diagnosis consumes my whole world even to this day. Although this patient did not have the severe cardiomegaly that Kaia had, the diagnosis still got to me. This baby patient, who did not have a cardiac compromise, was still in hospital at eight weeks old, never having left.

I miss Jude and Kaia more than ever as I am flooded with the reminder of them in the children of the families at work.

November 6, 2020: Missing

I feel like, and know that, my life really began once I had kids. I recognize that these moments with my children being so young and needing me are fleeting. I am convinced that my rainbow children have also been made extra special.

I am missing you, Jude, and longing for you. In my grief, my default setting has been to get pregnant again. With our past, I've learned to cope by balancing my grief with hope at the same time. Right now, I am not pregnant, and I have to sit with these deeply unsettling emotions. As I hold the babies of other moms, I sense something is missing in me. There is an endless love that oozes from the hole in my heart.

I worry about all the anxiety I will face during a next pregnancy.

I am finally feeling and denumbing myself, and it hurts. My navigation plan isn't working. We always go to what is comfortable, but sometimes we don't allow ourselves to sit with the uncomfortable pain. But pain doesn't have to be bad.

At times, it makes me sad to think I have written more to my dead babies than to my living children. I have to remember that it is because I am busy living and experiencing love and life with them. My only way to stay connected to my dead babies is through journals, prayer, and mindful reflections.

November 11, 2020: Creating

Today I took myself to the beach, wrapping up my grief-stricken, freezing, numb self.

A retired colleague once told me that in the moment, we can only see our lives like the back of a piece of embroidery. One day in the future, we will see the finished product, the masterpiece that is being created through our experiences. I think of the rainbow baby blanket I was making for our rainbow baby Jude, not knowing then, as I worked on it at the beach, that each stitch would turn into a blanket for myself. I needed its weighted warmth and bright colours to comfort and ground me. At the beach, with the waves behind me, the bright sun and calm pond ahead, I started to see more clearly the creation of our life experiences.

November 12, 2020: In Grief, There Is No Conclusion

The geneticist received our spit results and noted that there was nothing specific that caused Jude's Potter's syndrome. Based on the literature from old studies, we have a 3 to 4 per cent chance of it occurring again. Or a 96 to 97 per cent chance of having a healthy child, but that is not what I heard.

In an effort to find answers for ourselves, we had extensive testing done. The only thing found was that I have an extra X chromosome. I started to form a thesis, which I never shared with the geneticist, that perhaps one of my X chromosomes is normal, and the other is faulty. The outcome of the pregnancy would then depend on if the child received the normal or the faulty chromosome. If this was true (and I am making this up as I go, knowing little about genetics), we have a 50/50 chance to have a normal pregnancy.

The geneticist assured us that our file would be kept open, and the team would monitor for updates in the literature. She was sure we would have a healthy baby one day in the future as our risk for complications is low, about one in a thousand. "However," she compassionately said, "it doesn't matter what the risk is when it happens to you. Then you are that one in a thousand."

We had been that one in a thousand before.

November 14, 2020: Remembering

Today was hard. I have neglected myself and haven't been going for runs. I used to believe my pregnancies with Case and Maelie worked out because I never ran. I was paranoid of doing anything that could jeopardize the pregnancy, even at the expense of my own wellbeing. My self-worth was riding on my babies, and all my selfish and favourite pastimes could take a back seat. When hubby asked today if I wanted to go for a drink, I said no, thinking and wishing, *What if I am pregnant?*

I felt guilt, and we missed out on a fun time together because of my new anxiety/obsession that I cannot shake—that of desperately wanting to be pregnant. This has stopped me from living, in the hopes that something else will live. The self-blaming has begun once again. I sift through all the possible scenarios, searching for something I can do differently.

Today was also hard, as I was given a leave of absence at the hospital, a day off to be with my kiddies for Remembrance Day. Everyone was asking what I was doing with them. I was writing a diary to my dead babies instead of playing with my living ones. Obviously, I do it to help myself, my children, and others, but the mom guilt is always there. As I reflect, I actually open more space to remember (on Remembrance Day) and hold on.

I know that the pregnancy losses have robbed me of my naïveté and joy in being pregnant. I have to remember how I used to feel—like our losses had robbed me of being a mother. Although I know the innocence is something I can never get back, today I remember I am a mother.

November 18, 2020: Waking Up and Living

My anxiety is really acting up. It has always been there, but I am starting to accept and realize the constant spinning pushes me to organize pictures and work on projects strictly as a distraction. When Case pats me on the back and Maelie gives me a big hug, I am briefly snapped out of the low moments. It doesn't take long before there are more and more low moments; the outside world has no idea.

I know my hubby has polite concern for me. "Is there anything else you can do? I know you talk to a counsellor, but it has got to be hard on you when you get depressed," Phillip said. "You've been really good lately, but you still have those moments."

I know my short-tempered outbursts are becoming more frequent and it's tiring. I believe they are coming from tears I have held back, tears from so many beliefs formed over a lifetime. My losses have forced me to look at and chip away at that mountain. I think back to the time Phillip and I did the Machu Picchu hike and Phillip said, "Wake up! You have to climb a mountain today!"

It is time to wake up and rise.

Janice mentioned the drug Zoloft. I've fought this for a long time. I am getting tired of fighting, knowing full well that I need something. As Janice listed off my history, she said, "Cut yourself some slack. It is no wonder you need something; you are the perfect candidate."

Growing up, my dad, who has bipolar disorder, was quick to anger and had many outbursts that threatened our safety. As I see myself repeating these outbursts in grief, it scares me severely. Do I have bipolar disorder too? No, I am not my father, and my circumstances are much different. The grief is natural, and it brings me to a dark place. I remember when I started seeing my counsellor, my mother's exact words were, "Are you sure you need that? You can always talk to me." Although her intentions were good, my mother's generation seems to believe that to seek help is to show weakness.

Seeing a counsellor was the best decision I ever made and, I dare say, may even be one of the gifts that came out of my loss. Counselling allowed me to come face to face with my life beliefs and to start shifting my thinking. There is such a stigma with mental health. Pregnancy and loss definitely take a toll on mental health. I understand now; it is hard to function, and then you feel bad for being unable to do so.

Last week, as I headed to work, I ran into a vehicle at a stop light. I was so distracted by all the ruminating and intrusive thoughts. This was my lucky wake-up call. I realize I am never really hearing people, just going through the motions with my forever spinning mind distracting me from the present. It is debilitating. The truth is that my head was in a million directions and far from the car that was right in front of me.

Being a nurse, I know that the potential risks of taking anxiety medications in pregnancy are minimal. Heck, having a chill baby as a side effect would be a huge bonus. Many mothers are on anxiety medications; it's just not something that is openly talked about. I am learning that the strongest mamas are those who get the help they know they need and deserve. I lack assertiveness, a lifetime trait I am plagued with. I need people who boss me around and give me direction. I often feel weak, but for the first time, I am being assertive and asking for help. Interestingly enough, I have never felt stronger in my weakness.

After chatting with Janice and feeling motivated, I took a leap of faith, and I called the high-risk clinic for myself. I am not okay. It has been three months since I lost Jude, but in my head, it feels like forever. I am feeling judged, and at this point, I am not over it, and now I need even more help. The moment I pulled over to make the call, Case screamed on cue, "I gotta go pee!"

I wailed at the clerk over his screams: "I need anxiety meds!"

I can just imagine how that sounded to her. Desperate times. She must have sympathized, or I flat out scared her, because she said, "That is not something we usually do, but I will ask the doctor." In the end, prescribing anxiety medication was not within their scope. I had been shaking with nerves, but I knew I had made the first step.

Next, I called my family doctor to book a phone consult. As I pulled out my health card, the answer was right there on my driver's license—a photo taken one year ago to replace the license I lost in the chaos of delivering Jude. The evidence was there in my pained and aged face. It was time to stop pretending to be strong and finally get help for my severe anxiety.

Yes, my baby died, but I don't have to. I need to get my life back. Our life back.

Part 7
Landing

To land is to stop.
Landing hurts but you begin to heal in that place,
no longer needing to fear falling further.

Babe #9
Hope

Hope is the one thing that is stronger than fear.
—Buddha

November 21, 2020: New Life

Today, I learned Jess was in labour. This is the same friend that I hid my pregnancy from when she was unable to get pregnant. I hid my kids from her when she miscarried. Jude's due date was close to that of her daughter. When we lost him, she hid her growing belly from us (COVID-19 helped with this). I had been looking forward to maternity leave with my best friend.

Today, I also learned Phillip and I are pregnant. I had an inkling but have decided to keep this news to myself for now.

Conveniently, I was working when Jess was in the delivery room. I got to sneak in as a "helping nurse" to see the sweetest bundle and to witness the joy on the faces of both Jess and her husband. When asked how it felt, they both said in graceful harmony and with glowing eyes that it felt unreal.

November 22, 2020: Starting Fresh

When I think about this pregnancy, rather than joy, the same negative thoughts come rushing back. What if it happens again? There are many things I know that I cannot control. But I can control the love that I have for my family, and what I can do right now is love this baby.

I am already sidetracked thinking how I'm going to do things differently: no hot baths, no oils, no kombucha, no magnets, no sips of alcohol, and diminished cell phone use. Phillip has jokingly said he would wrap me in duct tape if I got pregnant again. I need to know and feel like I have control over something. Yet if this baby is healthy, I will continue to blame the problems with my previous pregnancies on all the things that I didn't do.

November 24, 2020: Sharing

I am so lucky I can get pregnant. Although I am unbelievably happy, I feel scared that I won't stay pregnant. I also get tearful thinking what another pregnancy may do to my body, which is able to handle less and less. Phillip also voices his fear when he mentions how we are getting older and older.

Today, I told my other best friend, Mamacita (Celina), that I am pregnant and due near Jude's birthday. We both had delighted and disbelieving tears in our eyes.

At the end of the day, Case handed me a purple and green Fruit Loop, the colours I associate with Kaia and Jude.

November 25, 2020: A Happy Pregnancy

As I booked my prenatal appointment, the nurse asked me if this was a happy pregnancy. I had never heard it put that way before; it never occurred to me that a pregnancy couldn't be happy. The truth is that I don't know. I have had my fair share of sad pregnancies, but they were always happy and hopeful pregnancies until we received the strike. I told the nurse that we were just scared as hell because we have so much riding on it. Of course, we had lots riding on Jude's pregnancy as well, wanting him so ferociously, but this time there was an ultimatum. We had both agreed we would try for a third baby one more time—the third child I want so desperately—and if that baby doesn't survive, we will stop trying.

November 26, 2020: Knowing

I made a nice meal for Phillip, and I ate the stinky broccoli that he wouldn't even try. I tried to convince him it wasn't that bad, but it was. Note to self: Never let broccoli sit in water for three days on the stove before cooking it. I handed him some damn hot Pepperettes.

"Oh, I'll give you my sausage," Phillip said.

"Nope, I don't need it anymore."

"I know you're pregnant."

"How did you know?"

"You have been acting normal lately."

Apparently, I act the most normal when I am pregnant, and that is a scary thought.

December 9, 2020: Bleeding Heart

As I write these words, I am bleeding. My worst fears have been confirmed.

Yesterday, while on break, a coworker asked me if there is a reason I keep having miscarriages. I love her honesty because no one wants to ask those hard questions. I sit here every day asking myself the same question. What is wrong with me?

"I've been told we are just unlucky," I told her.

But could they please just look again? Investigate further? Maybe we have a translocation (basically when the location of chromosomes changes) or hyperfertility that has been overlooked.

The same girl innocently asked if we would try again. I'm grateful I didn't tell her we were pregnant yesterday; today, would be another awkward story.

I could have called in sick, like I had for my previous miscarriages. Instead, I went to work as if nothing was happening. I wanted to work rather than be alone with myself, my hurtful thoughts, and the blood.

My heart breaks that I had to tell Phillip one more time. There was so much riding on this pregnancy because I was convinced we owed it to Jude and ourselves to try one more time for our wanted third baby. I had promised Phillip that if this one doesn't work out, I would know that we tried, and we could move on. Here I sit now, not wanting to recall the finality of my own words. I do not want to lose the hope of a future child. Not right now. At least I know we tried. Or maybe it's finally time to accept and let go. Only I can't. It absolutely wasn't as easy as I had thought.

In hearing the news, Phillip said, "We can still try one more time." I was surprised by these quick and sincere words and was greatly appreciative. A new promise. A new chance.

I just can't do it anymore. I can't keep trying, I am too fragile.

Phillip had already started talking about life with three kids in our future home. He encouraged me so gently to be careful about lifting weights with my sister and always reminded the kids not to jump on Mommy. He wanted to know about my bleeding during previous pregnancies, trying to reconcile its severity for himself. He was sincerely concerned for me and for our future baby.

I am forever grateful for sitting on the couch while immersed in the love of my family. Maelie patted my head gently, and Case took my hand on gentle reflex to wrap it around his belly.

I am still afraid to push when sitting on the toilet, for fear of the inevitable. I still grab my boobs and evaluate their sensitivity. I am still trying to hold on to some semblance of pregnancy.

December 18, 2020: Case's Third Birthday

Up until today, I was grieving, occupying my mind with preparing for this day, Case's birthday. Today marks close to the day we found out the devastating news about our daughter Kaia four years ago. Today is Case's third birthday. Today, as luck would have it, would have also been Jude's due date.

Today, I am celebrating the life I get to have with my son Case. Today, I am grieving the life I don't get to have with my son Jude, and I am missing him deeply.

Today, I am grateful. Today, I am hurting while I am healing. Today, I don't look to the future. I don't worry or fear what is to come, though thoughts of miscarriage and fetal anomalies are dancing in my head. I have so many emotions, lost hopes, and dreams. Today is and was supposed to be so many things.

Today . . . I am still pregnant.

A note about bleeding: As a woman who has lost pregnancies, I never stop checking for blood. My doctor told me how first trimester bleeding is relatively common in about 20 per cent of all pregnancies. For my first two miscarriages, blood was confirmation of an ended pregnancy. With Kaia, there was no bleeding, but there was a severe cardiac anomaly and confirmed DiGeorge syndrome. There were two very early pregnancies where I treated the bleeding like a period. With Maelie, the bright red blood I saw in the toilet is what saved her. In my pregnancy with Jude, there was bleeding that did not lead to a miscarriage. Later, we learned he had no kidneys.

Although the doctors have proven that my baby is still growing and my hCG levels are still climbing, I now fear the blood means the baby will have no kidneys. The fear of blood and what it can represent never goes away; it has saved me, and it has broken me.

Today, we learned I am measuring a little earlier, so our due date is August 2 (of all the days in the year), and so the cycle repeats.

December 20, 2020: Flip Flop

In reviewing my journal entries, I see that my feelings flip flop between elation and deep sadness. It feels like it could be bipolar disorder, but I believe it is the grief cycle. I have ironically learned and gained a new appreciation and acceptance of bipolar disorder and mental health in general. We all need to be kind to one another and gentle with ourselves.

My father has bipolar disorder; this was a script I had my whole life. Don't show any anger or pain for fear that emotion will cause a flare up. Don't do anything wrong that may trigger an outburst. We would hide in the shed or bike to Oma's. We dodged flying plates as we watched our parents fight, scared someone would become seriously injured.

We asked our mother why she never left our father. She said, "I vowed to be with him through sickness and health. Bipolar disorder is like cancer. It is a sickness."

Just like grief can be.

I have learned that my grief, with its highs and lows, looks much the same as my father's bipolar disorder. There are good days and bad days. One day, I want to flee, and another day, I want to never let go. I have worried that showing these feelings would mean that I might have bipolar, and it has always been easier to hide these highs and lows and be internally angry.

Growing up with a dad with bipolar disorder, we always had to have a Plan B. I couldn't have realized back then that always being prepared with a Plan B would end up being rather helpful to me in our situation. I am not saying you can prepare for any of this; however, at a deep level, I never really anticipated things would go as expected. I brought my childhood wiring and beliefs with me in grief, which is why each of my experiences has been so different.

December 25, 2020: Sleep in Heavenly Peace

I was scheduled to work on Christmas Day. A colleague (who is a true angel on Earth) asked if I wanted it off with my family. She has her own young family but sensed my need to be with mine. With tears in my eyes, I accepted and cherished how the world works.

Thank you, Jude, for working some strings to remind us that you are here and in giving us the gift of being all together with cherished family time. We got your memo and cherish all the good cheer. Case also says, "Santa is a very nice fellow!"

December 28, 2020: Beating Heart

To begin the ultrasound, the technician gently asked me if we had four kids at home. I realized she must have glimpsed at my chart and seen that I have delivered four times.

"Nope," I said, "I have two." This was met with silence for the entirety of the scan. I thought:

On this day, I apologized.
On this day, I prayed.
On this day, I saw the flicker of a beating heart.
On this day, I cried.
On this day, I am pregnant.
On this day, I have hope.

January 1, 2021: Goodbye

When I reflect on 2020, I recall the words the OB said when Jude was born: "He is beautiful." And he was. We will always remember what 2020 gave us rather than what it took from us. As 2020 comes to an end, so does the year that Jude was in it.

My elementary school friend Jenn recently told us that she is ten weeks pregnant. I couldn't hold back the excitement. Here is another chance to maybe be with a friend on maternity leave. I admired her bravery in making the announcement before the twelve-week gold standard. I reflected on how I once naively and eagerly shared the news of our first pregnancy at her birthday party those many years ago. Now, I am secretly in awe of her naïveté and excitement.

I fantasize about being on maternity leave when my boy starts school, about being on leave with my friend, and having our baby exactly a year to the day we had Jude. With the fantasy comes the deep pain of what we have lost, what we could lose, and why it all means so much more.

January 2, 2021: A Whole New World

The photographs of my living children will always change, yet Kaia and Jude will forever stay the same, a constant reminder of never-changing love.

Earlier, Case and Maelie held Kaia's picture together. Now they each have a picture to hold, Case holding the picture of a lost brother and Maelie holding the picture of a lost sister.

January 5, 2021: G9 T2 P2 A4 L2

This is my number: G9 T2 P2 A4 L2.

The number glares at me from the top of my prenatal chart at my doctor's appointments. I have memorized this number. The G signifies Gravida, every pregnancy I have ever had. I am pregnant with my ninth pregnancy. Where my next numbers land for term, preterm, abortion, or live birth is not up to me, but I know that every one of my pregnancies I have loved fully and that every pregnancy mattered in my life.

January 14, 2021: Curiosity

Out of curiosity, I started looking at what size the baby is at this period of gestation: a strawberry. I realized that I stopped doing this after our first miscarriage; it seemed to have lost its importance. Besides, babies are not the size of an olive. Babies are not fruits or vegetables.

January 19, 2021: Discovery

Phillip asked me today if I felt this tired with Maelie. I said yes, although I felt pukey with her, and I do not with this one. I could tell he was trying to determine if we are having a boy or a girl.

January 21, 2021: Hi Ma!

I was awakened by these words. It felt like they were shouted right into my ear, and I jolted up in bed. Expecting to find Case or Maelie right in front of me, I was surprised to discover they were in bed sleeping. Then I realized it was you.

I no longer shake off these experiences as being crazy. I did in the beginning, but now I keep an ear open for you always. Although I struggle with ever knowing which spirit baby of ours is visiting, I feel you all the same. This time I felt it was you, Kaia. It sounded like a young girl's voice, although young voices can sound similar. I guess it could have been any one of my spirit babies, but I felt in my heart it was you trying to reach me.

This brought comfort to me. You are okay. You came back to me. The words have reminded me that you are cheering me along and letting me know I am on the right path and that all is in divine order. I needed this reminder—that even with so much time unavoidably passing it doesn't stop you from reaching us. You are still here with us. Hi!

January 23, 2021: What We Couldn't Have Known

Today, my patient was Twin A of a pregnancy. I recognized the mom somehow. I am not great with faces, but hers I remembered. She was the mom who was there as we left the fertility clinic, when we were told we had a heartbeat with Kaia. She sobbed in her hubby's arms because they had been handed the opposite news. That was over four years ago, and now here she is with a twin boy and girl. If only I could have hugged that mama back then and told her that one day she would have twins. She wouldn't have believed me.

I thought about the question I had asked my high-risk doctor. "Why do you do this sad work every day?"

She said, "It is very hard work, but I see many families come back showing off their families down the road. One day, you will be here with your three babies."

I didn't believe her then, and nor would this woman have believed me if I offered her the assurance of a child, let alone twins, in the future. Yet recognizing that, here we are.

January 25, 2021: Masking

I wish I could say I went into room number seven with the hopes of debunking my superstitions and proving my pregnancy losses had nothing to do with the room number. Today, I was placed in room eight, and I focused on the fact that our baby is due in the eighth month of the year. I took this as a good sign.

My biggest trigger is the ultrasound room, where the news gets delivered, and you are rendered helpless and alone. Always alone. I packed my eye pillow and didn't even apologize for wearing it. I stated I needed it for my anxiety—my invisibility cloak—so no one would be able to see me and my emotions. I didn't need to pretend to be strong and force a smile. The mask worked great; I was fully covered.

The anxiety never goes away.

The tech said she had read my history and knew that I would be anxious. This tech was also pregnant and due in March. Talking with her about her pregnancy was extremely calming for me, as I could put the excitement, anticipation, and focus on her.

As I entered another room for my next appointment with the high-risk doctor, I felt my anxiety ramping up and taking hold. Everyone seemed so sympathetic and understanding, but all I saw was my whole history in big letters at the top of my records: G9 T2 P2 A4 L2. Seeing that number, I remembered why I was anxious, and I wanted my eye pillow back.

I was told I am twelve weeks and six days pregnant. I had not even registered that I had made it past the biggest risk-of-miscarriage phase. I knew it was too early to detect the kidneys, but I frantically looked for them. The flashbacks were coming back.

The resident asked, "Have you ever been diagnosed with post-traumatic stress disorder?"

Jokingly, I explained to the resident how being pregnant is a coping strategy for me—vitamin pregnant—and that not being pregnant causes me more anxiety. It may just be a weird new hope phenomenon. When she heard it, she chuckled and said it made sense.

The last time I saw this OB, at the six-week-post-delivering-Jude followup, I told her we would either cut our losses or wait for quite a while before trying again.

Today, she laughed and said, "Somehow, I thought I would see you soon. What a pleasant surprise." She told me she had meant to tell me we should not rush to get a vasectomy. A part of her knew we were not really finished.

We talked about IPS testing, as it can also give indicators about my placenta. Having had an abruption before, they offered for me to have a sixteen-week high resolution scan that shows the four chambers of the heart and the kidneys (the two things we most wanted to know about). I adored the OB in that moment; she wanted to help ease my greatest fears, without me having to ask for it. Today, our scan looked structurally good, and today I am taking that as a positive.

After the appointment, talking with Phillip on the phone, I reported that all was well with the test. I could hear the skepticism in his voice. He worries it may not be okay down the line. He got really quiet and said nothing. I thought he had hung up.

At night, while I was trying to let everything sink in about this pregnancy, Nola jumped up on the bed with me. She has been through all my pregnancies with me. Was she trying to comfort me? Did she sense that something was wrong?

February 2, 2021: What Starts with *M*?

A patient told a joke to a nurse. What starts with "m" and ends in "arriage?" She immediately replied "marriage," as most people would. When she posed the joke to me, I said "miscarriage" without hesitation. The word marriage did not occur to me. This goes to show that those who have lost remain in that dark-head place, and even time will not shift them out of it.

February 10, 2021: Touched

Today, I went for a massage, and I cried. The COVID-19 pandemic has left many of us craving for the touch of another human. Here I was taking time to love myself, to be held and cared for by another's therapeutic healing touch, and I cried. I cried for my body and how each area holds so much of my life experience.

One thing all of my babies had in common was that my body held them through every stage of their life. I focused on the different areas of my body as she massaged them.

In my tailbone (root chakra), I felt myself grounded every time I was pregnant—a knowing of who I am and how I continue to sit with the memories of my lost babies.

In my lower abdomen (sacral chakra), I remembered the moments Phillip and I were trying to have a baby and how I knew the moment I was pregnant, as there was a shooting star energy that always took place. I thought about the pain, the big and small babies I delivered, the clots, the missed periods, and the lack of vaginal deliveries. I also, on occasion, rejoiced in the periods I had. I knew my body was operating appropriately, each day preparing itself for pregnancy.

In my stomach (solar plexus chakra), I remembered the butterflies from when I told my family of the readiness I felt to be a mama. I felt the first kicks when I worked up north; I had not made it far enough before to feel kicks. Then I felt the emptiness of having to let Kaia go and knowing I would miss those precious kicks and still feel the phantom kicks after. I recalled the moments I would talk to her, touching my belly. With Case, I watched in awe as my belly moved and continued to grow. Phillip said it was like an alien was in there or that my belly was alive. Memories came to me of Case saying "baba" for baby and tapping my belly when I was pregnant with Maelie and the two of them doing the same with Jude.

In my neck (throat chakra), I noticed how my throat buckles, collapses, and chokes up when I think of Jude. I felt the tension, the stress, and the residual stiffness of holding on tightly, not being able to clear and release the knots within, always on guard.

In my mind (third eye chakra), I saw the big picture. I thought of Maelie and Case hugging, how they genuinely embrace each other as they sway and giggle, squeal and love. I could see them welcoming, holding this baby, and genuinely loving it. I can't erase the images of my babies from this spot. I look at other babies and think how I should have one right now or what age they would be had I not lost them or what they would be doing.

In my head (crown chakra), I at times could clearly envision the tactile touch of my babies and my tingling fingers where I felt their energy. I touched every part of them, wanting to remember it all; my fingers had gently cradled them and lightly caressed them while mindful of their fragility.

My body carries all of this and remembers. In it is everything. Everything I need to know, where I held and hold the loves of my life. Life can take a lot from me, but it can't take from me what I got to hold and what I still hold in my body and my mind.

February 15, 2021: Family Day

Phillip and I had a conversation about sharing the news of our pregnancy on Family Day. Phillip said, "Let's just wait until your ultrasound to be sure, which is just a few days away."

Regardless of the ultrasound, I know we have to tell family. If it is bad news, I will need their help to grieve again. If it is good news, then we will have made our announcement on a memorable day—one we had wished to use for our first pregnancy when we used to strategically plan announcing. I want this. Sadly, though, we can't live for planning cute memories. It's just not for us.

Okay, I need to let that wish go. I will wait for the ultrasound results.

I already told my sister Selena in confidence on her birthday. I confided in her how I would like to do a gender reveal, since it is something we haven't had the chance to do yet. Even she said not to talk about it until our ultrasound. But I want something to get excited about. My loved ones no longer show initial excitement because they are trying to protect me, and that hurts. I feel my history has tainted all of them in how they are to feel, so they also don't get too attached themselves. Deep down, I know I need all the protection I can get.

As the ultrasound looms closer, I am nervous. I worry about the same bleeding, the same room, hearing bad news alone, and possible changes to our lives. I realize the ultrasound is booked early for my own peace of mind, but if they don't see what they need to, it's another month before my anatomy scan. My mind will start spinning again.

February 17, 2021: Nightmares

Today, as I was making my final rounds on my shift, I came across a young patient puking. Her dad was with her and needed towels. Although she was not my patient, I stopped to help. She was a one-year-old girl with bright brown eyes and red-tinged hair. I knew from my coworker that she had cystic fibrosis and was in for an exacerbation (a flare-up or inflammation in the lungs, one that couldn't be controlled at home).

Her father told me they spent a month at the hospital after her birth because she was born with pyloric stenosis, a blocked small intestine, the same as her sister had. He went on to explain how her sister had been transferred at birth to different hospitals for surgery. While she was there, they learned her heart needed surgery. The surgery had been successful; however, when the doctor closed her up, the child went into cardiac arrest and died.

His daughter had now been born with the same problem, and it brought them back to the same nightmare. How could this happen twice? Unlike her sister, she had done really well, and they were proud of their strong and fiery redheaded girl.

I said I was deeply sorry, and before I was able to ask what their dead daughter's name was, I got pulled away to deal with a person who was actually my own patient. My patient from today is five years old and doing well, although his mama has stage-four cancer. She told me that if anything ever happened to her, she wanted us to know that she has a huge family to look after her son. Thoughts flooded my mind. At that age, would the child remember his mother? What a pivotal age to need your mama and know she is there supporting you in your development. It is freaking unfair.

These parents have come out the other side of unfairness and are still enduring and carrying on joyfully, though with an undertone of painful loving and appreciation. In their loss, they still remain hopeful and humbly kind.

February 18, 2021: Flooding

I woke up with a migraine. I sat by the window sipping tea and watched the flags flapping in the wind. It was a peaceful, calm morning, no snow falling and no sun either, just grey.

I arrived at the ultrasound appointment. The same pregnant technician who had done our thirteen-week scan called my name. It was nice to see a familiar face. I have to admit that if it had been the same technician who had done Jude, I would have had to pass, not because she wasn't kind but because it was all just too much already.

She asked, "Did you receive the IPS results?"

"No."

"That is odd."

I self-assuredly claimed that no news was good news or that maybe I would hear the results today, not letting myself go there. With our past pregnancies, the results often came right away.

The tech offered, "They should call you regardless. Hopefully, you get some answers."

The ultrasound tech and I talked the entire time about life with kids. We shared life's little hacks and hilarious pleasures. I told her that for sleep training, I coslept with my son and left a bottle in bed for my daughter to find when she needed it in the night. Yup, not the right thing to do nor what any parenting book will tell you. But it worked for us.

She asked if I wanted to know the gender of the baby. This question struck me as hopeful because when the news is bad, the tech starts to act weird and never talks about anything future oriented. I told her it would give the family something to look forward to during COVID-19 and to keep it secret for now.

She showed me my baby, and I looked at the little bean. I saw perfect kidneys, amniotic fluid, and a beating heart. The baby looked so cute. Phillip laughs when I say this; he believes that on the ultrasound, they all look the same.

The tech said she was going to check with the radiologist that all was okay. My heart sank. As I returned from an always needed trip to the toilet, the radiologist was not in the room waiting to deliver a blow. The tech said everything was good: "We got great pictures today, baby cooperated very well, and we got everything we need. We may have to repeat the brain scan in the future, as some features are just too small right now."

I heard, "The brain is too small."

The ultrasound tech gave me lots of ultrasound pictures and said they were great shots. She also said not to show anyone in the waiting room in case they got jealous. Deep down, I think she felt sorry for us, and that was how she was making up for it. I don't want pity, but in this case, I did appreciate her kindness. I took them.

I left knowing I was to meet with the doctor afterwards. I picked up the phone and messaged Phillip (whose phone was on) and my best friends—Celina, Jess, and Selena—to let them know the ultrasound was done. Now I needed to wait for the doctor. I called Janice and told her how I didn't have news yet, but I knew there were kidneys, and the images were really good. We rejoiced in that, but I still didn't feel completely relieved since I did not have my IPS results. I thanked her for her support, and as I hung up, there were texts from my best friends that both read "Yay for kidneys!"

I waited four hours to see my doctor. I sat with women just weeks away from delivery who continually repositioned themselves in their uncomfortable chairs. I was the only one with a tiny bump. A hot water pipe had burst that needed to be attended to straight away, and it caused a delay because it limited how many exam rooms were available. I laughed thinking that someone's water could have broken when they announced there was a problem with a water leak. While waiting, and to occupy my mind, I googled "small brain." Only then did I realize that it had likely meant that at sixteen weeks, the brain was too small to see what they needed to see.

Finally, the doctor called my number. I sat in a room with a round table that just felt like a table where bad news gets delivered. We sat at the same round tables in the conferences with the medical teams for Kaia and Jude. I clenched my eyes, waiting for an entourage to arrive bearing the bad news, but when I opened my eyes, they weren't there. Only the doctor was there, and she went through the pictures in front of me.

"Everything looks good," she said. "The only thing we would like a better image of is the brain, to capture the CSP. You can be very re-assured by this ultrasound. Would you like to know the gender?"

I was still. I didn't know what CSP was or meant. But I fumbled together an answer and asked if she could write down the gender in case we decided to do a reveal. As she left the room, I quickly searched "CSP brain fetus" on my phone: "Cavum septi pellucidi (CSP) is an important landmark in the prenatal ultrasound evaluation of the fetal brain, and its visualization provides reassurance of normal central forebrain development. Nonvisualization of the CSP is a prenatal sonographic finding, which in most cases is associated with neuro-anatomical anomalies that include..."

When she returned, she slipped me the gender in an envelope and was about to leave. I couldn't help but ask, as my words leaped before my brain, "Is it normal to not see the CSP at a sixteen-week ultra-sound?"

I had been briefed that in doing the scan early, there could be things they would need to rescan after more growth. She said it looked good to her, "but radiologists can be so picky." She politely reminded me that I should feel reassured.

"Oh, wait, one more thing. Do you have the results of my IPS?" I asked. "I'm assuming no news is good news?"

"I don't have them with me; they are in my office. I will give you a call if there is anything abnormal. I will also call if radiology needs further scanning." I thought of the water leak and how when it rains it pours. I felt like I was drowning in the unknown again. I was so focused on the kidneys and heart being okay that it never occurred to me that the brain might not be normal. Isn't it amazing what the grief brain can do?

I knew that after going through the scan, I needed some brain food. I pulled up to McDonald's, ordered everything I could dream of, and finished off with a shamrock shake. They didn't even ask me what size and ordered me a large. When I pulled up to the window the girl looked at me a few times and said, "I have to ask. You wanted the Big Mac, upsized fries, shake, and ice cream, right?" Umm, yes.

I quickly shot Phillip a message saying everything looked good and that they just needed to rescan the brain. As I texted this, I chucked the envelope with the baby's gender into the back seat and occupied my hands with food to avoid the extreme temptation that was in the car with me.

Phillip wrote back, "I hope the brain is okay." Both Phillip and I know we can never have full relief until this baby is in our arms.

That night Phillip and I talked, and we cuddled while holding hands. Our hands always seem to find each other in times like these. We talked about what to do with the gender information, and I could see it in him right away. Phillip's eyes twinkled when he said how much he loved the surprise of Maelie, and I wanted to honour his wish. That conversation flooded me with hope, as I saw the joy that was in Phillip.

I speed-dialed Selena and asked her over so she could steal the sheet of paper and strategically hide it from me. I joked that they could open it and have their own gender reveal at home when I went into labor. When we announced the birth, they could announce the gender from home. Fun!

That night, I felt your movement for the first time.

February 20, 2021: Revealing

I continued to think about a potential gender reveal. Could I just look in the envelope and not tell Phillip? No. I am the worst at keeping secrets, and I couldn't do that to my dear loving husband.

With Kaia, we found out so matter of fact after finding out the bad news.

With Case, finding out we were having a boy helped us with our grief process because had he been a girl, we might have associated the baby with Kaia.

With Maelie, we got to experience a surprise, welcoming her and what we had once envisioned for a girl.

With Jude, I always sensed he was a boy. He was a surprise but not in the conventional sense. They couldn't make out the gender on ultrasound due to the decreased fluid, and he was a surprise in a completely different kind of way.

I will never know what our other early losses might have been, although we named some and not others, and I hold on to those warm imaginations.

We don't need any more surprises. From a gender perspective, we don't have anything riding on this baby. When asked if we would prefer a boy or girl, we say we are happy with whatever we have as long as the baby is healthy. Every time we ask Case what the baby is, he says, "It's a Case baby, a boy," and as Maelie trails her dolls all over the house, feeding them and changing them and giving them baths, she says, "girl baby."

Comic relief: When I asked Case if he would be upset if we had a girl baby, he shrugged and said, "No. Mommy has two babies because she has two those things," as he pointed to my boobs. I had tears from laughing so hard. But maybe also subtle tears that I can't bring them both a brother and a sister, something in my mind I had actually already done.

After the loss of Kaia, I found out Case's gender. This helped to make him real because in my mind, I never truly believed he was real. I couldn't. Although I had wished for a girl after Kaia, in retrospect I was so happy to have a boy so that my son could be his own self and not have to fulfill the hopes, wishes, and dreams we had for Kaia.

There is a loss that comes with gender; let's be honest. Most moms want girls, and men want boys, maybe because it's what they know. For example, I have never peed standing up and always learned to wipe, so I taught Case to wipe. Case came running to me one day saying, "Daddy says don't wipe my pee-pee thing; just shake it." Lesson learned, son. I can say now, though probably would never say it out loud, that I would have been disappointed had Maelie been a boy. I would have loved my boy baby dearly, but there would have been some sadness there. I would have felt the weight of what I had been robbed of, my then only chance at a girl with Kaia.

There is also judgment when you have both a girl and boy. I've heard and experienced it. Why would we need to try for another when we've already got the perfect family? Families with two boys or two girls don't get faced with this question because naturally they are allowed to try for their girl or boy baby. Perhaps there is a smidge of disappointment in this pregnancy, as I think perfect would be a brother for Case and a sister for Maelie, the brother and sister that we lost for them. I know that a girl close to Jude's birthday would not be as triggering a reminder as a boy baby. Although a boy would not replace him, he may also be a haunting reminder of what we lost. I am also saddened that I cannot use the name Jude ever again—a name that we both loved and wished to call a living son one day.

Phillip says he doesn't need to know the gender. As the pregnancy progresses, I just may have to find out the sex to help me bond with this baby, something I want so desperately yet try so hard to avoid. For now, I feel at ease with the surprise.

At work, people have started to ask if we will try again for a third. I feel like saying that we have already tried for our third baby several times. Deep down, I feel so selfish for wanting three babies. I am nervous and tired of feeling like I have to constantly explain myself, as I did when we were pregnant with Jude. Even with loss, I am judged. People have said "Wow, you are just thirty and are having your third child," and "You are crazy to want three," and "Wow, you're pregnant again? You are not a dog." Someone actually said that to me. Or even worse, "You've already got two healthy babies. Why risk it for one with a syndrome?"

Many people often assumed I loved being pregnant. But the sad truth is that I've had more pregnancies than living babies, and if I didn't keep miscarrying or losing babies, I wouldn't always be trying to get pregnant. I also didn't love the PTSD that accompanied every one of my pregnancies.

In the city where I work, I am sometimes called crazy for having three kids at thirty. The mentality is that I should put my career first. But the farming community where I was raised is totally different.

There is surprise if you only have three kids by the time you are thirty. Everything becomes about the farm, and the women stay home to raise their children, ones who will also work the farm when they get old enough. I sometimes feel so torn between these two lives.

As women, we always feel we have to explain ourselves, and I really wish we didn't have to. Even with my hoped-for three babies, I never say I'm done. I am allowed to keep that door open, as that door brings hope. I don't ever have to finalize or say we're done anything.

February 23, 2021: Celebrating

Today, we visited Jess and her newborn. Her excitement for us and her curiosity about the pregnancy felt familiar. I have been pregnant for five-plus years with two incredible babies to show for it, but it wasn't supposed to be this hard. It wasn't supposed to be like this.

Jess insisted on taking a picture of my belly before I left, again reiterating her elation. It is something I have not yet done myself.

As I arrived home, I listened to a voicemail from my high-risk obstetrician's secretary.

It said, "When you come in for your repeat anatomy scan on March 1, you can go home after, and your OB will call you the following day with results."

Could this mean that she is actually confident enough that she can have this conversation with me over the phone, sparing the round tables? I appreciated that they would not make me wait six hours like last time. They had to wait for a radiologist to look at it anyways, but my ever-racing mind began to formulate negative thoughts. Ugh. Oh, how the mind wanders.

February 26, 2021: Protecting

Working back on the paediatric floor, I feel I need to protect myself even more as I deal with so many unfortunate cases with babies. I used to think that once I made it past the twenty-week mark, I would be out of the woods. I could breathe a little easier and make it to the end. But wait a minute Carmen, uh uh uh, not so fast. Don't forget about the premature infants, the sudden infant death syndrome (SIDS) babies, and even the metabolic syndromes that are determined after the baby's birth. Things I wouldn't normally think of keep exposing themselves to me in my line of work, and I can't look away.

A personal support worker (PSW) I work with talked to me randomly about how nice it is that I have two children, something she always wanted but never got to experience. The guilt crept in. This lady continued on and told me she has a boy, and when she was pregnant with him, she was sick enough to require hospitalization. Once she felt she could stomach another pregnancy, wanting one desperately, her husband left her. Years later she experienced extreme abdominal pain that resulted in her needing a hysterectomy, and when she woke up in the recovery room, she learned they had to remove her ovaries. She said she couldn't stop crying, remembering her primal screams of what was taken from her. She never had another baby.

Another PSW shared about her constant losses and how she couldn't carry a baby to term. It wasn't until her grandmother took her in, making her stay in bed as she fed her every day, believing in her and her baby, that she delivered her only son at twenty-nine weeks. Today, she is a huge advocate for pregnant women not having to do any heavy lifting or pushing while at work. I get it now.

I think back to when Maelie had been playing outside and decided to sunbathe. She was simply lying there on the ground looking up at the sky. I instantly thought she had choked on a rock when she was really lying still, looking up, and taking in the moment. I yelled, and she instantly jumped up and started hollering. This revealed where my mind goes sometimes. I find it has been harder to work after having kids, and I empathize more deeply with the unimaginable. The fear of loss grows stronger in me the more fiercely I love.

February 28, 2021: Exposing

As of today, Phillip is off work for two months for his final term of refrigeration schooling. Go figure he starts at school on the same day I go for the repeat ultrasound. Again, he will not be there when I need him the most but not by choice. He wants to be there; he will simply have to keep his phone turned on. In an effort to be positive, I tell myself that he doesn't need to be there because everything is going to be okay, just like it ended up being with Maelie.

I sometimes joke with the girls at work about being a newly single mom, but it is to hide the pain of how alone I feel. Before Phillip left, he said, "Look at that belly and how big it is." He kissed my belly and acknowledged the thing I have been desperately trying to hide from others, especially at work.

I only told one girl at work that I am pregnant, due to the fact she is moving to another hospital. I figured it was safe to do so, and she has also been trying to help me hide the pregnancy. Recently she gasped, "Carmen, you took your sweater off." I had been sweating through everything and kind of forgot myself and the reason I had been covering up, and without the sweater, I was exposed. I thought about how maybe I would be able to flaunt my belly one day, as I dripped profusely underneath my swiftly reapplied sweater.

I can sense that Phillip wants to believe this pregnancy is happening. Phillip sees new hope when he looks at my belly, something I wish to believe in, too. I can feel the fluttery movements, yet I still don't feel this baby is real. Though there is nothing I can do to make it happen for us, what I can do is move to the rhythm of the baby kicks and my current affirmation: One can only dream.

March 1, 2021: Eighteen-Week Repeat Ultrasound

Between shifts, I went to my ultrasound, and it was about to happen. We were about to go into the dreaded room, lucky number seven, but they moved me to another room. Maybe they just knew it was a room I could not be in. I needed a room where good news gets delivered.

The ultrasound tech did not talk at all. She let me listen to the heartbeat, and it was 143 beats per minute. I barely heard it, as I was waiting for her boss to coldly blurt something out at the end. Instead, she smiled (after what seemed like ten deep breaths) and said that they got everything they needed and good luck. My assumption was that everything they needed meant there was in fact a brain in this baby's sweet head.

That night at work, I had a patient with a degenerative brain disease who had a very sad prognosis. The student nurse asked me why this happens. Then she answered as she read the patient's history further, "Oh, maybe it's because—

"It can happen for no reason at all," I interrupted.

She looked at me with fear in her eyes and said, "Really? That scares me, as I think about myself and having kids one day."

I did not say this to scare her but to say that sometimes there are no textbook answers for why such terminal illnesses and tragedies occur.

As I frantically try to not think about how I will endure the long twenty-four hours before I get the news from the ultrasound, it is hard to shake my worrying mind, especially after having a patient with a degenerative brain disease. Is it another sign? I hope not.

No reason, remember.

March 2, 2021: Beautiful Chaos

Today marks seven months since Jude's due date. Today was also pick-up day for a package that I ordered, a "Mama" sweater, the same sweater Jess and many moms in this area have. I decided that I deserve it. Then I had an awful thought. What if I pick up this sweater and then get the bad news and never wear it? Even though, no matter what, I am still a mama, it's what it symbolizes—my first and finally accepting mama attire. I picked up the sweater, and I'm keeping it packed away, just in case I have to return it. I will wait until I receive the news.

After my night shift, I was trying to sleep while Oma watched the children. Of course, I could not sleep. They said they would call me at noon, and it was 12:00 p.m. exactly. Maybe they were having lunch, right? Then at 1:00 p.m., I realized that afternoon can mean anything before 5:00 p.m. I didn't want to be that person who calls asking if they had forgotten about me. After messaging to Jess, I settled on calling them at 3:00 p.m., since 4:00 p.m. is the time the clinic closes, and to wait another day would just be too nerve-racking. At 2:30 p.m. the phone rang.

"Hello, Carmen speaking." I started to shake. I had to steady myself, bringing my free hand to my lap.

"Hello, Carmen. May I say this is the best scan I have ever had in my entire career. The pictures are so clear. It is such an honour to get to have you as a patient," my doctor said.

"Oh, that's so sweet." (Cough, okay, go on.)

"As you know, we had a relook at the baby's brain." (Please spit it out.) "And . . . everything looks normal."

Feeling so grateful but not yet totally at ease, I asked about the results of my IPS testing.

"The testing shows you have less than a one in twenty thousand chance of Down's syndrome. Another thing that is interesting, we tested your placenta hormones due to your history of placental abruption, and they are all above the normal range, which is good to see."

We then bantered on about COVID-19 vaccines and being robots and next appointments, but holy shit (not something a robot would say), today our baby is normal and has perfectly working organs.

I told her what a pleasure it was to receive such good news, and as I hung up, the tears fell and rested in my mouth. I looked out the window at the beaming spring sun, and I reflected the light I could feel. I could hear the new life in the birds singing joyfully and matching my inner state.

I called Phillip, who said he knew it would be okay and that it was wonderful news. Then he said, "It is going to be chaos!"

He isn't wrong. This is a fact that I have allowed myself to forget. Sure, there has been definite chaos in our life. When hasn't it been in the growing of our family? But with three children, this chaos I can handle. This is the kind of chaos I have wanted all along. This is our beautiful chaos.

Second Entry: Telling

With Jude's pregnancy, Oma had been watching the children when I returned with the bad news. It was Oma who witnessed my true initial heartbreak. But today was different. I tried to act cool as I entered the room, but I couldn't keep focused on anything Oma was asking. (Yes, my sleep was good; wait, no it wasn't.) I was grateful when she said she had to go pee. I grabbed an ultrasound pic and had Maelie run it over to her as she came out of the bathroom, while Maelie yelled "baby" and Case (preorchestrated) said "surprise!"

With her hand clasped to her mouth, tears began to form in Oma's eyes, but this time, they were much different looking tears. Oma said, "I truly didn't think, with all your problems, you would ever try again."

My mom also came over, and I shared the news with her in the same rehearsed way. Yay for bladders and needing bathrooms . . . genius! She, too, began to cry. When I asked her to guess the due date, she guessed her birthday, July 7. I told her the due date was August 2, 2021, Jude's birthday.

Dear baby, you believed in us more than we believed in ourselves, as we have both gone through so much to create you and this sweet family. Thanks for believing in us when we needed something to believe in. You are teaching me that things can come back full circle. Even when we feel lost, or like we have lost everything, all hope is never lost.

As Phillip and I talked about the wonderful news that night, he said, as he always does now, "I will be happy when the baby's out."

Fair enough. We decided this time it felt right not to share on social media and to enjoy our pregnancy for ourselves. We both just want you safe and in our arms, at which point we will share you. But for now, you are all ours.

March 5, 2021: Of Course Your Baby Has a Brain

Today, we visited with Jess and her daughter. She casually gave us a onesie for our baby as I shared the exciting news. She had also got her daughter a matching onesie so our babies could wear them together on the beach on our maternity leave together.

I cried (something I do often these days with my raging hormones). Buying onesies is something I no longer do during pregnancy. I fear I will buy items that will never get used or that I will have to return. Or worse yet that I will regift and then have to see on another baby instead of my own.

I sent my mom a picture of my children, myself, and Jess's baby together. In the photo, I could see the new light emerging in my eyes. The joy was coming through again. This picture prepared me for what it could look like and for what our real life could be, and it made me happy. I could see the vision, the dream appearing in a real tangible photograph.

At night, Phillip and I found ourselves rambling off baby names: Hannah, Willa, Everett, Holden. Phillip eventually said, "Wow, there's actually a lot of your friends having babies around the same time as you." I liked that he was taking notice of this and not frantically changing the topic as he always did. Perhaps he considers this baby as real, and he is looking forward to it. We are winning.

April 4, 2021: Thirty

The children woke up happy. The sun was shining brightly on the "Some-bunny is 30" sign placed on our front yard by my darling family, along with thirty bunnies. The kids sang "Happy Easter Birthday" to Mommy. Since it was Easter, they were also excited to hop around on their morning indoor Easter egg hunt. Phillip and I drank our tea together on the couch as the kids hopped and yelled and kind of shared their eggs together. Our day's bunny trail led us to the beach, where we found a peace sign made of stones in the sand. The kids rolled around in the sand and threw rocks in the water while Phillip and I held hands, listening to the shrills of excitement from the kids. This is thirty, and I am in hoppy peace, warmed, comforted, and hatching in many wonderful ways.

Along with our families, we later watched a video on a projector of the story of my life, starting with my deceased grandparents holding me and announcing my arrival. I remember thinking how amazing it was to see how many lives were transformed by the life of a baby, always marked. Crying and watching my mom watching me as a baby while the tears rolled down her eyes, I could see my children in these videos and how she once saw me. I feel the magic of these moments, the moments with our forever babies, our little angels.

April 7, 2021: Seen

It's a bird. It's a plane. It's a bald eagle soaring overhead. Together Case, Maelie, and I spotted it as we pulled over for Case to go pee. This was our first official sighting during this pregnancy.

April 9, 2021: Maelie's Second Birthday

My dear Maelieboo,

If I had one word to describe you it would be fierce! You hysterically run away from my kisses on purpose to torment me while turning around to growl at me. Your raspy growls are seriously amazing. You may not hug me on demand, but you will call out Mommy anytime I am not in your sight. Yet you will surprise me with a hug or a kiss when I seem to need it most. It is like you can sense those kinds of things.

You have such a beautiful voice when you are singing to yourself in the morning. When you are screaming, we say you can reach unreachable octaves. You will literally randomly start screaming because you know it is your deadliest weapon and smile while doing it and giggle afterwards, and we always join in the fun and scream back as you genuinely think it is so funny.

Watching you walk with your dollies around the house, kissing them and tucking them in and changing them with baby powder everywhere, has been the ultimate joy. I know in your second year you are going to be the best big sister, as you are the best sister to Case and Nola with your endless hugs and cuddles.

We love you so much, our girl. You are the best daughter we could ever ask for, and every day your fierce independence and love makes us the proudest parents.

All of our love, forever and always,

Mommy and Daddy

April 16, 2021: Unwrapped

I unwrapped a gift we received from Becca. In keeping with tradition, inside I found a rainbow blanket for you, sweet baby, just like the ones we received for Case and Maelie, the ones made with so much love. I cannot wait to wrap you in your own special blankie.

April 18, 2021: I Have Received

You are the balloon, connected by my string,
easy to grasp but hard to let go of.

This morning, as the kids played with me in bed, Case said, "Baby loves tickles and will plop out in the toilet." Instead of recognizing that this is how three-year-olds think (as we mamas are known to poop our babies out), it brought back a horrible recollection and brought me to a fearful place.

I decided to get up, get dressed, and get moving. I cuddled the kids a little longer on the couch for encouragement. I then took myself for a walk to my spot. Normally on weekends, I use any extra time to tidy up the house, organize for the week ahead, attend to emails, and all the other errands. But today, I was feeling exhausted and in a funk. Jess responded to my message saying, "Yay for feeling exhausted AF! That means baby is taking all of your energy to grow big and strong." I appreciated this little reminder, even though my confidence in this pregnancy has been growing along with this baby.

As I walked towards my tree, always secretly looking for the locket I lost somewhere on that path, I saw a bright, large shimmer in the tall grass. I walked towards it. I crouched down to find it was a pink heart helium balloon. I settled down on my knees, trying to stabilize myself as I started to weep, remembering the single blue helium balloon that was rising as I thought of Jude. And now this single pink heart helium balloon, arriving to me from above, had finally landed here, holding on in that tall grass just then for me to see. I am convinced these moments are no longer mere coincidence; they come when I need them most. My babies always sending me love.

I cried about how hard this pregnancy has been. Remembering how excited my children were for Jude, patting my belly, and how excited they are for this baby, tickling my belly, giving it kisses and endless zerberts. To them, I have been pregnant all along. Time does not pass the same way for them as it does for adults.

I cried about how, up until this point, I have struggled my whole life. From a young age, I struggled with being the oldest and trying to be a good role model and support my younger siblings. I struggled with bearing the weight of our struggling family farm, always trying to clean to prevent an outburst from my bipolar dad.

I cried about how I would write in my room for hours about how stupid, ugly, and horrible I was and how everyone hated me. I will spare you the countless entries here. I cried about how I used to obsess over counting calories, and lose my mind when I could not exercise, and how I would run with garbage bags on to lose weight. It was a way that I could feel in control. Then I started to eat a lot when I felt I was too skinny and everyone who was beautiful had boobs, only my boobs never grew.

I cried about how I was often teased for my high voice and smiling face, the seemingly perfect image I hid behind while always trying to convince others that all was well for me and for my family.

I cried for the pain I endured on this pregnancy journey. It has been so painful. I would not wish this pain on anyone. And I cried for how I used to think I deserved it.

I cried as I realized the struggle has been me all along. With the help of these lost pregnancies, I now cuddle my kids longer, maybe in small part due to the exhaustion and being unable to move, but I love it just the same. I do not clean like I used to, although that may be due to no one setting foot in my house because of COVID-19. Winning. I eat what I need to nourish my body. I am genuinely happy, as I have begun to let go and to not sweat the little things. Thank you anxiety meds! I still worry that other people dislike me but no longer cry all night long recounting who I pissed off or feeling like I constantly have to give to be liked. I just listen, live, and check in on people when the spirit moves me.

I will say, through this experience, I have received many things.

I have received a new outlook and not one that is overcome by to-do lists (and there were endless to-do lists even before having kids). To-do lists that would leave our relationship strained, as I was always asking Phillip to do this and do that, so we could never relax together. I was always busy, always running around, always trying to please and be perfect. Today, I feel the most perfect, relaxed, grateful, loving, and beautiful peace and feel as loved as I have ever felt in my life.

My kids gained a mom who has slowed down, as I no longer worry about missing everything. (We can't take it all in; let's be real.) It has been such a process but no longer a struggle. I know if I would have continued with that life, I would have blinked only to find out that all of it never mattered; nobody really cares that much. I would have wept for all that I lost through my years at battle with my own internal struggle.

I have received your message. I ended up walking the whole way home holding on to the string of that helium balloon, which swayed right next to me, not struggling to rise or fall, but right beside me, carried by the breeze. This balloon was with me, grounding me in the gifts that are always exposing themselves to me. The gifts of my babies. Gifts I had never seen or felt before in my previous struggling life.

May 10, 2021: Butterflies and Fluffs

Today is Phillip and my twelve-year anniversary.

At the end of my shift, I decided to take the long way back to my car. The weather was lovely, so I made sure to loop by the healing garden; I had a special family and their baby on my mind. As I began to walk in the garden, a fluff greeted me, just floating at eye level in the middle of the garden on the paved path. I continued to walk towards it and began thinking of our babies. The tears started to form as I continued to walk and the fluff stayed exactly where it was, so still. I came towards it and it graced my cheek. The fluff stuck for a moment on my moistened cheek and then, just like that, was gone with the wind.

I thought about how our lost babies and their memories never ever go away. We will live with them for the rest of our lives. There are no drugs to erase their memories, as it goes so much deeper than that. But if given the chance, I would never want their memories to dissipate, although some days I do wish for them not to affect me. Their beautiful memories stay with us and come and go like the butterflies and the fluffs. I am lucky to know these moments.

May 21, 2021: Unprepared

I completely understood when my counsellor had to postpone our session to obviously help out a family who had their first loss, but it still hurt and felt like I was pushed aside because my loss wasn't as fresh. And it was true. There is a natural progression of things—one that reinforces all the pressure from society to "get over it" when you lose a baby, especially once you're pregnant with your rainbow baby.

June 4, 2021: Found

Together with my sister Kerrie, I packed up the kids and went on a trip to Lake Superior Provincial Park. I had vacation days stacked up, and since Phillip was busy with air conditioning season during this heatwave, we hit the beach. Now this mama does not have to wear clothes and can live in the water because, wow, that's enough dear heatwave. Sincerely, Pregnant Carmen. Most importantly, though, I wanted to have a little baby moon with my babies before the full-moon baby comes.

While Kerrie played with the kids (Maelie trying to pet butterflies and Case jumping on a rock he found in the water that he called Case Island), I decided to meditate. That is, I closed my eyes and felt the breeze through the heat at a gorgeous beach called Katherine Cove. This place had what seemed like a chair made just for me: a straight rock backing and a carved out bum spot eloquently moulded in the rock beneath me. As I started the meditation, I looked out to the calmness that was the lake and heard only the gentlest waves. They gradually reached me on top of the slanted and inclined smooth rocks right next to the slowly encasing water.

Midmeditation, I opened my eyes to take in the view and look at my children in their purest glory, playing and splashing in the water, only to see one lone loon in my plane of vision. This is a bird we don't see back home, so I found it had a certain enchantment. The bird looked lost, peeking and jolting its head hither and thither, jigging around the water. I closed my eyes again and hoped for that crazy loon to find where it was going.

As I ended my meditation, I bowed forward, and to my surprise, I saw the same loon was suddenly surrounded by babies. It never occurred to me that this loon could be frantically looking for her babies.

I can't say with complete certainty how many babies there were, as they were so fast and flocking together, but I counted nine baby loons. I noticed how with that calculation, there were about six that travelled on top of the mother loon's back (something I never knew they did), and three following close behind.

The meaning of this was so symbolic to me. It is not about the story but the meaning we attach to it. That loon was lost without her babies, both the living and those that lived on, inside her and carried by her. We all find a way to travel through life with our lost heavenly angels and living angels, trying to navigate it all, always together.

Then I thought of something my granny has always said, about how she always wished for a picture of a mother duck with her seven ducklings following behind her. She could never find this portrait in stores, always looking but never finding the right number of ducklings. To her, the seven ducks were her children who had lived life, but she didn't include the number of her five other miscarriages.

Today, I envision my own duck picture just like that loon with her six babies travelling on her back with the three following close behind. How times have changed. Where my granny only wanted to somehow remember the ones she birthed alive, the ones that had life, I want so badly and so desperately to remember how the lives that didn't live continue to guide me and how with them I am found. They have made me the best mama loon for her living babies, sharing their story, which has now become ours.

June 19, 2021: It's a Girl

Dear Hope,

Writing to you makes it feel more real. I know I haven't written to you much, and I promise it is not because you are the third child. You are extremely important to me and all that I do.

I will admit that chasing your siblings around makes it hard to write about every doctor's appointment, kick, or measurement, but that doesn't make them any less special to me. Although everything I do with you is so precious, I know one day, it will not be the notes I took at the doctor's appointments that are important. The privilege, pleasure, and honour of being your mama, to me, are the most important things to note. Your pregnancy has filled me with hope again and taken me out of my head. You've given me purpose: to get help by way of anxiety meds, to give a speech at an end-of-life workshop on early loss, to paint just because I want to, and also to sing and dance with your siblings and even to buy you things with your name on them, something I never did for your siblings. Your father and I, for the first time in history, have picked out and agreed completely on a name for you, so we are extremely pumped about that.

When I think of your name (the one we plan to give you) which means, a visitor returning and purity, I think of the pink heart balloon you sent me and the book you allowed me to write, grounding me in hope. I do this all for you, Maelie and Case, with your heavenly angels guiding us.

You are everywhere, and you're all that I am and more. I hold you now and will hold you my entire life. Thank you, my pure and returning visitor, for the gift of you and for coming into our lives at a time when we needed you most.

Love your adoring Mama

June 22, 2021: Dear Jude

I haven't allowed myself to think like this since you left us, as I've been through this before, and it's too painful. You're gone, and there's nothing I can do about it, so why put myself through more suffering, I should know better. But today is a month shy of a year to the day that we found out the news of your terminal diagnosis. You would be six months old.

As I try to imagine my life with you in it, I only know what I know. What I know is that after we lost you, I signed up for an advanced asana yoga course, which reminded me of my strength and vulnerability. I then ran a rainbow hat campaign, and while writing to you every day, it sparked an idea to write a book. I have started a new position on the paediatric floor, leaving the paediatric ICU in June. I didn't love it in the start, and I took some time off in my favourite months of summer—healing with Oma at the cottage, talking with mom, going for swims, and enjoying beach days with the kids. I am beginning to find myself again, figuring out the process alone, the only way I can.

I have lost some close friends, but as I begin to pick up the pieces of my life—crying almost every day, confronting old demons of past hurts, and finally accepting the help of anxiety medications—my world has changed.

I've started doing things because I want to do them, and I enjoy them. Your Daddy and I continue to grow closer, something I didn't think was possible. Had we not lost you, we wouldn't have this little rainbow coming, due right on the unexpected date you were born.

I miss you unabashedly and want the little, brown-eyed boy that I have imagined, the one I dreamed of from the very start of this journey. But I also desperately want this child inside of me.

I wouldn't have known all of this if not for losing you, Jude, as I would be raising you and loving you. I would have never known this other side of my life. But this is my reality, the gifts that you, my son Jude, gave me and continue to give me. This has been hard to say because at the time, how could this all have possibly seemed like a gift, when I was cursing the universe and asking the moon for help. Today, I'm thanking that same moon, although it feels both wrong and wonderful. When I look back on my year of loss, one in which I was blind, I now see what I have gained. I do hate saying that, as it was not a blessing to have lost you, dear Jude, but I am beginning to see the blessings in it.

There are many other wonderful things that may not have happened. I would not be talking at an end of life workshop in front of five hundred people. The recent loss of you made the committee think of me as a speaker, and they wanted me to talk about how I honour my babies through both my hat campaign and my book.

I also would not have been working right now, as I would have been on maternity leave and would not have saved the money we needed to buy a farm with my family—a place that we plan to have as an oasis for our littlies one day.

Jude, I miss you, but I believe your soul has evolved in mine. I'm not perfect, and I still worry about what others think of me. I can become easily overwhelmed and have anxiety issues and a smiling disorder to hide and disguise my pain. I still ask for a lot of help, but these are all deep-rooted themes in my life, and with you, Jude, I learned to be totally and completely myself with my family. I do what speaks to me and moves me, and I believe those things come from you. I've never felt more alive.

Jude, this is my year without you physically, but you have been with me spiritually; of this, I am certain, and you have made my life whole.

June 23, 2021: Playmates for Life

Late last night, I woke to a new toy that I had bought, as per Case and Maelie's request, "for the baby." Before going to bed, I placed the chicken train toy on our coffee table for the kids to play with in the morning and turned off the sound.

This toy started playing in the middle of the night. I must have heard it roughly six times spaced out in an hour. It's hard to judge when you're half asleep, and when I listened more deeply, I could hear giggles. I was imagining it was Kaia, four and a half years old, and Jude, six months old, playing together to welcome this baby. The more I thought, the more I became frightened they were trying to haunt me, but it also felt calming, like a greeting of sorts. I had to check in the morning, with goosebumps on my arm, that the sound button was still off on the toy. Maybe it was imagined, maybe dreamed, maybe it was comforting myself through my fears, or maybe it was a combination of many things, but it happened.

When I mentioned this to Phillip, he told me he had been woken up through the night by the sound of a piano randomly playing, one that is in a box and not played. Perhaps we are both whacked! I think maybe Kaia and Jude wanted to make sure we both experienced their playing. Thanks kids! It means a lot that you included your Daddy, so your Mommy does not feel completely nuts. Or maybe Mommy and Daddy are the only two nuts in the world who found each other . . . now that would be nuts!

June 25, 2021: Hearts Sent

Like most summer days, today, we headed to the beach. While sitting on the sand, a lady crossed my path, and we exchanged pleasant hellos. On her walk back, she said, "Look at this sea glass I found. It looks like a heart, doesn't it?" And it really did. She said, "I want you to have it."

I couldn't express my thanks enough, as she kept on walking. I clutched that heart hard and held it to mine. I then realized I was not wearing my Kaia and Jude heart locket today (which I had replaced again); the latch had recently broken, and so it remained open, unguarded. My new sea glass heart that was once sharp and jagged was now smooth and almost aqualike in its new colouring; transformed by the water, it was no longer clear but now filled with a colour. It was like a new formation unlocked, with an appreciation for its beauty that needed to be cracked open in order to be shared.

July 6, 2021: Releasing

Today, I answered the call. I accepted an invitation to join in a circle meditation at the lake. There was a free spot that opened, and I took it. The lady leading the meditation was the same lady I found leading me in the yoga studio where I also taught. Also joining the meditation was the same reiki lady I had during my time at the cottage. This circle and community of woman, answering the call, replenished what our souls needed and deserved.

Finding ourselves in this space, seated in a circle and united again, we breathed. The sounds of children playing on the beach did not ruin my quiet experience; instead, they brought joy. My worries about the pregnancy and birth dissipated with the sounds of their squeals; they were washed away, let go. This time to be at the beach and meditate, like I did with Jude before his birth, was a releasing moment for me. I let myself be—scared and alone. Yet I felt blissfully connected to my baby and to something more.

Ayda Catherine Grover's Birth Story

Ayda: returning visitor, inside the moon, happy, angel of love.

Catherine: Pure (in honour of Kaia, and for your grandma, her middle name).

July 19, 2021: Pink Sun, Clear Skies, and Calming Fluffs

Dear babe,

Pregnancy after loss is very emotional. I worry every day for your life, and I haven't been able to enjoy you as I should. I shake my belly constantly to make sure you're still moving. Even today at the finish line, I am fearful of your delivery, something I know all women fear, but I've never feared it in this way. Tonight, I found myself desperately saying the same prayer I did with your brother Jude—to please let you come naturally and how you are meant to come. I again find myself jealous of those who can have normal births, whatever that means. With my history, all I want is to have a normal-ish delivery just once, and as I pray, I see the fluff float past and the butterfly fluttering in the tree in the distance, working hard to make sure all things go well for us.

As you know, you follow the same timeline of Jude's birth and short life, which has currently been very difficult for me. I keep recounting how we didn't know anything of the sad news until July 22, so I was still blatantly naive at this time last year.

As we left for home after Opa's birthday celebration today, we took notice of the sky on our drive home. The kids were admiring how the sun seemed to be following us the whole way home, and they wanted me to stop and take a picture of it. The sun was completely coral, alone in the sky with not a single cloud or a single worry; all that cannot be controlled was erased away in that perfect, clear sky. We then passed a field that was spewing endless fluffs that flew past us. I know it was Jude telling us we will receive.

That night before bed, Maelie hugged my belly as she always does and patted it, saying "This is Mommy's big belly," and then patted my boobs, saying "These are Mommy's little bellies." I laughed so hard, and let's just say that I think the hypnotic happiness of the night may have kickstarted something.

July 25, 2021: We Have Received

> *When we lose one blessing,*
> *another is often most unexpectedly given in its place.*
> —C.S. Lewis

My darling girl Ayda,

You came into our life on July 20, 2021. It was a clear-skied, sweet-breezy summer Tuesday. The clearest weather we've had in forever. Corn as high as we've ever seen it, with a vivid green colour full of life itself.

Your birthday was one of the last days a year ago that I remember joy, the day before receiving the news that changed our world forever. I have to believe in these synchronicities and that you wanted to come on a date where we remember being the most purely happy, naive, hopeful, and completely in love with our family to be.

We dropped off the kids at Gramma's, and as we were leaving, they ran to me to say goodbye. Maelie rubbed my belly and then laid her head on it, and Case said, as he hugged me and his arms reached directly under my belly, that he wanted to hold me forever.

You are here, and even still I cannot believe it! This entire pregnancy I held my breath. I talked to others about the thought of you yet never allowed myself to fully give you much thought when on my own. My thoughts often turned dark fast when not in the presence of others. Keeping you in the light and love of others was often the best thing I could do for us, although I only shared you with those in our immediate circle and colleagues who took note of my swollen basketball belly.

You came into our life after I completed my rainbow hat campaign for Pregnancy and Infant Loss Month. From that moment forwards, I worried. I never worried about my love for you, as that has always been one constant. But I worried about you the whole way until you were in my loving arms.

Your Birth Story

I saw the high-risk OB the day before my labour started, the one who looked after us with Kaia and Case, as she was covering for my own OB. It was such a perfect moment of closure. I greeted her by saying, "Well, here we are, our family with three children." She paused, took a deep breath, and said it was her greatest reward, and that if we happened to want eight babies, she would be our OB for all of them.

The following morning, I had started having contractions. I took a bath, and the contractions became more regular and frequent. Off to the hospital we went. I was four centimetres dilated when they checked me. I worried when they didn't know what end of the baby was presenting, so they checked with ultrasound to make sure it was the head that was down. I knew it was there just the day before, but what if the baby had flipped, like my insides in anticipation.

We had a prebooked C-section scheduled for July 30, since it was better to be safe with our history, although I selfishly prayed for a normal delivery. I know, what even is normal at this point? I wanted this one to be my lasting reminder, concluding our story with perfection, as our story has been far from perfect in many ways yet completely perfect in others.

So . . . we had the best nurse. We chatted about our love for the nursing profession and the many similarities we shared, really enjoying our chats together. My contractions were regular, every four minutes and lasting thirty seconds. The epidural went in, and we adopted a paramedic who wanted to watch this seemingly normal, chatty, pain-controlled birth. Then I looked outside at the sun, the pink and blue skies greeting you, and then at my belly and drifted off with thoughts of the baby circulating in my head. This day that we were told would come was happening, and everything was going swimmingly. For once I felt in control and at ease. I tried so desperately to hold on to this peace, snapping a photo of it in my mind.

Since coming in the doors, we had been monitored. The nurse said they were going to keep the monitor on the baby the whole time. I was okay with this, as I loved hearing the strong, beating heart. Then it was time, and the resident came in to break my water. Your heart rate on the monitor was always a beautiful and consistent 143 glorious beats per minute. I would startle when the rhythm that was music for my soul would dip to 138 at times. I felt it all, and the rhythm was sustaining me.

After they broke my water, I no longer heard a whoosh on the monitor, no beats. They moved me side to side to see if baby had just moved—nothing. I noticed I had also stopped breathing. Maybe the baby's absent heart rate was my own? The kind nurse was no longer laughing or chatting but staring me in the eyes, telling me I would be okay. She asked me to listen to her as she grabbed my hand. I knew this was not how it was supposed to be.

Everything is all fine and good until it isn't. Phillip and I know this too well. These were skilled professionals, and when they are not freaking out, you know you are okay, but Phillip knew what was coming. The doctor asked for clips to put on the baby and told me they wanted to monitor the baby more closely. The clips were on and then there it was:

Blip... Blip...... Blip......... of the monitor. I felt like puking.

I yelled out loud, "Guys, I don't like this." (This still echoes in my mind.)

I remember hearing: "You're going to be okay. You're going to be okay. We can't get babies heart rate up. Phillip, we need you to stay here. We are taking your wife to the OR to prep her for a C-section."

I didn't—I couldn't—even look back at my dearest best friend, left behind me, alone. I, on the other hand, had this baby inside me and thoughts of earth-shattering fear erupted inside me. The body remembers.

They brought me in to the operating room and told me their names and how they were going to take care of me, never once saying anything about the baby. One nurse squeezed my hand and told me to look at her, but I couldn't with my eyes clenched tight with tears constantly streaming down my face. My eyes simply could not focus or open. Once again, "you're going to be okay..."

I heard the surgeon loudly and boldly state they were ready to go in five. They prepped my belly, and the last thing I remember doing was taking my hand and placing it directly on my clean and prepped belly. The team, still being kind, sternly asked me to stay still. Let's just say it wasn't long after that incident that I was out. Yet what they hadn't known was that I had looked over at the monitor to my right prior to that moment and saw the single green number zero next to a flat line on the screen.

In a desperate last mama bear attempt, I tried to feel what I thought was left of my baby's life, feeling for a subtle movement, anything. I never got that confirmation. I fought the sedation, but once my eyes closed, I tried to think of something nice—this time last year, the sun at the window, the pink and blue helium balloon flying past our window. "Take care of her" I kept begging the images of helium balloons.

I learned that you come out of sedation just how you go in. I came out screaming like a wild bonobo: "Where is she? Where is my baby?" They knew exactly what to say and repeated it to me several times: "She is okay. She is okay. She is okay." She had cried right away and was with Daddy in his arms. I think I screamed a toe-curling scream. I will never know that fact but felt such a surge of screamlike energy release from me. And the tears flooded.

The nurse that was with me when I woke up kept telling me that I did great and that although this was not expected or wanted, she was here, and she was safe. She told me that she knew I had put on a brave face before, but that I needed to release it all. I cried. Again I was unable to see my daughter right after birth or hear her cry. I tried really hard to squint through my swollen and heavily drugged eyes, observing the room. A resident quickly came by and said that my daughter sounded quite grunty and that I had an arrhythmia and heart block on the operating table and that is why it took longer to wake me up. Oh, is that all? Yet these were such miniscule asides to me. We were safe, and I was endlessly grateful.

I laugh that I used to think Case's birth was dramatic. Each birth of ours has topped the next in some way, with even more shock factor. We get it universe, loud and clear: We are lucky to all be here. The honour is mine to get to bring these beautiful beings of light into this world and to be their mama.

What transpired after the birth is only accounted for with endless baby snuggles. She had been placed in my arms, and after that moment, I never let her out of them, holding on for dear life.

The following morning, having processed nothing and still trying to wrap my head around our daughter actually being here, a resident who was in on the surgery and birth of our daughter came to see me. I've been through this before, the aftermath. How are you? How's your pain? The normal sign-off questions, so I followed suit. When she asked how I was, I answered tired and sore but overall no complaints. The resident paused and asked, "I mean, how are you emotionally?"

In all the years, I had never been asked this simple question. It was like when I would get hurt in soccer, and I would continue on, bravely wobbling until someone would ask how I was, and, boom, I would choke up, unsure even how to answer or proceed. How am I emotionally? I was unable to say any words and the resident said she thought I might want to know the events that transpired. She recounted everything that happened from the moment my water broke, answering every question I was unable to ask.

Again, sadly, there was no explanation as to why her heart rate dipped for so long, as was also the case with all my living babies. There was no cord wrapped around her neck, no placental abruption that they could see, although they would send my placenta off for sampling to be sure. But they got her out as quickly and safely as they possibly could have.

When the resident left, I wept for what Phillip informed me was only an hour, but it felt like a never-ending cry session with no pauses. It felt like I was crying for the six years of all of it, unleashing it all. Right after this, my counsellor called me at the hospital, as I had quickly shot her an email telling her of our little wonder's arrival and our scare, hoping it would help me process it all. This all helped tremendously, and I would have been in a much different place had these conversations and unleashings not happened in the timely matter that they did.

We have been so unlucky yet so lucky. Every one of our living children is healthy. It all could have been much worse. The fears all disappear now that she is with us, but the thought is still there, and it still hurts—of what could have happened.

When we got home after being in the hospital, we were welcomed by our Rose of Sharon tree in full bloom. We had been gifted this tree from a friend last year after losing Jude, and we noticed it was just starting to bud when we left for the hospital. On our return, the tree was blooming in pink. A blooming pink tree greeted our newest member, which I am sure Jude, with Kaia's help, sent us. I find such comfort in this.

My kids came running to greet me and halted as soon as they saw their sister in the middle of the room with Daddy. They have taken their sister Ayda in full heartedly. Case really loves Ayda's super soft head, never getting enough of head rubbing and laughing at her yawns and cat purrs and how she keeps sucking like a hungry hippo when he feeds her. Maelie keeps yelling that there's a baby in the house! As she hugs her, she says that she loves her and that "Baby is booty (beautiful)." Every morning, Maelie wakens and asks to see the baby and if she can pet her. These moments give me strength, awe, and wonder and heal my heart of all the missing parts, bruises, and holes that had developed along the way.

I wonder if my heart had stopped or had simply given up at the thought of losing this baby. How could it possibly go on if the outcome was different? Or was my heart super recharged by the endless love that it feels for our family, the one we have today and get to keep? Perhaps it experienced a rebirth for our current life and next chapter.

Ayda is our whole world. I know that is something every parent says, but I just feel like she is so sacred and protected. I look into Ayda's wide and bright blue eyes, and I can see such clarity in them. I get lost in her eyes, as I see not only myself in the pure reflection but also Kaia, Jude, and all her siblings before her. It's an extraordinary "returning visitor" phenomenon to me; she is here when they couldn't be, and she is here for them as they are here for all of us. She has been sent and perfectly picked by Kaia and Jude. Ayda really needed to be here, with angel prints all over her.

This is not entirely how I wanted this story to end. I wanted to portray the normal, easy birth of our baby, the one who completes us. I'm not going to downplay or sugar coat our experience. Unfortunately, our girl's birth was by far the scariest birth I have ever had, although this story still ended happily with tears and joy in my heart. This is our real story. Pregnancy until the finish line is scary no matter what. But it is also incredible. I will focus on the intense love we feel at this moment and forevermore—a love of purity and astonishment.

Naturally, Ayda is safe in our loving arms, and in the end, that is all that matters. But there is nothing like the trauma of thinking you have lost your baby, your biggest fear. Waking up to her alive in her Daddy's arms reminded me of how incredibly blessed we are to have what we have. It is still hard for me to look at my girl and imagine her being placed in my arms in other circumstances. We tiptoed through this whole pregnancy together, not really believing she could actually happen. We still do not entirely believe she is here.

Our girl needed some aid, and it is my belief that she has already provided aid by giving new hope to our family. I feel she will spend her life aiding all of those she meets. She clearly needed to be here. The hope of her has helped us to remind others to remain hopeful, even in the depths of no-hope moments. Our lost babies are always aiding us in many ways through life—ways we can't always see but do end up feeling.

To our little angel of love, Ayda, who was sent with so much love from her angels above. You place your warm head in the nook between my neck and collarbone and clutch and hold on tight to my sea glass heart necklace. We love you so much.

We have received.

August 1, 2021: Remembering You I Will on This Hill

Dear Jude,

I write to you today as I still do not believe I can stomach it tomorrow.

Today, I bathed your darling sister Ayda, something I didn't get a chance to do with you, although I did not think this moment possible a year ago.

The morning is grey and a calming, comfortable kind of cool.

I sit on our hill, snuggling your sister as I write, with thoughts of you on my mind. I remember playing on this hill with the kids when the geneticist called about the negative Harmony prenatal test and the tiny bleed that was seen on the ultrasound, the one that I decided not to get checked as I was so unconcerned. I had no reason to think there was any worry.

I think of this hill, where I taught yoga while pregnant with you and later held a tribute class to you, playing "Hey Jude" as the students lay in Savasana and I hid behind the hill and wept.

I think of this hill, where friends gathered to sit next to me to talk and listen and simply be there for us.

The hill where I dreamed of and crocheted rainbow hats as the kids rolled down it, giggling around me.

The hill where I danced, and I watched the single sunflower emerge, the twirling leaves falling overhead and the fluffs floating by.

The hill that was always there for me and supporting me when I heard vehicles whiz by, and the world around me spun madly on when I couldn't.

The hill where occasionally walnuts fell aggressively around me, where I sometimes wished one would hit me and awaken me from this seemingly real life that was mine.

The hill where I watched the sun rise, listening to morning doves and the sounds of crickets and watching the fireflies sparkle in the predawn hue.

The hill where we set up and slept in our tent.

The hill where Phillip and I watched a silver balloon float by as we marvelled at our family playing under it, our very own silver lining.

The hill where I sobbed, prayed, remembered, smiled, and spilled my soul out onto these pages. This is the hill where I meditated and thought about collecting all of my diary entries of my babies into a life story for family and friends.

Thinking about this hill, where we hosted many slip and slides for adults before we had kids, I wouldn't have believed that today I would watch my own kids using it as a bike ramp and a toboggan hill. It is a place we continue to all gather at every stage of life, through the sorrows and the joys, the sorrows and joys all mixed into one and shared on this very hill.

The hill where we took a picture to announce to friends and family about baby Kaia—our first official announcement.

The hill where we took family pictures when I was pregnant with Jude.

The hill where I now hold your sister Ayda and hold the memories of all my babies. I must believe this moment was made possible because of you.

As I write these words, a squirrel fearing nothing runs and leaps from one tree to the next, totally trusting with full faith it will arrive at its planned destination. And it does. Our family has arrived, though not always trusting the process in which we got here. I feel and look up to see the sun peeking through the trees. I whisper, "I love you" and "I miss you" to the sun. Although I can't see you, we continue to feel you and all our angel babies with us.

You will always be part of our completed family. Although I still find it hard to say, I wouldn't have our family any other way. I appreciate more deeply the miracle of all our babies.

Just before the sun goes away again and you say goodbye for a while, I collectively say thank you to you and all my forever babies. I look down at Ayda, and she smirks, knowing her angel siblings have sent her and that they are now surrounding her. I peer into her sky-blue, wondering eyes, and I am released.

My kids are all the beaches, tall grass, sunflowers,
fluffs, trees, butterflies, balloons, bald eagles, rainbows,
ducks, loons, spiders, hummingbirds, yoga, running,
twirling leaves, my spot, meditation, and stars.
They are every delight in this world.

Afterword

August 2, 2021: Home

Today was Jude's first heavenly birthday. I woke up with thoughts of him and thoughts of sending the announcement of Ayda's arrival. Just as I posted on social media, our fire alarm went off, flickering on and off for an hour—our fire alarm that has not gone off for years. There was no fire. Jude, please know you never need to feel like we need an alarm to think of you.

Today, I also needed to write a letter to all my babies to release and be at peace because I've found my way home. With a new sparked flame inside, I've landed.

My dear babies,

May your time with us live on in these diary entries of our time together and in our hearts and the many others who you have graced. I sometimes still can't believe that this is our life. In writing everything down along the way, I can see it all. Had I done it from memory, I would not have remembered the conversations with people, the single helium balloon or sunflower, every star and duck along the way, the healing practices, the lessons of people in our life at that exact timeline, and the kind gestures of others. These beautiful moments that were planted especially for me, to heal and to now find comfort in, would have all escaped into the oblivion of grief.

Although we did not grow our family as we had planned, we did grow together through all of this. We are the lucky ones who got to have what we always wanted, and we know that is not true for many. Everyone adjusts to their fate in their own way. We learned more about life, honour, and appreciation than we ever could have had these events not happened. It took us off course, but we learned to persevere and adjust to our new normal. After much grieving and hardship, there came a time when there was hope towards life again.

This book is my baby, and it is the gift of all my babies. This project is my purpose, the story of your lives. You were here, and you mattered. May my story give the topic of pregnancy loss a resonating voice. Sadly, I know people will likely only read this if they have also gone through loss. For that, I am deeply sorry that they were pregnant or wanted to be pregnant, and it has led them here.

My story is nothing special, nothing more than anyone else's. This project was cathartic for me in terms of my own personal healing, and I hope it will serve to be invaluable to you, my children, one day. In time, I expect to gain a fuller perspective, one with even greater understanding and insight. The power of being able to look back and reflect cannot be overstated.

In releasing the story of growing our family, we can now go on living our current story with our completed family, continuing to grow together. Although this story ends, our grief story will go on and so will the story of all my babies. We will continue making our story together.

August 2, 2022: Peace

With each passing year you are always with
our family in our hearts and thoughts.
You are with us in our children's twinkling
eyes and glowing spirits.

Dear Jude,

Today, I glimpsed an old ultrasound picture of you to be reminded of your realness and our excitedness for you over two years ago.

I look over at your active sister Ayda, who is always getting into trouble in the best ways as she throws her head back showing her two bottom teeth as she giggles, hyperventilates, and head bangs any time she gets excited, claps at anything that is going on around her, and makes us laugh all day long. Right now as I write this, she smacks the keyboard—jl/'|41239/99/9/—and whips me with my power cord. She shakes her head no in a joking way and sways her hips. She can't stop herself from being goofy and busy, and just like that, she's off to the next thing, which is currently trying to put a whole toy car trailer in her mouth.

It is odd on these days to be grieving my precious angels and parenting my beautiful living ones.

Yesterday on your second birthday I started out by honouring you by taking myself for a swim to look after me first, something I have learned to do on this grief journey of healing. I noticed the birds around me, the clear gloom sky, and the weltering sunflowers. I tried to swim under water, holding my breath to try to find some exhilaration. Your siblings and I then met my best friend Celina and her littlies at the sun-flower fields. I looked for you there, watching our children run through the sunflowers emitting their brightness as they giggled on this overcast mourning. We searched for you at our "Happy Time Place" (our cabin at our farm).

Later, Phillip insisted on showing my Oma our cabin. As we walked to the site, I watched the several varieties of butterflies dance around us and pointed each one out to my Oma to make sure she noticed. She loved it and was so proud.

After that, I detoured home. I took myself to the other side of the farm—"to look at the corn" I said—but really to try to find the two balloons I had observed stuck in the trees earlier that spring. The wild turkeys were hidden in the tall grass, a home they had made thinking it was a place that no humans go. But I greeted this secret place with generosity, gratitude, and a quest for love. Yet the turkeys still fled from my approach.

I had to find those balloons today! This became my mission, one that I created for myself.

The land that was once dead and barren was alive and lush with new growth. I pushed the tall grass down, crushing native plants below my feet only for them to jubilantly shoot back up. Glancing behind me I was unable to track my path. I was pricked and then held in place by the thorns. All cut up, I unrestrained myself from each individual pick and kept going a little more cautiously. I then found one opening. I took a breath in that space before noticing I was being consumed by this forbidden Garden of Eden.

I tried to find an exit route while bugs ate me alive, only to glimpse another new place. Each new place felt like a rebirth. It was the same place but looked different. Nothing was familiar, as I couldn't even imagine where the tree with the balloons would be in this sea of green. I quickly caught a glimpse of something red in the bush line. It ignited me and reminded me of my passion in always trying to come back to that place where Jude was—where I confirmatively know he is with me.

I mumbled to myself as I found my way back to the turkeys' previous home, where they all had fled. Only one remained, flapping and fleeing as I came closer. Please let me see or send me those two balloons I said to that lone bird. I have to see them or find them in some way today!

I knew there was no chance of me actually finding the balloons, as this is where I went hoping almost forcing to find something planted there for me, a sign from you. I mindfully looked for these balloons in desperation, needing proof of you and your continual existence in our lives while deep down knowing the place where they were could not currently be accessed.

I came home slightly defeated to finished supper plates and to Ayda dancing to Daddy playing the fiddle. He had never played it for her yet and said how easy it is to "forget simple tunes"—ones that had once come almost automatically.

My mom came over to watch the kids as I had planned to see the Elvis movie with Phillip tonight. I didn't say anything else about to-day's significance, even though I knew Phillip knew what today was, as he allowed me time to go to the farm with Oma.

"Oh yeah," Phillip said. "The movie is today." I watched the movie and totally forgot about my blue balloons wish. Why had I wished for it? Was I just trying to distract myself from what today once was and still is—a day of joyful heartbreak?

In the middle of the movie, when the colonel was in the hospital, two balloons appeared: one bright blue and one darker blue. Once I spotted them next to the flowers in the scene, I kept seeing them dart around as if they were dancing for me. It was all I could see. I cried, not for the colonel, but for the place in me I so desperately searched for and needed to uncover today. Constant fear arises on the anniversaries of losing the space where I can always find the peace of you my son, in the supernatural, bigger-than-life otherworld. But on these special days, I am always gifted access to our secret welcoming garden that we've created. It means so much. It is a confirmation...a sign.

Thank you, Jude, for showing me the power of you when I needed it most. I will not forget this happened, but if I do, I will dream as Elvis did: "Every dream I ever dreamed has come true one hundred times." And then I will feel you, say hello and know you again.

Thank you, Jude, for always reassuring us that something greater exists. Until we meet again; same time next year? It is a date I can always count on 1 year, 2 year, 10 years, 20 years, forever—a date you will always find me waiting for. You are with us always sending us signs, confirmation that our story never ends. You and all our babies are my reason.

Though I wish I could take away baby loss from every person experiencing it, we are on a path that feels so unlucky but in other ways more beautiful to spend our lives walking with angels and catching their angel droppings.

Forever & Always, Love mama xx

Changing the Script

I end by asking "What is your number?" This is mine:
G9 T2 P2 A4 L3.

Maybe you can write a part of your story before handing this book on to the next woman. We can start a movement and create the next book of stories, sharing them and our babies' names and brief lives to offer support for the next generation to come. Pregnancy and infant loss will never go away, but our communication on the topic can change the script and the struggle forever.

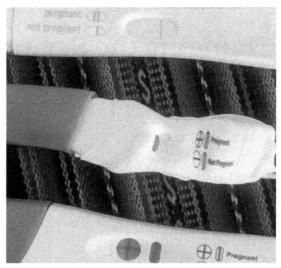

The melted pregnancy test.

Phillip and I in the East Coast at Gros Morne.

Grover's First Pregnancy Announcement.

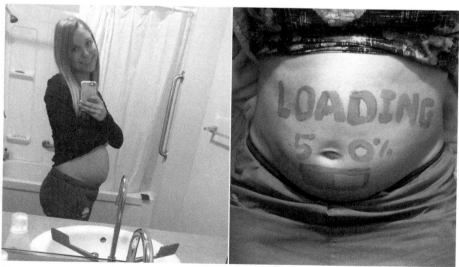

20 week belly pose.

50% loaded belly.

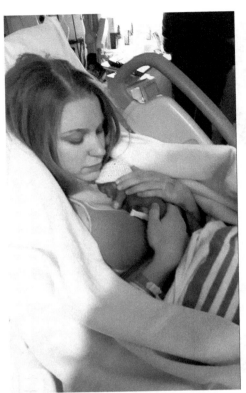

Kaia Belle, born January 2nd 2017 at 6:56 p.m.

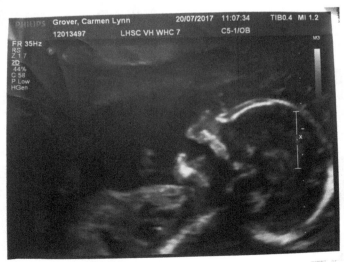

Case laughing on ultrasound.

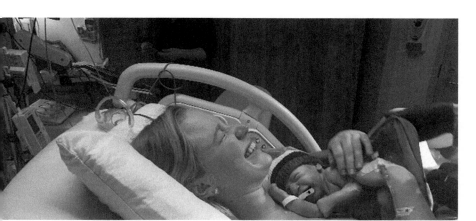

Holding Case for the first time.

Maelie at one month old.

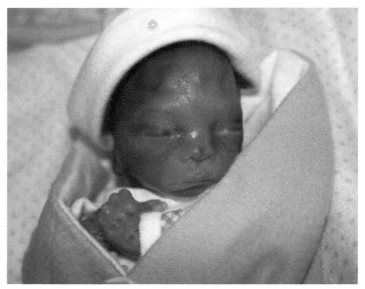

Jude Simba Joy, born August 2nd 2020 at 9:49 p.m.

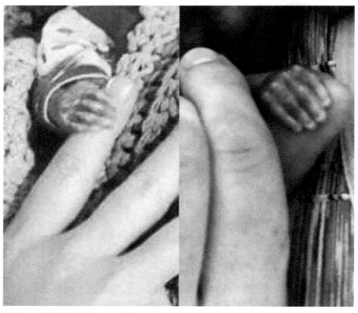

Kaia and Jude holding my finger.

Watching the Duck with angel footprints around us.

Case and Maelie holding their Sister and Brother.

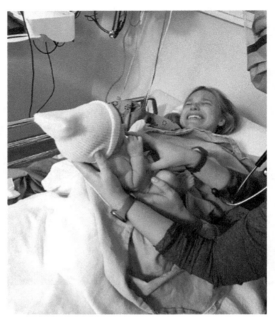

Seeing Ayda for the first time.

The Grover Five.

A painting by me of a loon holding 6 babies on its back and 3 babies following close behind, representing our angels.

Acknowledgments

To My Babies: To Amity Ella Lynn Grover, Will, Kaia Belle Grover, Babe #4, Babe #7, and Jude Simba Joy, it will always be for you, as I carry you with me each day. To Case Emerson Grover, Maelie Lynn Grover, and Ayda Catherine Grover, you are my forever and always loves. For all of our babies: May we give praise to our powerful journey of the purest beauty, triumph, and joy.

To My Husband: Phillip Grover, you are my life's love and favourite travel companion. You are the supportive, wise man responsible for the many philosophical Phillipisms along the way.

To Anne Hobbs: Thank you for your help in bringing this project to the manuscript stage and for encouraging me to follow this dream. I sincerely could not have done this important and intimate project without you.

To My Mama: You are the woman who gave me life and who has believed in me and loved me since I came to be. You have supported me even though you have never had to deal with pregnancy loss in your own life. You are always ready with a kind ear and a helping hand.

To My Oma: You are my greatest motivating force. I know you want to read my story one day so you can try to understand.

To My Family: Who has been with us the whole time on this long road. May our angels, Kaia and Jude, who are forever in our hearts, guide and protect you. Their light shines through all of you.

To My Friends: I do this to heal myself. Hopefully my healing will help you and others on your journey.

To Myself: When I didn't have the strength to tell it, I could always write it.

Sources

Ayuda, Tiffany. "How the Japanese Art of Kintsugi Can Help You Deal With Stressful Situations." *NBC*, 25 April 2018, www.nbcnews.com/better/health/how-japanese-art-technique-kintsugi-can-help-you-be-more-ncna866471. Accessed 15 Oct. 2020.

Angelou, Maya. Forgive Yourself Quote. *The Mind's Journal,* theminds journal.com/forgive-yourself-for-not-knowing-what-you-didnt-know-before. Accessed 10 Aug. 2020.

Baby Names. "Baby Names and Meanings." *Baby Names,* babynames.com/. Accessed 9 Dec. 2015.

Bible Gateway. "Luke 127–38, King James Version." *Bible Gateway,* www.biblegateway.com/passage/?search=Luke%201%3A27-38&version=KJV. Accessed 11 Sept. 2020.

Buddha. "Hope Is the Only Thing That Is Stronger Than Fear." 21 March 2018, hwww.oldandwisemonk.com/2018/03/hope-is-only-thing-stronger-than-fear.html. Accessed 28 Sept. 2021.

Chernoff, Angel. *Pinterest,* www.pinterest.ca/pin/345088390171004348/. Accessed 8 Mar. 2021.

Cox, Franchesca. "A Mother is Not Defined by the Number of Children You Can See, But By the Love she Holds in Her Heart." *Today's the Best Day,* www.todaysthebestday.com/letter-daughter-infertility /a-mother-is-not-defined-by-the-number-of-children-you-can-see-but-by-the-love-she-holds-in-her-heart-franchesca-cox/. Accessed 8 Aug. 2020.

First Cry Parenting. "Foetal Pole—What if it is Missing on an Ultrasound?" *FirstCry.* 7 April 2018, parenting.firstcry.com/articles/fetal-pole-what-if-it-missing-on-ultrasound/. Accessed 23 Aug. 2020.

Harris, Elena. "Hummingbird Spirit Animal." *Spirit Animal,* www. spiritanimal.info/hummingbird-spirit-animal/. Accessed 11 Aug. 2020.

Healthline. "The Next Steps After a Two-Vessel Cord Diagnosis." *Healthline,* 7 March 2016, www.healthline.com/health/pregnancy/2-vessel-cord#:~:text=A%20two%2Dvessel%20cord%20is,risk%20for%20not%20growing%20properly.Accessed 16 Nov. 2018.

Hosseinzadeh, K., et al. "Non-Visualization of Cavum Septi Pellucidi: Implication in Prenatal Diagnosis?" *Insights Imaging,* vol. 4, no. 3, 2013, pp. 357-67.

Iriye, Brian. "Two-Vessel Cord." *The Bump,* 2 Mar. 2017, www.thebump. com/a/two-vessel-cord. Accessed 16 Nov. 2018.

Jones, Sarah. "Your Quote." *Quotes,* 30 Nov. 2017, www.yourquote.in/ sarah-jones-iaqd/quotes?page=2&sort=. Accessed 22 July 2020.

Joy Number. "333 Angel Number—Hidden Truths Most People Don't Know About." *Joy Number,* 4 April 2020, joynumber.com/333-angel-number/. Accessed 18 Dec. 2017.

Keyes, Marian. "My Truth Is That What Doesn't Kill You Makes You Weaker." *Independent,* April 2013, www.independent.ie/entertainment/ books/my-truth-is-that-what-doesnt-kill-you-makes-you-weaker-2919 3556.html. Accessed 15 Sept. 2020.

Lama, Dalai. *Philosiblog,* 16 June 2013, philosiblog.com/2013/06/16/just-as-ripples-spread-out-when-a-single-pebble-is-dropped-into-water-the-actions-of-individuals-can-have-far-reaching-effects/. Accessed 10 Oct. 2020.

Lewis, *C. S. Letters to an American Lady.* Wm. B. Eerdmans Publishing, 2014.

Make Fun Of Life! "A Butterfly Lights Beside Us." *Animals,* 18 July 2018, www.makefunoflife.net/animals/a-butterfly-lights-beside-us-by-author-unknown. Accessed on 19 July 2019.

Makichen, Walter. *Spirit Babies: How to Communicate With the Child You're Meant to Have.* Random House Publishing Group, 2005.

Mayo Clinic. "DiGeorge Syndrome: (22q11-2 deletion syndrome)." *Mayo Clinic,* www.mayoclinic.org/diseases-conditions/digeorge-syndrome/ symptoms-causes/syc-20353543. Accessed 22 December 2016.

National Gallery. "Gabriel, Archangel." *The National Gallery*, www.nationalgallery.org.uk/paintings/glossary/gabriel-archangel. Accessed 11 September 2020.

Native Voices. " Medicine Ways: Traditional Healers and Healing." *Native Voices: Native Peoples' Concepts of Health and Illness*, www.nlm.nih.gov/nativevoices/exhibition/healing-ways/medicine-ways/medicine-wheel.html#:~:text=The%20Medicine%20Wheel%2C%20sometimes%20known,and%20the%20cycles%20of%20life. Accessed 24 Aug. 2017.

Petkus, Shelby. "Hyperfertility and Too Much of a Good Thing." *Pregnant Chicken*, pregnantchicken.com/hyperfertility/?fbclid=IwAR1-2NTbsAGTbRpcFUrAd3SD_wBOZ2ssWD6NwVBfTTDi4wDljgLPS Edd854. Accessed 9 Dec. 2020.

Phillips, Trish. "Fly Like the Eagle." *Facebook*, 9 Feb. 2017, www.facebook .com/SAMSONADEBOGA/posts/1402646479807357:0. Accessed 18 April 2017.

Richo, David. *The Power of Coincidence: How Life Shows Us What We Need to Know*. Shambhala Publications, 2007.

Ross, Tracee Ellis. *Black Girls Rock!: Celebrating the Power, Beauty, and Brilliance of Black Women*. Atria Publishing Group, 2017.

Sunnybrook Pregnancy and Infant Loss Network. "Pregnancy and Infant Loss Network." *Sunnybrook Hospital*, pailnetwork.sunnybrook.ca/. Accessed 2 Sept. 2020.

Tauscher, S. "Training English Language Teachers U& Zumbini Instructors Blog." *Wordpress*, 20 Aug. 2016, vanessareillytelt.wordpress.com/2016/08/20/we-worry-about-what-a-child-will-be-tomorrow-yet-we-forget-that-the-child-is-already-someone-today-stacia-tauscher/. Accessed 15 Jan. 2017.

The Gathering Place. "Butterfly Poems." *The Gathering Place*, 22 June 2006, www.thegatheringplacehome.com/butterfly-poems-t487.html. Accessed 6 Jan. 2017.

The Name Meaning. "Baby Names." *The Name Meaning*, www.thename meaning.com. Accessed 9 Dec. 2015.

Unknown. "The World Pursuit." *Rainbow Quotes*, theworldpursuit.com/rainbow-quotes/. Accessed 20 Aug. 2020.

Weil, Sharon. *ChangeAbility: How Artists, Activists, and Awakeners Navigate Change.* Archer Publications Limited, 2016.

What to Expect. "What to Expect: The Number #1 Pregnancy & Parenting Brand." *What to Expect*, www.whattoexpect.com/. Accessed 28 Jan. 2016.

Wilder Poetry. *Nocturnal.* Andrews McMeel Publishing, 2019.

Zuba, Tom. *Permission to Mourn: A New Way to Do Grief.* Tom Zuba.com, 2014.

Deepest appreciation to
Demeter's monthly Donors

DEMETER

Daughters
Rebecca Bromwich
Summer Cunningham
Tatjana Takseva
Debbie Byrd
Fiona Green
Tanya Cassidy
Vicki Noble
Myrel Chernick

Sisters
Amber Kinser
Nicole Willey

Grandmother
Tina Powell